JOHN DONNE, BODY AND SOUL

JOHN DONNE, BODY AND SOUL

RAMIE TARGOFF

THE UNIVERSITY OF CHICAGO PRESS

CHICAGO AND LONDON

RAMIE TARGOFF is associate professor of English at Brandeis University and the author of *Common Prayer*, published by the University of Chicago Press.

The University of Chicago Press, Chicago 60637
The University of Chicago Press, Ltd., London
© 2008 by The University of Chicago
All rights reserved. Published 2008
Printed in the United States of America

17 16 15 14 13 12 11 10 09 08   1 2 3 4 5

ISBN-13: 978-0-226-78963-7 (cloth)
ISBN-10: 0-226-78963-2 (cloth)

An earlier version of chapter 3 was published as "Traducing the Soul: Donne's *Second Anniversarie*" in *Publications of the Modern Language Association (PMLA)* 121, no. 5 (October 2006): 1493–1508, and is reprinted with permission. Parts of chapter 6 were included in "Facing Death," in *The Cambridge Companion to John Donne*, ed. Achsah Guibbory (Cambridge, UK: Cambridge University Press, 2006), 217–32, and are also reprinted with permission.

Library of Congress Cataloging-in-Publication Data

Targoff, Ramie.
  John Donne, body and soul / Ramie Targoff.
    p. cm.
  Includes bibliographical references and index.
  ISBN-13: 978-0-226-78963-7 (alk. paper)
  ISBN-10: 0-226-78963-2 (alk. paper)
    1. Donne, John, 1572–1631—Criticism and interpretation. 2. Donne, John, 1572–1631—Religion. 3. Donne, John, 1572–1631—Philosophy. 4. Body and soul in literature. 5. Christianity and literature—England—History—16th century. 6. Christianity and literature—England—History—17th century. I. Title.
  PR2248.T37 2008
  821'.3—dc22

                                                          2007024574

♾ The paper used in this publication meets the minimum requirements of the American National Standard for Information Sciences—Permanence of Paper for Printed Library Materials, ANSI z39.48-1992.

FOR HARRY

So leben wir und nehmen immer Abschied

So we live, forever taking leave
—Rilke, *Duino Elegies*

CONTENTS

ILLUSTRATIONS

ACKNOWLEDGMENTS

This book began in the Houghton Library at Harvard, where I spent a year reading Donne in his earliest editions and manuscripts. The bulk of the book was written while I was a fellow at the Wissenschaftskolleg in Berlin, where I enjoyed the tremendous generosity and intellectual vitality of this fine institution. I want to thank the excellent librarians at the Houghton and the superb staff of the Wissenchaftskolleg for providing me with the ideal contexts in which to think and write. The invitations to present my work at the University of Strathclyde in Glasgow, the University of Wisconsin in Madison, the Freie Universität and the Humboldt Universität in Berlin, the University of Munich, Florida State University, Columbia University, and Harvard University produced many rich exchanges that have enhanced these chapters, and I am grateful to the many people who made these visits possible. I also want to thank Brandeis University for giving me the time and support I needed to finish this book.

I am greatly indebted to the many colleagues and friends who helped me bring this project to fruition. Annabel Patterson has been the most loyal and dedicated of mentors: she read the complete manuscript with her characteristic rigor and intelligence, and spent hours with me poring over it page by page. Gordon Teskey read each chapter as soon as it was drafted, and pushed me repeatedly to grapple with both minute details and abstract ideas that I would not have come to myself. Michael Schoenfeldt reviewed the manuscript in both its early and final formations, and gently but firmly pushed me towards many of my most important revisions. Richard Rambuss helped me initially to formulate the shape of the project when we organized an SAA seminar together on the Renaissance soul, and his unswerving support and advice in the ensuing years have been incredibly important to me. Arthur Marotti generously read several chapters on Donne's poetry; Peter

McCullough was an invaluable resource for my chapter on the sermons; and Jeffrey Knapp provided a strong, final reading of the finished manuscript. My mother, Cheri Kamen Targoff, who was my first editor, remains one of my best. I am very grateful to her, and to my father, Michael Targoff, for their continued dedication and generosity.

Many others have read or discussed parts of the book with me, and have helped me in ways too numerous to detail. Among these colleagues and friends, I want to thank in particular Amy Appleford, Sarah Cole, Jeffrey Dolven, Tobias Döring, Jorie Graham, Dayton Haskin, Anselm Haverkamp, M. Thomas Hester, Susan James, Joseph Koerner, Thomas Laqueur, Yoon Lee, Verena Lobsien, Paul Morrison, Molly Murray, John Plotz, Leah Price, Catherine Robson, Beate Rössler, Peter Sacks, Quentin Skinner, and Michael Witmore. I have been very lucky in my research assistants, Beatrice Kitzinger, Nathaniel Hodes, Timothy Robinson, and above all Benjamin Woodring, who began as my undergraduate student at Brandeis, and has become a truly remarkable navigator of the early modern period, answering questions of any magnitude with incredible authority and ease. Alan Thomas, Mara Naselli, and Randy Petilos have been wonderful editors, and I want to thank the entire staff of the University of Chicago Press for bringing this book into the world.

My final and deepest gratitude is to my husband, Stephen Greenblatt, who is my finest reader, and my dearest companion. In ways that Donne would no doubt have understood, he has both sustained me while I wrote this book, and inspired me to write it in the first place. My son, Harry, who spent the nine months of his gestation in the Houghton Library, has been a source of pure joy from the day he was born. I dedicate this book to him.

Among John Donne's contributions to the English language is the word "valediction." From the Latin *vale*, the imperative of *valere*, "to be strong," or "to be well," and *dictio*, an "utterance" or "saying," "valediction" translates literally as the act of saying farewell. Four of Donne's love lyrics are entitled "Valediction," but his interest in valediction is by no means limited to his treatment of love. Donne's fascination with parting runs throughout his poetry and prose, and provides the occasion for his most imaginative writing.

There are many contexts in which Donne ponders what it means to say good-bye. In his immensely varied collection of works, he bids farewell to his spouse, his friends, his lovers, his children, his patrons, and his neighbors. Each of these valedictions is tinged with sorrow and regret, and some—as in his epitaph for his wife, Anne—are deeply moving. But however painful Donne's expressions of loss for his loved ones may be, the single most agonizing farewell for him is not between two people. It is between the body and the soul.

For Donne, the relationship between the body and soul—a relationship he regarded as one of mutual necessity—was the defining bond of his life. His experiences of friendship and love, health and illness, work and leisure, were all conditioned by the interactions between the two parts of the self. "In the constitution and making of a natural man," he declares, "the body is not the man, nor the soul is not the man, but the union of these two makes up the man."[1] When Donne preached these words in 1619, he was giving voice to his deepest and most passionately held belief.

The question of how body and soul relate to each other had plagued philosophers and theologians since ancient times. If we substitute—as Donne himself often does—the word "mind" for "soul," it is a question that continues to plague us today.[2] What is striking about Donne is not his decision to address the subject per se, although there are few early modern poets or priests who did so with his level of attention and seriousness. What is striking is the emotional charge that he brings to bear upon it, the way in which a set of seemingly abstruse metaphysical concerns become for him vivid, lived experiences.

This braiding together of the metaphysical and the experiential is what T. S. Eliot famously described as Donne's unified sensibility. "Tennyson and Browning are poets," Eliot remarks, "and they think; but they do not feel their thought as immediately as the odour of a rose. A thought to Donne was an experience; it modified his sensibility."[3] Donne's thoughts about the body and soul do not belong to a realm separate from his thoughts about his lovers or his friends. He approaches the parting between body and soul and the parting between two people with the same structure of feeling. The only difference is that the parting between body and soul is for him more intense, more fraught, more poignant.

To read Donne's collected writings is to bear witness again and again to the difficulties of this particular valediction. As we watch Donne suspend and evade and confront and lament the moment that the soul leaves the body, we realize how profoundly his imaginative life was organized around the challenges that this moment posed. The parting between body and soul is, I will argue, the great subject of Donne's writing. By understanding how he envisions this supreme separation, we learn something fundamental not only about his imaginative and psychic life—what he most feared and desired. We learn something fundamental as well about the complexity of saying good-bye in any of the circumstances of our own lives. Whether we believe that we have souls, whether we worry about our fate after death, Donne's lifelong brooding on these subjects teaches us something powerful about the act of parting. Above all, it teaches us what it means to leave, or to be left behind.

Before turning to Donne's own thinking about the relationship between the body and soul, I want to begin by explaining how something so crucial to nearly all of his writing—his letters, love lyrics, elegies and obsequies, meditations, devotional sonnets, and sermons—has not been fully acknowledged by centuries of readers and critics. This is not to say that no one has recognized the importance of this relationship in isolated poems or works, but the absolute centrality of the body and soul's union, and Donne's preoccupation with its inevitable rupture, has largely escaped our attention. For a poet who has spawned entire schools of criticism, how can this have happened?

The simplest answer is that literary history has developed a particular

bias against considering Donne as a poet with serious theological or philosophical interests. However much Donne has been admired for the terrific
wit of his conceits, the drama of his voice, the sheer beauty of his lines, he
has also been maligned as an author who lacked a real focus or purpose. This
is in many ways ironic, because Donne was from very early on credited with
having invented metaphysical poetry, which is generally understood to have
expanded the scope of poetic language by incorporating ideas and metaphors
from other disciplines—philosophy, astronomy, medicine, theology—into
its imaginative realm. No sooner was Donne's association with metaphysics pronounced, however—first by his contemporary, William Drummond of
Hawthornden, and some decades later, by the late seventeenth-century poet
and dramatist John Dryden—than it was qualified as an affectation rather
than a serious intellectual pursuit.[4]

The idea that Donne's metaphysics are on the surface rather than in the
depths of his writing has persisted for centuries. In his late eighteenth-century
Lives of the Poets, Samuel Johnson criticized Donne for forcing relations
and resemblances between things that had no business together. "The most
heterogeneous ideas," he famously complained, "are yoked by violence together." According to Dr. Johnson, Donne's perverse practice of *"discordia
concors"* had no serious philosophical purpose; it was driven merely by the
desire "to say what [he] hoped had never been said before."[5] Donne fared
little better in the nineteenth century: the Romantic poets by and large re-
belled against his intellectual language and difficult conceits;[6] the Victorians
were intrigued by Donne's personal history as a rakish lover-turned-priest,
but had little patience for his verse. Anna Jameson captured the long
nineteenth-century's opinion of him in her 1829 *Loves of the Poets:* Donne
was "more interesting," she remarks, "for his matrimonial history . . . than
for all his learned, metaphysical, and theological productions."[7]

A serious identification of Donne with metaphysics did not come until
the early twentieth century, when it was once again invoked as a high value
only to be dismissed. In 1921, Herbert J. C. Grierson published a new edition of Donne and his contemporaries entitled *The Metaphysical Lyrics and
Poems of the Seventeenth Century.* This was a strong title, and the volume
carried with it the explicit claim, as Grierson lays out in his introduction,
that Donne was to be counted as "metaphysical not only in virtue of his
scholasticism, but by his deep reflective interest in the experiences of which
his poetry is the expression, the new psychological curiosity with which he
writes of love and religion."[8]

Grierson's case for Donne's metaphysical seriousness was at once ex-
ploited and undermined, however, by T. S. Eliot's review of Grierson's vol-

ume in the *Times Literary Supplement*, and Eliot's much lengthier exposition of Donne in the Clark Lectures at Cambridge on the subject of metaphysical poetry five years later.[9] Although Eliot praised Donne, as we have seen, for possessing a "unified sensibility" of feeling and thought, he did not identify this sensibility as particularly metaphysical. Indeed, he announced that the "invention and use of the term metaphysical" to describe Donne's poetry sprung "from what . . . is hardly better than an accident." In a separate essay published in 1927, Eliot concludes that Donne's writings reveal no signs whatever of "any thinking, but only a vast jumble of incoherent erudition on which he drew for purely poetic effects."[10]

In the eighty or so years since Eliot's assessment, literary critics have generally embraced the notion that no sustained interest in metaphysics lay behind Donne's works as a whole. This is not to say that all aspects of Donne's intellectual engagement with his world have been ignored: his ambivalence about the "new philosophy" and advancements in medical science; his inheritance from his poetic predecessors, especially Petrarch; his complex relation to the devotional practices of Catholicism; and his absorption of Protestant ideology and theology have to varying degrees been documented.[11] The idea, however, that Donne had metaphysical concerns that were not limited to individual works or genres, but that pervade his works as a whole, has gone almost entirely underground.

In recent decades, critics have focused attention primarily on the social and political motivations that lay behind Donne's writing, without accounting for any deeply held philosophical or theological beliefs. There have been a number of important studies in this category—among them, Arthur Marotti's *John Donne, Coterie Poet*, and Jonathan Goldberg's *James I and the Politics of Literature*—but none so influential as John Carey's 1981 study, *John Donne: Life, Mind and Art*. Carey's central argument is based on a biographical observation: that Donne's erotic and religious works are shaped by a combination of apostasy and ambition. According to Carey, Donne's guilt in abandoning the Catholic faith into which he was born explains the poetry's central preoccupation with betrayals, infidelity, and impermanence; Donne's political and social ambition, itself responsible for his apostasy, produced both the agitation and egotism that suffuses the satires, the love poems, and many of the religious lyrics.

By offering an account of Donne's career that traverses the divide between its secular and religious periods, Carey's book has informed nearly all subsequent accounts of Donne's collected writings. And yet, the reduction of Donne's life to these two central "facts"—apostasy and ambition—has come at a cost. It is difficult to find critics or readers who consider Donne's career without impugning his motives and accusing him of bad faith. The sentiments of the love poems are discounted, while the religious poems are often regarded as theologically confused and sophistic. Studies of the sermons tend to distance them from the poems, as if consideration of the latter risks contamination of the former, and the project of reading Donne as an author with deeply held beliefs or preoccupations has been almost entirely obscured from view.

It is not my intention to argue that Donne was a metaphysician. But I shall argue that Donne's writing is fueled by a set of metaphysical questions, and that these questions coalesce most persistently around the nature of the soul and its relation to the body. Donne's expression of his belief in the mutual necessity of body and soul, and his obsessive imagining of their parting, is the most continuous and abiding feature of his collected works. It lies behind some of his most celebrated images—the description, for example, in "The Relique" of the two lovers reduced to "a bracelet of bright hair around the bone" (6).[12] The power of this image can be traced both to the poetic achievement that Eliot admires ("the sudden contrast of associations of 'bright hair' and of 'bone'"), and to the startling metaphysical claim that the image makes for the lovers' reunion on Judgment Day when each soul will come searching for the missing parts of its body.[13] Donne's concern with both the union and the separation of body and soul also lies behind the very striking first sentence of his Last Will and Testament: "First I give my good & gracious God an intire Sacrifice of Body & Soule with my most humble thanks for that assurance which his blessed Spiritt ymprintes in me nowe of the Salvation of the one & the Resurrection of the other." Unlike the will of Donne's father, which begins with a conventional disposition of body and soul—"I geve and Comend my soule into the hands of Allmightie God . . . and I commytt my bodie to the earth to be buried"—Donne insists that his final "sacrifice" will consist of both matter and spirit.[14] Not only does he affirm his belief that God desires equally both parts of the self. He also seems to elide the period of separation—when the body is buried in the earth and the soul rests in heaven—by imagining salvation and resurrection as concurrent events, "ymprinte[d] in me nowe."

In works that range from his erotic lyric "The Extasie," in which Donne explores what happens when two lovers' souls leave their bodies in pursuit of a shared ecstatic experience, to his mock epic, *Metempsychosis*, in which he traces the fate of a single soul as it is serially reincarnated; from *The First Anniversarie*, where he considers the effect that the loss of a single, exceptional soul has on the world-corpse left behind, to *The Second Anniversarie*, where he chronicles the soul's reluctance to leave its mortal flesh; from his Holy Sonnet, "At the round earths imagin'd corners," in which he describes the frantic rush of souls to locate their "scattered bodies" on the last day, to the *Devotions*, in which he tries to gauge, and improve, the health of his soul by carefully tracking the symptoms of his bodily illness; from his personal letters, which attempt to transcend periods of physical absence through the epistolary transmission of souls, to his sermons, which attempt to alleviate his and his listeners' fears surrounding death: Donne reveals his obsession with what connects, and what severs, the body and soul.

To uncover the nature of Donne's obsession—an obsession whose metaphysical nature cannot be separated from its emotional and spiritual underpinnings—it is crucial to understand the intellectual materials with which Donne actively grappled. There is no early modern poet for whom theology and philosophy were more important to the creative process, and we do Donne a disservice when we fail to recognize how much his learning penetrated his writing. In what follows, I will sketch what it was about the soul and body, respectively, that mattered so deeply to Donne, and how we might account for his lifelong fascination with imagining both the moment they part and the prospect of their coming together again.

I. The Soul

In a letter to his closest friend, Sir Henry Goodyer, Donne confesses that he suffered from a "Hydroptique immoderate desire of humane learning and languages."[15] Both his poetry and his prose reflect this insatiable thirst for knowledge. By the time of Donne's death in 1631, his first biographer and possible acquaintance Izaak Walton records that Donne had in his library a total of "1400 Authors, most of them abridged and analysed with his own hand."[16] Walton's observation that the authors were "abridged and analysed" suggests that Donne kept notebooks or commonplace books in which he digested the texts. No books of this sort are ever mentioned by Donne, and the 200 or so volumes from his library that remain today have no marginal notes of any substance—only occasional stars, or squiggly lines.[17] But Donne's writings overflow with learned references to ancient and contemporary authors, and there can be little doubt that he read with the kind of scrutiny and attention that Walton describes.

What were the books that made up Donne's personal library? The wide range of references in his writings suggests that he was entrenched in the theological and philosophical debates sweeping both the continent and England, and there are few obvious limitations to his scope of inquiry. We can nonetheless identify a handful of topics that seem to have engaged Donne more than others. Many of the texts are of a polemical religious nature, and would have informed his research for his 1610 attack on the Jesuits, *Pseudo-Martyr*. But besides the polemical texts, there is a sizable collection of metaphysical and philosophical treatises that address one subject of particular importance to Donne: the subject of the soul.

The sheer variety of books that Donne owned about the soul suggests that the topic had an unusual urgency for him. This urgency led him to read far beyond the obvious works of the Latin church fathers and biblical scholars whom he cites regularly in his sermons. The surviving texts from his library include several conventional defenses of the soul's immortality, such as the thirteenth-century Spanish theologian Ramon Llull's *Duodecim Principia Philosophiae*, which affirms that the soul is unaffected by death and corruption; or the sixteenth-century Italian physician and philosopher Antonio Bruno's *Entelechia seu De Animae Immortalitate Disputatio*, which rehearses traditional Aristotelian notions of the soul's simultaneously incorporeal and substantial nature. Donne also owned works that contained more eccentric accounts of the soul's relationship to the body, such as the sixteenth-century German Jesuit Petrus Thyraeus's *De Demoniacis Liber Unus Inquo Daemonum obsidentium conditio*, a work on demonology that explores the conditions under which the spirit may function independently of the body during mortal life; or the sixteenth-century Frenchman Claude Prieur's *Dialogue de la Lycanthropie*, whose treatment of wolf-men includes lengthy considerations of metempsychosis.

Donne's readings on the soul were not limited to obscure foreign authors—he also kept abreast of contemporary works on the subject. Two of the volumes that he owned were written by fellow Englishmen, who take diametrically opposed positions on the corporeality of the soul. The first was Nicholas Hill's *Philosophia Epicurea, Democritiana, Theophrastica proposita simpliciter, non edocta*, a heretical text published in Paris in 1601 that blended classical atomism with Christian metaphysics to defend the incorruptibility of the soul's matter. (Donne's copy of Hill's text was previously owned by his friend Ben Jonson, who presumably gave or sold the book to him, and whose signature on the title page Donne chose heavily to score out in a frenzy of possessive pleasure—the deleted signature was then covered with a paper slip upon which Donne inscribed his own name.) The second, *The Differences of the Ages of Mans Life*, combats the implications of Epicurean materialism for the Christian understanding of the immortal soul. The author of this text, Henry Cuffe, was an acquaintance of Donne's—he had accompanied Donne on his Cadiz expedition with Essex in 1596 (unlike

Donne, Cuffe became one of Essex's closest allies, and was executed for treason in 1601).

It is not clear what Donne made of any of these works in particular—with the exception of Hill, whom Donne mocks in his early work *The Courtier's Library*, few of these authors are explicitly discussed in his writings.[18] But it is clear that questions surrounding the nature of the soul engaged Donne throughout the different phases of his career, and that he put few, if any, limits on his restless exploration of the subject. Some of the theories about the soul that he considered were no more than occasional interests—ideas that he found amusing or convenient for particular purposes, but never entertained as serious possibilities. In this category belongs, for example, his curiosity about metempsychosis. Donne experimented with the notion that a single soul might be serially reincarnated in different bodies in his early poem, *Metempsychosis* or *The Progresse of the Soul.* But that this satiric poem was left unfinished reflects, I believe, his ultimate distaste for its conceit. The idea that each soul belongs to an individual body was of the utmost importance to Donne—there is perhaps no single idea more important to his metaphysics. "It is not perfectly true," he writes to Goodyer, "which a very subtil, yet very deep wit Averroes says, that all mankinde hath but one soul, which informes and rules us all, as one Intelligence doth the firmament and all the Starres in it; as though a particular body were too little an organ for a soul to play upon" (43). In a funeral sermon delivered in 1626 for his friend Sir William Cokayne, Donne states his opinion of metempsychosis unambiguously: "that the soule departing from one body, should become the soul of another body, in a perpetuall revolution and transmigration of soules through bodies . . . hath been the giddinesse of some Philosophers to think" (7:257).

Other theories about the soul seem to have interested Donne on and off throughout his life, but neither fully seized his imagination nor persuaded him of their truth. One such theory was mortalism: the idea that the soul died with the body and then is resurrected with the flesh at the last day. In sixteenth-century Europe, mortalism was at the center of multiple controversies and debates. The Catholic Church denounced it as a heresy in the Fifth Lateran Council in 1513, arguing that the soul was immediately received either in heaven, hell, or purgatory, and the Protestant Church of England includes in its 1553 Articles of Religion: "The soulles of them that departe this life doe neither die with the bodies, nor sleep idlie."[19] Although the Protestant Reformers William Tyndale and Martin Luther both avowed a sort of mortalism or psychopannychism—the idea that the soul did not die, but slept with the body—these beliefs were largely associated with the radical Protestant sect of Anabaptists, whom the English authors of the 1553 Articles had expressly intended to attack. Calvin himself took up the anti-mortalism and anti-psychopannychism cause in his 1542 treatise, appropriately entitled *Psychopannychia*, in which he rejected the idea that the soul would die with the body, but declared that "it is neither lawful nor expedient to inquire too curiously concerning our souls' intermediate state."[20]

Despite its heretical status in the English church, mortalism seems to have held out a strong appeal for Donne. Indeed, he may well have wished that he were a mortalist—such a belief would have resolved many of his deepest anxieties. For mortalism meant that soul and body would never have to part, a possibility that eliminated the horrible period of posthumous separation that Donne dreaded above all else. But although he refers to the "sin-burd'ned soules [that] from graves will creepe, / At the last day" in his verse epistle "The Storme,"[21] and although he mentions souls both rising from death and waking from sleep in several of the *Holy Sonnets*, he never suggests that he found mortalism or psychopannychism theologically convincing. There is not a single work in which he sustains these ideas for any length of time, and in a 1624 Easter Day sermon preached at St. Paul's he denounces mortalism explicitly: "Now a Resurrection of the soule, seemes an improper, an impertinent, an improbable, an impossible forme of speech; for, Resurrection implies death, and the soule does not dye in her passage to Heaven" (6:74). We could say, of course, that Donne was merely voicing the orthodox view of his church, and that his private beliefs lay elsewhere. But his position in the sermon corresponds to the account he gives of the soul's departure from the flesh at the moment of death in nearly all of his devotional writings.

Another theory of the soul that surfaces from time to time in Donne's writings, but which he never seems fully to embrace, is that the soul comprises three parts: vegetable, sensitive, and intellectual. The vegetable soul was responsible for growth, the sensitive soul for movement and feeling, and the intellectual soul for thinking. This conception of a threefold soul derived from Aristotle and was adapted for Christian theology by Thomas Aquinas, who learned about it from his teacher Albertus Magnus. Aquinas was clearly attracted to the Aristotelian idea because it allowed him to postulate an immortal part of the soul—the intellectual or rational soul—which came directly from God and which differentiated humans from other forms of life. In response to the question of whether the intellectual soul is produced from human seed, Aquinas answers that the "body has nothing whatever to do in the operation of the intellect," and therefore "the power of the intellectual principle, as intellectual, cannot reach the semen." The intellectual soul "cannot be caused through generation," Aquinas concludes, "but only through creation by God."[22]

In Donne's poetry, the idea of the threefold soul is irregular. He adopts it, for example, in "A Valediction: of my name, in the window," but he does so to make a romantic, not theological point: "all my soules," he tells his beloved, "bee, / Emparadis'd in you, (in whom alone / I understand, and grow and see)" (25–27). In a verse epistle to his friend and patroness, Lucy Harrington, the Countess of Bedford, Donne rehearses the idea that "our Soules of growth and Soules of sense / Have birthright of our reasons Soule, yet hence / They fly not from that, nor seeke presidence" (34–36), meaning that the vegetable and sensible souls preceded the intellectual soul in their creation, although the intellectual soul, once created, assumes the rights, as it were, of the firstborn. Likewise in an epistle to Catherine Howard, the Countess of Salisbury, he writes: "Wee first have soules of growth, and sense, and those / When our last soule, our soule immortall came / Were swalloed into it, and have no name" (52–54). Outside of these examples, however, Donne's lyrics generally work from the assumption that the soul is single and indivisible. When he refers to souls in the plural, as he does in "The good-morrow," "A nocturnall upon S. Lucies day," "The Relique," and "The Expiration," among many other poems, the reference is not to his multiple souls. It is to the combination of his soul and the soul of his beloved. Even in Holy Sonnet XIV, "Batter my heart three-person'd God," the invocation to God as "three-person'd" does not prompt Donne to draw the obvious connection between God's tripartite nature and his tripartite soul.

In his devotional prose, Donne does endorse the idea of multiple souls on several occasions. Preaching at the royal palace of Whitehall in 1620, Donne explains the theory as if it were an orthodox truth:

> First, in a naturall man wee conceive there is a soule of vegetation and of growth; and secondly, a soule of motion and of sense; and then thirdly, a soule of reason and understanding, an immortal soule. And the two first soules of vegetation, and of sense, wee conceive to arise out of the temperament, and good disposition of the substance of which that man is made, they arise out of man himselfe; But the last soule, the perfect and immortal soule, that is immediately infused by God. (3:85)

Likewise he declares in a 1621 sermon, also at Whitehall, that the bodies that make up the kingdom of heaven have "one vegetative soule, head and members must grow together, one sensitive soule, all must be sensible and compassionate of one anothers miserie; and especially one Immortall soule, one supreame soule, one Religion" (4:47).[23] And in the 1623 *Devotions*, he writes that "Man, before hee hath his *immortall soule*, hath a *soule of sense*, and a *soule* of *vegitation* before that: This *immortall soule* did not forbid other *soules*, to be in us before, but when this *soule* departs, it carries all with it; no more *vegetation*, no more *sense*."[24] But these references to our threefold souls are vastly outnumbered by the countless references in the sermons and *Devotions* to the soul as a singular entity, a soul whose integrity would be threatened by even the suggestion of its being composed of multiple parts.

The theories about the soul that engaged Donne most deeply were those that addressed the soul's creation and immortality. His earliest sustained discussion of these subjects comes in an unusually philosophical letter written to Goodyer sometime around 1607.[25] This letter, which is the closest Donne comes to a treatise on the soul (we might call it his own *De Anima*), begins with his expressing his frustration that the nature of the soul's origins is surrounded by so much uncertainty in Christian theology. Although, he writes, there is nothing more worthy of reflection and meditation than the soul, yet "all sects of Christians, after long disputations and controversies, have allowed many things for positive and dogmaticall truths which are not worthy of that dignity."[26] The Christian church has two dominant traditions in explaining how the soul is made, and neither can be regarded as definitive. "Hence it is," he complains, "that whole Christian Churches arrest themselves upon propagation from parents, and other whole Christian Churches allow onely infusion from God."

The idea that the soul is formed inside the body through "propagation from parents" is known as traducianism or *ex traduce*. It derives from the Latin noun *tradux*, which originally meant a vine trained for propagation, and suggested something cultivated rather than divinely made. *Tradux* later came to be associated with the idea of a family tree. The noun shares the same etymological root with the verb *traducere*, which carried both the neutral meaning "to lead across" (*transducere*) as well as the pejorative meaning "to disgrace or betray." The *ex traduce* or generative theory of the soul's origins stands in opposition to a theory known as *ex nihilo* or infusionism, which holds that souls are not made from human generation but are created by God "from nothing"—from no pre-existent human substances or materials—and are then infused individually into the fetus before birth. According to the infusion theory, the soul is not related in substance to the flesh it inhabits.

Over the course of his career, Donne wavers between these two positions. In a verse epistle to Lady Bedford composed around 1609, he propounds the infusion theory: "As men to'our prisons, new soules to us are sent / Which learne vice there, and come in innocent" (59–60). In the *Anniversaries*, written several years later (1611–12), he places traducianism at the very center of his poetic project. Later in his career, as a preacher, Donne generally endorses the infusion theory upheld by the Church of England. Among many other examples, he preaches in a 1618 sermon at Whitehall that his listeners should consider "what he was when he was but in the list, and catalogue of creatures, and might have been left in the state of a worm, or a plant, or a stone" had God not "created, and infused an immortal soul into him" (1:274).

In the letter to Goodyer, however, Donne is interested less in taking sides on the origins of the soul than in conveying the theological muddle that surrounds the question. "For whosoever will adhere to the way of propagation [*ex traduce*]," he exclaims,

> can never excite necessarily and certainly a naturall immortality in the soul if the soul result out of matter, nor shall he ever prove that all mankind hath any more then one soul: as certainly of all beasts, if they receive such souls as they have from their parents, every species can have but one soul. And they which follow the opinion of infusion from God, and of a new creation, (which is now the most common opinion), as they can very hardly defend the doctrin of original sin (the soul is forced to take this infection, and comes not into the body of her own disposition), so shall they never be able to prove that all those whom we see in the shape of men have an immortall and reasonable soul, because our parents are as able as any other species is to give us a soul of growth and of sense, and to perform all vitall and animall functions, and so without infusion of such a soul may produce a creature as wise and well disposed as any horse or Elephant, of which degree many whom we see come far short; nor hath God bound or declared himself that he will always create a soul for every embryon. (17–18)

This is a dense passage, and its density reflects the seriousness with which Donne tackled the subject of how the soul gets into the body. It begins with his identifying two obvious problems in the propagation theory. First, he argues, since this theory assumes that the soul is created from human generation, it provides no assurance of the soul's immortality—how can we know if the soul is made from divine substance if it is generated, like the flesh, in the womb? Second, if the soul is composed of multiple parts—as Donne assumes it is in this letter—propagation cannot account for anything but the "one soul" that comes from the parents directly. It is not altogether clear what Donne means by the "one soul"—typically the vegetable and sensitive souls are both understood to be made through human propagation, and it may be that he lumps the two together for purposes of his argument. It is clear, however, that his primary concern is with the intellectual part of the soul, and he voices his fear that there will be nothing to differentiate men from beasts if we do not allow for the idea that God separately infuses this immortal soul into our human flesh.

If the *ex traduce* theory has two obvious shortcomings in its logic, so does the theory that the soul is created outside of the flesh and then infused into the body by God. First, Donne questions what guarantee we have that God has created an immortal soul for "every embryo," when many human beings show no more evidence of possessing such a soul than do horses or elephants. (The identification, that is, of the infused soul with the highest intellectual function fails to apply to all human beings, and hence suggests that many people might have no immortal soul at all.) Second—and, I would argue, more seriously—he observes that the infusion theory complicates the question of where original sin is contracted. For those who believe that the soul is made inside the body, there is no problem in explaining how the soul becomes tainted by original sin: it is simply passed on through human generation beginning with Adam and Eve. (It is according to this logic that infants are baptized—even at birth they are already contaminated.) The infusion theory, by contrast, raises the heretical possibility that God contaminates each soul with original sin before placing it in the body.

Donne rejects the idea that God deliberately created tainted souls in a 1618 sermon delivered at Lincoln's Inn (where Donne himself had studied law, and where he assumed the role of Divinity Reader in 1616). "Here's no sin in *that* soul, that God creates," he preached before the learned members of this society, "for there God should create something that were *evill*" (2:58). The alternative to this idea, however, is equally problematic: that the soul voluntarily came into a body in which it knew it would contract original sin. For one of the crucial features of original sin according to the Latin fathers is that it is willed and voluntary—"original" in this sense means not that our sin is inherited, but that it is "original" in each soul, which chooses to sin right from the start. "There can be no sin that is not voluntary," Augustine declares in *Of True Religion*, and original sin is no exception.[27] The complexity of Augustine's explanation for the voluntary nature of original sin exceeds our inquiry here, but it is adequately summarized in *The Literal Meaning of Genesis*, where Augustine argues that if the infusion theory is correct, "we will admit also that the soul was not originally created so as to know its future works whether good or evil. For it is quite unbelievable that it could have tended of its own free will to life in the body if it foreknew that it would commit certain sins by which it would justly incur perpetual punishment."[28]

Donne was certainly familiar with Augustine's writings on this subject, and he recognized that the willfulness of original sin posed a problem for the infusion theory.[29] This recognition is implicit in his *"De Anima"* letter to Goodyer, where he remarks parenthetically that one of the problems with the infusion theory is that "the soul is forced to take this infection, and comes not into the body of her own disposition," as if the infused soul would need to make a willful decision to enter the contaminating flesh. He explains this more fully some fifteen years later in the *Devotions*, in which he admits that it is "hard, to charge the *soule* with the guiltinesse of *Originall* sinne, if the *soule* were infused into a *body*, in which it must necessarily grow *foule*, and contract *originall sinne*, whether it *will* or *no*" (91).

At times Donne abandons the Augustinian position that the infused soul willed its entry into the flesh, declaring instead that the soul was compelled by God to do so. In one of his first sermons preached before James I, in April 1616, he inquires whether "Gods judgement [was] executed speedily enough upon thy soul, when in the same instant that it was created, and conceiv'd, and infus'd, it was put to a necessity of contracting Original sin?"[30] In the *Devotions*, however, Donne reaches a conclusion that seems more compatible with both his theology and metaphysics: that the contraction of original sin cannot be blamed on either the body or the soul, but lies in the conjunction of the two. "My *God*, my *God*," he asks, "what am I put to, when I am put to *consider*, and *put off*, the *root*, the *fuell*, the *occasion* of my *sicknesse*? What *Hypocrates*, what *Galen*, could shew mee that in my *body*? It lies deeper than so; it lies in my *soule*: And deeper than so; for we may wel consider the *body*, before the *soule* came, before *inanimation*, to bee *without sinne*; and the *soule* before it come to the *body*, before that *infection*, to be *without sinne*. . . . It is in the *union* of the *body* and *soule*," he exclaims, "and O, my *God*, could I *prevent* that, or can I *dissolve* that?" (118). There is no question that Donne was troubled by the theological uncertainties surrounding the soul's creation and its contraction of original sin, and that he thought seriously about these uncertainties throughout his life. But underlying his concerns about the soul's creation lies an even greater concern about the soul's immortality. At the conclusion of the passage from the *Devotions* in which he considers the problems besetting the infusion theory, he declares his ultimate indifference as to how the soul was created so long as he can satisfactorily explain its immortal fate. After quoting Augustine,

who in a similar moment of frustration declared that so long as "the departure of my soule to salvation be evident to my faith," he cared not "how
darke the entrance of my soule, into my body, bee to my reason," Donne
remarks: "It is the *going out*, more than the *coming in*, that concernes us"
(91). The "*going out*," and not the "*coming in*": this is the preference that
also governs the letter to Goodyer, in which Donne ultimately puts aside
the question of the soul's origins and contamination by original sin in order
to weigh the possible explanations for its immortality. As with the earlier
questions, however, whose answers have "such infirmities as it is time to
look for a better," he finds the hypotheses for the soul's immortality to fall
short of the mark. Indeed, Donne confides to Goodyer, although all Christians believe in the immortality of the soul, he is "ashamed that we do not
also know it by searching farther."

In a 1627 sermon for the wedding of the Earl of Bridgewater's daughter,
Lady Mary Egerton, to the son of Lord Herbert of Cherbury, Donne preached
that "there are so many evidences of the immortality of the soule, even to a
naturall mans *reason*, that it required not an Article of the Creed, to fix this
notion" (8:97). This unflinching conviction of the preacher does not apply,
however, to the younger Donne who searches in vain to justify the soul's
immortality according to "reason," not mere belief. At the end of the letter to Goodyer, he appoints himself the task of attempting some resolution
lest he leave his friend in a dangerous state of unknowing. "Because I have
meditated therein," he concludes, "I will shortly acquaint you with what I
think; for I would not be in danger of that law of *Moses*, That if a man dig a
pit, and cover it not, he must recompense those which are damnified by it:
which is often interpreted of such as shake old opinions, and do not establish new as certain, but leave consciences in a worse danger then they found
them in" (18). Unfortunately for our purposes, there is no further record in
the letters of Donne's meditations on the matter—either the promised letter
was lost, or it was never written—and hence in this respect his pit remains
dangerously open.

In another respect, however, Donne's poetry and prose testify to a lifelong commitment to thinking through the questions raised in this early letter to Goodyer. This is not to suggest that he in any way resolved the theological problems concerning the soul's creation or its immortality. But it is
to suggest that his writings attest to his profound concern with the nature
of the soul, and that taken as a whole, they provide some explanation as to
why the subject was so important to him. This explanation requires that we
turn away from the soul as an isolated topic to explore its relation with the
flesh. However much Donne worries about the posthumous fate of the soul,

he worries equally if not more about the posthumous fate of the body. When he frets about keeping his own soul in heaven, he also frets about keeping his own body in heaven. And when he celebrates the prospect of an eternal life, he celebrates the prospect of an eternal marriage between the two parts of the self. Donne's intellectual, devotional, and emotional life is shaped not only by his obsession with the soul's immortality. It is shaped equally by his obsession with the body's resurrection.

II. The Body

Donne's attitude toward his earthly body has been the subject of a number of fine studies, but little attention has been paid to his preoccupation with the body he will assume in heaven.[31] This preoccupation with his resurrected flesh surfaces throughout his written works—where we most, and where we least, expect to find it. It is in the verse epistles written as a young courtier, in which he compares receiving a letter from his friends to being resurrected from the dead. It is in his lyric "The Funerall," where he describes his mistress's "subtile wreath of haire" as a substitute soul that "keepe[s] these limbes, her Provinces, from dissolution" until God re-collects him (8). It is in his elegy "The Autumnall," where he expresses his disgust for those withered old men or women "whose every tooth to a severall place is gone, / To vexe their soules at *Resurrection*" (41–42). It is in the poems he wrote for the dead, like his "Obsequies to the Lord Harrington," in which he brings up the problems raised by cannibalism:[32] even if "man feed on mans flesh, and so / Part of his body to another owe, / Yet at the last two perfect bodies rise, / Because God knowes where every Atome lyes" (53–56). It is, above all, in the many sermons that seek to convince his listeners that however unlikely or difficult it may seem, God will reconstitute them in body and soul.

What was it about the resurrection of the flesh that compelled Donne to return to it so regularly in his works? We will return to this question in chapter 6, but I want to propose some preliminary answers. On theological grounds Donne finds the resurrection so compelling because among the many mysteries of the Christian faith, it seemed to him the hardest to believe. Unlike the immortality of the soul, which may lack scientific proof but, as he argues in the 1627 wedding sermon, stands to a "naturall man's reason," the resurrection of the flesh defies human understanding. More than anything else, this is the aspect of Christian eschatology that requires further proof—this is the pit, to return to the letter to Goodyer, which desperately needs to be filled. No article of belief is required, Donne contends, for the immortality of the soul: it is so deeply taken for granted. But all three of the Creeds that the Church of England upholds (Athanasius's, Nicene, and Apostles') need to state unequivocally that the dead will be resurrected.[33] Yet, even so, Donne exclaims in a 1623 sermon, this is the "hardest Article of the Creed" because it is the most difficult to teach to believers. It was for this reason that Jesus raised Lazarus from the dead: "this Miracle Christ meant to make a pregnant proofe of the Resurrection, which was his princi-pall intention therein" (4:327, 326).

The idea that the resurrection of the flesh requires either a "pregnant proofe" or a leap of faith is the subject of Donne's 1625 Easter day sermon preached at St. Paul's on John 5:28 and 5:29—"Marvell not at this; for the houre is comming, in the which, all that are in the graves shall heare his voice; and shall come forth." Donne explains that the meaning of Christ's warning, "Marvell not at this," refers to John 5:24, in which Christ declares that those who "heareth my word and believeth on him that sent me" shall have "everlasting life." This promise of spiritual resurrection, Donne insists, is not worthy of marvel. The real subject of wonder lies in the prospect of bodily rebirth at the last day. "And therefore," he commands, "be content to wonder at this":

> That God would have such a care to dignifie, and to crown, and to as-sociate to his own everlasting presence, the body of man. God himself is a Spirit, and heaven is his place; my soul is a spirit, and so proportioned to that place; That God, or Angels, or our Soules, which are all Spirits, should be in heaven, *Ne miremini*, never wonder at that. But since we wonder, and justly, that some late Philosophers have removed the whole earth from the Center, and varied it up, and placed it in one of the Spheares of heaven, That this clod of earth, this body of ours should be carried up to the highest heaven, placed in the eye of God, set down at the right hand of God, *Miramini hoc*, wonder at this; That God, all Spirit, served with spirits, associated to Spirits, should have such an affection, such a love to this body, this earthly body, this deserves this wonder. (6:265–66)

Why would God, who is all spirit, want to be accompanied by mere bod-ies? And what can our "clod[s] of earth" bring to the glory of heaven? In the Easter day sermon, Donne does not answer these questions, but he returns to them in a sermon preached at St. Paul's later that spring. Here he argues that God did not create mankind to compensate for his loss of the fallen an-gels. He created mankind because he wanted to have embodied creatures in heaven. "Man cannot deliberately wish himselfe an Angel," Donne remarks, "because he should lose by that wish, and lacke that glory, which he shall have in his body" (6:297). "He should lose by that wish": to be an angel is to diminish the splendor of human creation. Christ may say that "we shall be like the Angels" (Mark 12:25), and to the extent that we can refine the faculties of our souls, we might ultimately earn the comparison. But, Donne concludes, in a sublime moment of human chauvinism, although we may succeed in transforming our souls to be like angels, the angels "shall never attaine to be like us in our glorified bodies" (6:297).

If we compare Donne's account of the relation between angels and humans to John Milton's account in *Paradise Lost,* the difference in emphasis is glaring. In Milton's poem, the angel Raphael visits Adam and Eve before the fall, and tells them that if they remain obedient, they will eventually become more like angels: "Your bodies may at last turn all to spirit, / Improved by tract of time, and winged ascend / Ethereal as we."[34] For Milton, to be all spirit is to be "improved" from the human condition of embodiment. For Donne, there is no advantage whatever to the angelic constitution. Bodies as well as spirits are essential inhabitants of heaven. Donne states this clearly in *Pseudo-Martyr* (1610), where he affirms that "it is the intire man that God hath care of, and not the soule alone; therefore his first worke was the body, and the last worke shall be the glorification thereof."[35] He declares it with full rhetorical force in a 1621 sermon preached at Whitehall:

> We begin with this, that the Kingdome of Heaven hath not all that it must have to a consummate perfection, till it have bodies too. In those infinite millions of millions of generations, in which the holy, blessed, and glorious Trinity enjoyed themselves one another, and no more, they thought not their glory so perfect, but that it might receive an addition from creatures, and therefore they made a world, a materiall world, a corporeall world, they would have bodies. (4:47)

However happy the members of the Trinity may have been before the creation of human beings, something was lacking in their glory. It was for this reason, Donne argues, that God made a "materiall world, a corporeall world: There must be bodies, Men, and able bodies, able men. . . . They are glorified bodies that make up the kingdome of Heaven" (4:47).

The idea that the kingdom of heaven will be filled with glorified human bodies was not in itself controversial, nor did it need the authority of the Creed for its support. What was controversial, and what Donne struggles to prove repeatedly in his writings, is that the glorified bodies in heaven are essentially identical to the bodies we possess on earth. There is a long history

of debate in Christian theology over this question, and I will treat this at
some length later in the book. For now, I want to look briefly at two sermons
delivered at Lincoln's Inn during the 1620 Easter term, in which Donne
considers two of the crucial verses from scripture on the identity of the resurrected body: Job 19:26, "And though, after my skin, wormes destroy this
body, yet in my flesh shall I see God," and I Corinthians 15:50, "Now this
I say brethren, that flesh and blood cannot inherit the kingdome of God."
These sermons show Donne hard at work in reconciling the two seemingly
contradictory positions, and they also reveal how important it was for him
that the resurrected body would be his own.

Job 19:26 may have been the single verse of scripture Donne embraced
most passionately in his writings, and in his 1620 sermon he struggles to
answer those who claim that it does not in fact address the posthumous resurrection of the flesh. He begins by conceding that in the entirety of the New
Testament, the book of Job is never cited to support bodily resurrection. He
acknowledges as well Calvin's argument that this verse signified only that
Job will return to God's favor in his mortal life, and not that he will be reborn after death. In response to these charges, Donne supplies a list of church
fathers who base their justification of the resurrection on Job 19:26; he also
adduces a number of Protestant theologians, such as Osiander, Tremmelius,
and Piscator, who share his own interpretation. In a final effort to bolster his
case, he turns to the authority of the Jews, for whom, he claims, "this place
of Scripture, which is our text, hath evermore been received for a proof of
the Resurrection" (3:102).

The bulk of this sermon justifying Job 19:26 is not, however, solely an exercise in biblical hermeneutics: it is also an exercise in rhetorical persuasion.
Donne desperately wants to convey to his listeners that however implau-
sible or incredible the idea of the resurrection may seem, it is nonetheless
the case that they will be resurrected with their own flesh, and that this is
what Job avows. "That that soule," Donne begins,

> which sped so ill in that body, last time it came to it, as that it contracted
> *Originall sinne* then, and was put to the slavery to serve that body, and
> to serve it in the ways of sinne, not for an Apprentiship of seven, but
> seventy years after, that that soul after it hath once got loose by death,
> and liv'd God knows how many thousands of years, free from that body,
> that abus'd it so before, and in the sight and fruition of that God, where it
> was in no danger, should willingly, nay desirously, ambitiously seek this
> scattered body, this Eastern, and Western, and Northern, and Southern
> body, this is the most inconsiderable consideration. (3:109)

When Donne wants to stress the soul's suffering in the flesh, he blames its contraction of original sin squarely on the body. But he does this to emphasize the longing that the soul feels all the same for its corporeal home. "And yet," he continues,

> *Ego, I,* I the same body, and the same soul, shall be recompact again, and be identically, numerically, individually the same man. The same integrity of body, and soul, and the same integrity in the Organs of my body, and in the faculties of my soul too; I shall be all there, my body, and my soul, and all my body, and all my soul. (3:109–10)

Despite the soul's liberation from the body that contaminated it, and despite the scattering of the body's remains throughout the globe, the soul will find its body again, and he shall be "identically, numerically, and individually" the same.

Donne's insistence on the "identical" nature of his resurrected body in the sermon on Job 19:26 provides the background for his sermon that he preached the same Easter season on the Pauline verse: "Now this I say brethren, that flesh and blood cannot inherit the kingdome of God" (1 Cor. 15:50). Like the sermon on Job, this sermon rehearses the interpretive history of its scriptural verse, beginning with the story of Eutychius, the sixth-century Patriarch of Constantinople, who late in his life "maintained that errour, That the body of Christ had not, that our bodies, in the Resurrection should not have any of the qualities of a *naturall body,* but that those bodies were, *in subtilitatem redacta,* so rarifyed, so refined, so attenuated, and reduced to a thinness and subtlenesse, that they were *aery bodies,* and not bodies of flesh and blood" (3:114). (The language of this passage echoes that of "A Valediction: forbidding mourning," although in the poem it is the souls, and not the bodies, whose substance is likened to "ayery thinnesse.")

Donne recounts that the emperor (Justin II) arranged for a debate between Eutychius and Gregory the Great on the subject, and that "the Emperour was so well satisfyed [with Gregory's position] that hee commanded *Euthycius* his books to bee burnt." Eutychius based his argument on 1 Corinthians 15:50, to which Gregory had responded with this interpretation: "sinfull flesh shall not, but naturall flesh [shall inherit the kingdom of God]; that is, flesh indued with all qualities of flesh, all such qualities as imply no defect, no corruption, (for there was *flesh* before there was *sin)*" (3:114–15). But on his deathbed, Donne relates, Eutychius died by affirming Gregory's position: "*In haec carne,* in this flesh . . . I acknowledge, that I, and all men shall arise at the day of Judgement" (3:114).

After narrating this story in some detail, Donne catalogs the history of heretics on the subject of personal resurrection, naming, among others: Simon Magnus, who denied the resurrection altogether; the Gnostics, who believed only in the resurrection of the soul, and not of the body; the Arabians, who were mortalists, advocating the temporary death of the soul; the Armenians, who had the extraordinary idea that all would rise as men, including women; and Origen, who thought the resurrection would last only one thousand years after which we would all be annihilated or absorbed into God's essence. Several of these heretics, Donne declares, perverted the Pauline scripture, and this perversion "occasioned those *Fathers* who opposed those heresies, so diverse from one another, to interpret these words diversly, according to the heresie they opposed" (3:116). Donne then proceeds to discuss each of these Fathers' interpretations, weighing the opinions of Jerome, Aquinas, Peter Lombard, and Augustine, among others, as to what kind of bodies shall arise on the last day.

The opinion most compatible with Donne's own belongs to Tertullian, the early third-century church father whom Donne quotes with great regularity throughout his sermons, and especially in his sermons on the resurrection. According to Tertullian, 1 Cor. 15:50 refers not to the flesh and blood of the resurrected body, but to the flesh and blood of humans on earth. Paul did not mean to describe our final resurrection, Tertullian contends, but spoke instead of our spiritual or "first Resurrection, our resurrection in this life" (3:116). "Leaving then that acceptation of flesh and bloud," Donne declares, "which many thinke to be intended in this text, that is, *Animalis caro*, Flesh and bloud that must be maintained by eating, and drinking, and preserved by propagation and generation," that flesh, he admits, "cannot inherit heaven." But Paul says nothing to contradict the resurrection of our flesh cleansed of its corruptions, and yet our "true, and reall body" all the same (3:118). "There is one flesh of *Job*, another of *Saint Paul*," Donne concludes, in a sweeping reconciliation of the two texts, "And *Jobs* flesh can see God, and *Pauls* cannot; because the flesh that *Job* speaks of hath overcome the destruction of skin and body by wormes in the grave, and so is mellowed and prepared for the sight of God in heaven; and *Pauls* flesh is overcome by the world. . . . And therefore, that as our texts answer one another, so your resurrections may answer one another too" (3:132–33).

III. Body and Soul

Why did it matter so much to Donne that his resurrected flesh would be identical to its earthly counterpart? The answer has little to do with the theological reassurances he offers to support the idea of bodily resurrection—that God loves human bodies, or that humans will enjoy a proximity to Christ which even the angels are not granted. The answer is more personal in nature: it comes from his desire for absolute continuity between his earthly and his heavenly self. Donne worries about how he will remain in his afterlife the person that he currently is. He worries that his soul will not locate all the parts of his flesh at the last day, and that he will end up incomplete. He worries that the mere substitution of someone else's knee bone or joint will undo the integrity of self that he treasures. He worries that his "I" will no longer be his "I" unless he keeps his spiritual and material parts together. The point is not, in other words, simply to be embodied, but to be embodied as John Donne.

We might speculate that Donne's desire to be identically in heaven as he is on earth was driven by his desire to rejoin his wife, Anne, who died in childbirth in 1617, and to whom Donne seems to have remained passionately devoted.[36] But more important than the longing to be reunited with Anne is his longing to be reunited after death as a self. Donne was haunted throughout his life by feelings of the awkward dissociation between his body and soul: the tensions that arose between their respective needs; their irreconcilable states of health or illness; the occasional discrepancies between their objects of desire. At the same time, however, he was fully convinced of his body and soul's mutual dependence, and strove to create as harmonious and intimate a relationship between the two as possible. Donne was not what philosophers call a hylomorphist—someone who adheres to Aristotle's idea that bodies and souls cannot be severed from one another any more than the form of a sculpture can be separated from its bronze or an impression can be separated from its wax. He was a dualist, but he was a dualist who rejected the hierarchy of the soul over the body, a dualist who longed above all for the union, not the separation, of his two parts. Although he perhaps never fully satisfied his desire to know what constitutes, as he puts it in "The Extasie," the "subtile knot that makes us man," he expended terrific imaginative energy in attempting to understand that knot. And if on earth he could not experience what it might be for body and soul to be perfectly joined, he held out the hope for such a marriage in heaven.

The fullest expression of Donne's desire that his heavenly life might realize the seamless union between body and soul that eludes him in his mortal life comes toward the end of the sermon on Job 19:26. Donne interrupts one of his most gruesome descriptions of the putrefied body and the miracle of resurrection to remark aloud on his own current state of distraction. "I am here now preaching upon this text," he announces, "and I am at home in my

Library considering whether *S. Gregory* or *S. Hierome*, have said best of this text, before. I am here speaking to you, and yet I consider by the way, in the same instant, what it is likely you will say to one another, when I have done" (3:109–10). He follows this confession by turning the tables on his listeners. "You are not all here neither," he exclaims,

> You are here now, hearing me, and yet you are thinking that you have heard a better Sermon somewhere else, of this text before; you are here, and yet you think you could have heard some other doctrine of downright *Predestination*, and *Reprobation* roundly delivered somewhere else with more edification to you; you are here, and you remember your selves that now yee think of it, this had been the fittest time, now, when every body else is at Church, to have made such and such a private visit; and because you would bee there, you are there. (3:110)

The point of this exercise, it becomes clear, is not to condemn either himself or his congregation, nor is it strictly to demand a concentration of the mind that has so far escaped both parties (although no doubt this startling interruption went some way toward achieving this). What Donne means to communicate is that the difficulties in preventing the mind from wandering—from reviewing the day's events, from recalling errands that have not been run or secret meetings that could have been had, from wishing above all to be elsewhere—are shared by minister and congregation alike. What Donne wants to convey is that it is not until we are resurrected that we shall really experience what it feels like to be perfectly ourselves. "I cannot say," he concludes, "you cannot say so perfectly, so entirely now, as at the Resurrection, *Ego*, I am here; I, body and soul" (3:110). Donne's deepest fantasy about being in heaven is not only to sit beside Christ or to see his God. His deepest fantasy is also to be fully present in both parts of the self.

This fantasy of being fully present is not limited to Donne's posthumous existence—it pervades his mortal life as well. What gives his poetry and prose its tremendous vitality derives to no small degree from his desire to seize this moment and not the next, to isolate and then luxuriate in a particular instance in time, to be all there in body and soul. Hence in the *Songs and Sonnets*, he fervently if futilely tries to make time stand still; in the *Holy Sonnets*, he positions himself again and again on the brink of this world and the next; in the *Devotions*, he declares in his very first sentence, "this minute I was well, and am ill, this minute" (7). But the closest earthly equivalent to the presence he longs for in his resurrected self may come when he is engaged in the act of writing. Compared to some of his roughly

contemporary poets—Jonson, Herbert, Milton—Donne seems to be indifferent to poetry as a vocation: he more or less abandons the medium of verse
once he enters the church; he never publishes his collected poems; and he
never presents himself in either private or public as a dedicated poet.[37] But
these facts do not answer the underlying question of why Donne wrote with
such fervor throughout his career.

Toward the end of his life, Donne confesses to a friend that he continues to suffer even in old age from what he describes as "this intemperance
of scribling."[38] Whatever his circumstances, Donne never stopped writing.
Neither during his own illnesses, when he describes the physical pain of
putting pen to paper but writes all the same, nor during the illnesses of his
loved ones, when he sneaks away, for example, from his wife's bedside to
compose a quick letter to a friend. Neither when he knows that what he is
writing might dissuade those who need convincing that he has embraced
his new vocation, nor when he knows that what he is writing might jeop-
ardize his relationship to a patron. Neither when he imagines that he is on
his deathbed and wants to chronicle the process of dying, nor when he is in
fact on his deathbed and wants to compose a sermon of valediction to the
world. Donne never seems to have felt more alive than when he was either
putting his thoughts on paper or speaking them aloud from the pulpit. And
this feeling of heightened aliveness is the closest he comes to tasting the
fruits of what he calls "inanimation"—a neologism that emphasizes the act
of putting the spirit *in* the body. Writing is Donne's experience of making
the word flesh.

CHAPTER ONE

Letters

With a characteristic mixture of exuberance and idiosyncrasy, Donne begins a verse epistle to his friend Sir Henry Wotton: "Sir, more then kisses, letters mingle Soules" (1). In making so extravagant a claim for the power of letters, he draws upon the ancient understanding that the soul resides in the breath, so that a kiss between two people would naturally involve an exchange of the two parties' souls. This image of kissing as a transference of souls can be traced back to an ancient Greek fragment: "Kissing Kate / At the gate / Of my lips my soul hovers / While the poor thing endeavours / To Kate / to migrate." Petronius similarly describes an embrace in the *Satyricon:* "We clung, we glowed, losing ourselves in bliss / And interchanged our souls in every kiss." And, among other classical examples, Achilles Tatius, the late second-century AD author of a Greek romance, writes that "When lovers' lips meet and mingle together, they send down a stream of bliss beneath the breast and draw up the soul to meet the kisses."[1] In the last decades of the sixteenth century, Christopher Marlowe revived this ancient idea with Faustus's desperate plea to Helen: "Sweet Helen, make me immortal with a kiss. / Her lips suck forth my soul!"[2]

When Donne wrote his epistle to Wotton—probably in 1597 or 1598—he depended upon his friend's familiarity with the conceit in order to do something unprecedented to it: he replaces the embodied kiss with the disembodied letter as the site for mixing souls.[3] In doing so, he at once playfully overturns centuries of received wisdom, and raises a potentially serious question about the nature of letters. How could a letter, so physically detached from the breath of both writer and reader, perform the kind of intimate exchange to which the kiss so naturally lays claim? What do letters have to do with souls?

A preliminary answer to these questions comes in the second line of the epistle: "Sir, more then kisses, letters mingle soules / For thus friends absent speake." For Donne, the letter was not primarily a means of exchanging information, nor was it a forum for philosophical contemplation. Instead, it was an alternative to physical intimacy. In an epistle to Goodyer, Donne explains his persistence in writing so regularly.[4] "If you were here," he begins, "you would not think me importune, if I bid you good morrow every day; and such a patience will excuse my often Letters. No other kinde of conveyance is better for knowledge, or love." "What treasures of Morall knowledge," he continues, "are in *Senecaes* Letters to onely one *Lucilius?* And what of Naturall in *Plinies* . . . how much of the storie of the time, is in *Ciceroes* Letters?" (105). However much Donne admires these classical authors for their delivery of knowledge, his own epistles belong in the second category. "It is the other capacity which must make mine acceptable," he affirms, "that they are also the best conveyers of love."[5]

"I send not my Letters, as tribute, nor interest, not recompense, nor for commerce," Donne continues his letter to Goodyer, "for my Letters are either above or under all such offices; yet I write very affectionately, and I chide and accuse my self of diminishing that affection which sends them, when I ask my self why: onely I am sure that I desire that you might have in your hands Letters of mine of all kindes, as conveyances and deliverers of me to you" (109). There is no ulterior motive—no bid for social or economic advancement, no hope for reward or compensation—behind his regular writing. Even the act of reflecting upon why he writes letters threatens to diminish the "affection which sends them." He wants to write letters of all kinds so that his friend might possess as much of him as possible: the letter is quite simply a "deliver[y] of me to you."

Why did Donne's craving for intimacy take the form of a longing to write and receive letters? There are certainly biographical explanations available: he seems to have written most frequently and passionately during his years of social exile with his wife and growing family in their small house in Mitcham, which he refers to as a "dungeon,"[6] and where he certainly lacked the social stimulation he had grown accustomed to during his time as secretary to the Lord Keeper, Sir Thomas Egerton. But he continued to write personal letters throughout his career, and seemed equally committed to their importance long after his difficult isolation, not to mention his lack of professional advancement, was far behind him. The letter was not simply a useful, if lesser substitute for actual personal contact, nor was it primarily a means of generating social connections that were otherwise outside his reach. Donne wrote to Goodyer, for example, even when they seem to have been in close proximity to one another, and continued to write to him long after his friend's career had all but failed.

Donne never published his letters, nor with a handful of exceptions did he keep copies of the letters that he sent. (A collection of 129 letters, compiled from friends and acquaintances by Donne's son, John Donne Jr., was published twenty years after Donne's death with the title *Letters to Severall Persons of Honour*; awaiting the publication of a modern, scholarly edition, this 1651 volume remains the most authoritative and complete version of these texts.)[7] Unlike his poetry, however, which he also never published and toward which he felt great ambivalence, Donne expressed nothing but pleasure in writing letters. This pleasure was not superficial, nor can it be separated from the satisfactions he most longed for throughout his adult life. For letters seemed to Donne to offer a series of tantalizing possibilities, at once physical and metaphysical, which otherwise seemed to elude him. In letters, he felt he could overcome the problems of separation and absence that haunt him throughout his life. In letters, he felt that he could convey aspects of his body and soul to friends without needing to be physically present. In letters, he felt he could create physical and spiritual modes of intimacy that would endure beyond the immediate moment. In letters, he felt that he could "inanimate" dead matter—making the corpse of the paper come alive through the sheer act of writing.

I

One of the most striking and underappreciated features of Donne's letters is that they contain an extensive theory of letter writing. This theory is informed by, but hardly dependent upon, the epistolary treatises circulating at the time. To understand Donne's epistolary practice, it is useful to situate his letters in the larger context of early modern treatises on the subject. There were two great humanist texts on letters: Erasmus's 1521 *De conscribendis epistolis*, and Juan Luis Vives's 1534 work of the same title. Each of these texts sought to recover the genre of personal letters written by the ancients, overturning the medieval practice of a style of writing known as the *ars dictaminis*, which was originally designed for chancery officials and employed a highly formal and artificial mode of address.[8] Following Petrarch's discovery of Cicero's frank and intimate letters to Atticus in 1345, Renaissance humanists began to write and publish similar volumes of their own correspondences. By the time Donne would have picked up pen and ink, personal letter writing had achieved a real vogue in England, and epistolary guides began to flourish as they had several decades earlier on the continent.

The first English manual of letters, *The Enimie of Idlenesse,* was written by William Fulwood, and published in 1568. Fulwood's treatise, which was itself largely a translation from a French treatise, *Le stile et maniere de composer, dicter, & escrire toutes sortes d'epistres,* begins its instructions on "how to indite Epistles and Letters of all sortes" with some dedicatory verses defining the letter:

> By which most needful thing we may
> communicate our heart
> Unto our friend, though distance far
> have us remov'd apart.
> By letter we may absence make,
> even presence selfe to be,
> And talke with him, as face to face,
> together we did see.[9]

Behind Fulwood's clunky ballad meter lie two of the fundamental principles that shaped both the classical and humanist art of writing letters. First, echoing the principle that can be traced back to the classical dramatist Sextus Turpilius, who defined letters as "the one thing which makes the absent present," Fulwood declares that letters "may absence make / even presence selfe to be."[10] (Ben Jonson repeats this idea in *Timber, or Discoveries,* where he quotes Justus Lipsius's definition of the letter in his 1591 treatise, *Epistolica Instituto,* as "a message of the mind [*animi nuntium*] to someone who is absent.")[11] Second, Fulwood suggests that letters should simulate real conversation to make one feel "as [if] face to face" with one's friends.

The idea that letters resemble a spoken conversation has many antecedents in classical literature, but perhaps its most famous articulation comes from Seneca's Epistle 75 to Lucilius. "You have been complaining," Seneca writes, "that my letters to you are rather carelessly written. Now who talks carefully unless he also desires to talk affectedly? I prefer that my letters should be just what my conversation would be if you and I were sitting in one another's company or taking walks together—spontaneous and easy."[12] Letters should not, he continues, be "strained or artificial"—they should reproduce as naturally as possible the dialogue between two friends. This prescription for a natural, conversational style was wholeheartedly embraced by sixteenth-century humanists. Erasmus declares that the "wording of a letter should resemble a conversation between friends," and Vives similarly describes the letter as a "conversation . . . invented to convey the mental concepts and thoughts of one person to another as a faithful intermediary."[13] In both of these instances, writing serves as a substitute for speaking. As Vives explains, the primary function of letters should be "to reproduce as closely as possible the tone of conversation and familiar speech" (97).

Classical and humanist authors do not imagine that letters transmit only conversations, however. In transmitting conversation, they also transmit the writer's spirit or essence. In his dedicatory epistle to Señor Idiaquez, the secretary of Charles V, Vives approvingly quotes a letter of Saint Ambrose to Sabinus in which the fourth-century bishop of Milan declares: "The purpose of the letter is that though physically separated we may be united in spirit. In a letter the image of the living presence emits its glow between persons distant from one another."[14] This language of personal glow—the Latin original uses the verb *refulgere* (to shine or glisten)—corresponds to what Seneca says in Epistle 40 to Lucilius, in which he declares his preference for a letter from his friend over his painted portrait. "I thank you for writing to me so often," he begins, "for you are revealing your real self to me in the only way you can. I never receive a letter from you without being in your company forthwith. If the pictures of our absent friends are pleasing to us, though they only refresh the memory and lighten our longing by a solace that is unreal and unsubstantial, how much more pleasant is a letter, which brings us real traces, real evidence of an absent friend!"[15] Unlike the painting, whose solace is "unreal and unsubstantial," the letter carries "real traces, real evidence of an absent friend [*vera amici absentis vestigia, vera notas*]." This emphasis on the "realness" of the letter versus that of the painting is somewhat counterintuitive: surely the two-dimensional representation of the portrait conveys the person's likeness in a manner that the mere words of the letter cannot. But what Seneca longs for is not an external resemblance but an internal and intimate recognition, a recognition that is best achieved through the spirit of the words, not the expression of the face.

Because the emphasis here and elsewhere falls on delivering spirit rather than matter, it is not surprising that neither ancient nor early modern accounts of letter writing seems preoccupied with the actual content of the epistle. The notion that a letter must contain important "news" lies outside of these traditions, which stress instead the value of spontaneous, unstudied expression. Cicero urges Atticus to write to him often—"If you lack a topic," he adds, "just put down whatever comes into your head."[16] On a later occasion, he confesses that he himself has "nothing to write about, having heard no news and having replied to all your letters yesterday." Nonetheless, he has begun yet another letter, "just in order as it were to talk to you, which is my only relief" (53).

Fulwood's *Enimie of Idlenesse* considers letters initiated by the desire to write, without any news, as a legitimate category in itself. Among his specific sections on letters of different kinds—"How to write when one friend comforteth another in an injurie received," "How to write of some small affaires, businesse or newes," and so forth—he includes, "How to visit our Frend with Letters, not having any great matter to write."[17] "Often times it chaunceth," he begins, "that we have no matter to write to our frend, & yet we would gladly visit him with our Letters." He then provides an example of such a letter, which declares at its onset that the "great love equall betwixt us will not suffer me to lette passe any messanger that I know goeth towards you, without sending you Letters by him, for I beleve verily that you have as great joy to rede my Letters, as I have to reade yours" (73). To have nothing to say ("no matter") and yet to desire to write all the same—this is the urge that letters can satisfy.

"This conversation with you has been very pleasant," Petrarch concludes a letter to his Flemish friend Ludwig van Kempen, whom he addresses as "Socrates," "it has brought back your face across lands and seas; it has kept you beside me since morning, when I picked up my pen, until now, when evening is falling."[18] For Petrarch, the pleasure of writing is not to convey his own presence to his friend, but to feel his friend's presence—to transport his "face across lands and seas"—while he addresses him in a letter. So intense is the experience of writing to a friend that he claims it can at least temporarily erase their distance altogether. "While I have been talking with you," he exclaims to Giovannia Colonna di San Vito, "I forgot that I was writing a letter" (67). The notion that to forget one's medium is itself the medium's highest praise points to one of the deepest paradoxes about the genre of letters. Petrarch enjoys writing letters in part because it carries him to another place, and sometimes even to another time. Writing letters allows him to escape from his immediate physical circumstances, enabling him to enjoy the intimacy of his friend without leaving his own chambers.

II

"This writing of letters," Donne writes to Goodyer, "when it is with any seriousness, is a kind of extasie, and a departure and secession and suspension of the soul, which doth then communicate it self to two bodies."[19] With this declaration, he begins the long letter that I have referred to as the equivalent of his *De Anima*: Donne's letter about the soul is simultaneously a letter that shares his soul with his closest of friends. Readers of Donne's love poem "The Extasie" will know already that he was interested in ecstatic experience, and that counter to all earlier uses of the term, which assume a rapturous state of the individual's soul, he understood ecstasy as something shared between two people.[20] Donne was no doubt aware of the unorthodox nature of his understanding. He was familiar with the work of Plotinus, whom he quotes in his sermons, and whose description of the soul's ecstasy in the *Enneads* served as the *locus classicus* for medieval and early modern Platonists.[21] "Many times," Plotinus writes, "it has happened, lifted out of the body into myself; becoming external to all other things and self-centered; beholding a marvelous beauty; then, more than ever, assured of community with the loftiest order; enacting the noblest life, acquiring identity with the divine."[22] Plotinus's account of his soul's departure from the body and subsequent elevation depends upon his contact with the divine. Donne's understanding of ecstasy, by contrast, turns on the connection it creates between two lovers.

Donne's letter to Goodyer includes a variation on the erotic fantasy described in "The Extasie." In place of the mingling of the lovers' souls and their eventual physical consummation, we find the satisfaction of a disembodied exchange (Donne sought this satisfaction from his friend on a weekly basis—he wrote to Goodyer every Tuesday). The act of writing separates the soul from the body: the soul undergoes a "departure and secession and suspension" to infuse the letter with its spirit. The logistics of this procedure are far from clear—how, we might ask, does the single soul "communicate it self to two bodies" without either dividing or leaving one person behind? These complexities notwithstanding, it is clear that Donne wants to emphasize the unusual capacity of letters to share souls between friends without the constraints or demands of physical intimacy. A single letter enables a soul to be twice embodied, to pass as if in metempsychosis from one person to the next, but then miraculously to come back again.

At the same time that Donne relishes the prospect of sharing his soul with his friends, the experience does not always depend upon his friend's actual receipt of the letter. "If we write a friend," he tells his close friend, George Garrard, with whom he corresponded for over twenty years, "we must not call it a lost letter, though it never finde him to whom it was addressed: for we owe ourselves that office, to be mindefull of our friends" (286).[23] Donne's language echoes Petrarch's description of experiencing his friend's presence simply through writing to him. Regardless of the letter's delivery, the act of writing performs the "mindefulness" so crucial to the "office" or duty of friendship. In the letter about the soul that compares letter writing to an ecstatic rapture, he confides that he does not even always send the letters he has composed:

> And as I would every day provide for my souls last convoy, though I know
> not when I shall die, and perchance I shall never die; so for these extasies
> in letters, I oftentimes deliver my self over in writing when I know not
> when those letters shall be sent to you, and many times they never are,
> for I have a little satisfaction in seeing a letter written to you upon my
> table, though I meet no opportunity of sending it. (11)

The pleasure Donne takes in preparing the letter, like the pleasure he takes in preparing the soul for death, depends in part upon the fantasy of a potentially endless deferral. Barring the possibility of his being alive on the last day (a possibility that must lie behind his musing, "perchance I shall never die") the reality of his mortality was not one that he could escape. But he clearly relishes all opportunities to rehearse his death—we will see this in both his secular poems and in his religious writings—and he finds a similar satisfaction in releasing but not parting with his soul in letters. The unsent letters upon his table not only remind him repeatedly of his beloved friend. They also hold out the alluring promise of future exchanges that may or may not be realized.

Donne's career was marked by a series of dramatic changes—most spectacularly from Catholicism to Protestantism and from courtier to priest—but his commitment to friendship remained a constant throughout his life. He refers to friendship as its own religion, whose central rite was the exchange of letters. "Writing," he explains in another letter to Goodyer,

> is a sacrifice, which though friends need not, friendship doth; which hath
> in it so much divinity, that as we must be ever equally disposed inwardly
> so to doe or suffer for it, so we must sepose some certain times for the
> outward service thereof, though it be but formall and testimoniall: that
> time to me towards you is Tuesday, and my Temple, the Rose in Smith-
> field. (116)

Like a purified animal on a classical or biblical altar, the letter becomes the sacrifice offered at the temple of friendship (Donne jokingly assigns the temple of friendship to the Rose Tavern, from whence he often sends his letters—composed with liturgical regularity on Tuesdays—with the so-called Smithfield carrier).[24] In a more distinctly New Testament idiom, he elsewhere describes his letters as "friendships sacraments," and hastens to add that like sacraments, "wee should be in charyty to receave [them] at all tymes."[25]

What does it mean that we should willingly receive our letters, "like sacraments," whenever they should come our way? He explains to Goodyer on another occasion his indifference to the actual dating of the letters that he receives. "In letters that I received from Sir H. *Wotton* yesterday from *Amyens*, I had one of the 8 of *March* from you, and with it one from Mrs. *Danterey*, of the 28th of *January*; which is a strange disproportion." But, he hastens to add, "if our Letters come not in due order, and so make not a certain and concurrent chain, yet if they come as Atomes, and so meet at last, by any crooked, and casuall application, they make up, and they nourish bodies of friendship."[26] Donne was familiar with the central tenets of Epicurean atomism, as evinced by his comments about Hill's 1601 book on the subject, and his brief reflections on Epicurus in the sermons.[27] Although these responses to Epicureanism are entirely negative in character, he adapts the idea of matter as a random and accidental organization of atoms to suit his purposes in the letter to Goodyer. There need be no divine plan, he suggests, behind the sequence of letters: just as a "casuall" clustering of atoms forms a human being, so letters received out of all order nonetheless constitute "bodies of friendship."

It should come as no surprise that Donne does not bother to date the vast majority of his own letters. This has been endlessly frustrating to his biographers, and has certainly contributed to the difficulty of publishing a modern edition of his letters. But it is important to recognize that it does not reflect a failure or oversight on Donne's part. For he deliberately chooses not to date his own letters, as he explains to Lady Bedford. "It makes no difference," he writes, "that this came [to you] not the same day, nor bears the same date" as the letter from her brother, the second Lord Harrington: "For though in inheritances and worldly possessions we consider the dates of Evidences, yet in Letters, by which we deliver over our affections, and assurances of friendship, and the best faculties of our souls, times and daies cannot have interest, nor be considerable, because that which passes by them, is eternall, and out of the measure of time" (23). Whereas the date of a last will and testament may determine whether or not one inherits property, the inheritance of "affections" does not depend upon legal niceties like the "measure of time." Because letters deliver "the best faculties of our soul," their gifts of inheritance are "eternall."

In a letter anonymously addressed "to your selfe," Donne similarly writes that his correspondent was "subtile in the disguise" of the letter that he had sent: "for you shut up your letter, thus, *Lond.* 22, in our stile, but

I am not so good a Cabalist, as to finde in what moneth it was written."[28]
Yet, he continues, even if he has already learned elsewhere the news that
the letter contains, its datedness is of no concern to him. "In the offices of
so spirituall a thing as friendship," he declares, "so momentary a thing as
time, must have no consideration. I keep [your letter] therefore to read every
day, as newly written, to which vexation it must be subject, till you relieve
it with an other" (246).

What is it about friendship that Donne values so deeply? In an epistle
addressed "To all my friends: Sir H. Goodere"—as if Goodyer either incorporated all of his friends in his single body, or were his only friend—he
discusses the human need for companionship. "I think sometimes that
the having a family should remove me farre from the curse of *Vae soli*
[Alas, alone]," he confides. "But in so strict obligation of Parent, or Husband, or Master, (and perchance it is so in the last degree of friendship)
where all are made one, I am not the lesse alone, for being in the midst of
them" (44–45).

Donne expresses the sentiment of feeling alone when he is among his
own family on several occasions, and this sentiment helps to explain the persistence with which he pursued his personal correspondences even at the
busiest moments of domestic life. In another letter to Goodyer, he explains
the circumstances of his writing:

> Sir, I write not to you out of my poor Library, where to cast mine eye
> upon good Authors kindles or refreshes sometimes meditations not unfit
> to communicate to near friends; nor from the high way, where I am con-
> tracted, and inverted into my self; which are my two ordinary forges of
> Letters to you. But I write from the fire side in my Parler, and in the noise
> of three gamesome children; and by the side of her, whom because I have
> transplanted into a wretched fortune, I must labour to disguise that from
> her by all such honest devices, as giving her my company, and discourse,
> therefore I steal from her, all the time which I give this Letter. (137–38)

This is one of the loveliest portraits we have of Donne's life at home: the
"gamesome children" frolicking in the parlor while husband and wife con-
verse before the fire evoke the pleasures of family, pleasures we too seldom
remember when pondering his difficult circumstances during the years at
Mitcham. The sweetness of this image, however, is complicated by Donne's
own admission that he has done some grievous harm to his young wife,
whom he has "transplanted into a wretched fortune." His guilty sense of obligation to Anne, and not his genuine desire to be in her company, prevents

him from withdrawing to his library, where he could "kindle or refresh" those thoughts that he longs to share with his friend.

In the letter addressed "To all my friends: Sir H. Goodere," the solution to the loneliness that Donne describes lies in what he calls *oleum laetitiae*, the oil of gladness. "Therefore this *oleum laetitiae*," he writes, "this balme of our lives, this alacrity which dignifies even our service to God, this gallant enemy of dejection and sadnesse . . . must be sought and preserved diligently" (45). The phrase *"oleum laetitiae"* can be traced to the Vulgate translation of Psalm 45:7, where the Psalmist declares, "Dilexisti iustitiam, et odisti iniquitatem / Propterea unxit te Deus, Deus tuus, Oleo laetitiae, prae consortibus tuis" (Thou lovest righteousness, and hatest wickedness: therefore God, thy God, hath anointed thee with the oil of gladness above thy fellows). What the Psalm regards as a divine reward for loving righteousness that elevates the worshiper "above thy fellows" becomes in Donne's hands a benefit earned through friendship.

The source of our oil of gladness—which he repeatedly glosses as "alacrity"—emerges from having friends. "This alacrity," Donne insists, "is not had by a general charity and equanimity to all mankinde, for that is to seek fruit in a wildernesse: nor from a singular friend, for that is to fetch it out of your own pocket: but the various and abundant grace of it, is good company" (47). The letter's address—"To all my friends: Sir H. Goodere"—may mean, as one early twentieth-century editor proposes, that the letter was intended as a "sort of circular letter" to all of Donne's friends at home while he traveled on the continent.[29] It may also mean, however, that Goodyer stands in for all of the "good company" that he so desperately needs—the multiple rather than "singular" friends whom he seeks to constitute his life force.

If friendship rather than family life provides the "alacrity" so crucial to Donne's well-being, letters are his central means of sustaining this source of vitality. In this regard, Donne might be seen as upholding the classical understanding of letters as a substitute for the real desideratum: human conversation. At the beginning of the letter "To all my friends," for example, he tells Goodyer that he is not weary of writing, for it is the "coarse but durable garment of my love," but that he is "weary of wanting you" (42). The letter serves as a "coarse" but enduring substitute for Goodyer's personal presence, and hence seems to lie on the outside of his love—it is a garment designed to preserve the relationship, but does not constitute the relationship itself. He says something similar in another letter to Goodyer, which opens with a discussion of the nature of friendship: "Sir, In the History or style of friendship, which is best written both in deeds and words, a Letter which is of a mixed nature, and hath something of both, is a mixed Parenthesis: It may be left out, yet it contributes, though not to the being, yet to the verdure, and freshnesse thereof" (114). The ostensible purpose of this passage is to contain—literally, to put in parentheses—the role that letters play in creating or sustaining friendships. At the same time that he concedes that letters are not essential, however (in theological terms they would be categorized as *adiaphora* or "things indifferent"), he seems tentative about this assertion, an impression confirmed by the double "*yets.*" Far from minimizing the role of letters, Donne concludes with one of his strongest affirmations of their importance. Letters, he declares, do nothing less than keep friendship alive—they supply its healthy greenness.

Examples in which Donne, however reluctantly, qualifies the importance of letters are greatly overshadowed by occasions in which he discusses the advantages of written exchanges over live conversations. One such advantage lies in the status of letters as unalterable records of the writer's voice. Hence he explains to Goodyer, letters are not the equivalent of everyday speech, but "have truly the same office, as oaths." The comparison he draws next is an odd one: he compares lying in letters to authorizing one's servants to lie on one's behalf. Just as he never authorizes his servants to lie on his behalf, so, he declares, he allows his letters

> much lesse that civill dishonest[y], both because they go from me more considerately, and because they are permanent; for in them I may speak to you in your chamber a year hence before I know not whom, and not hear my self. They shall therefore ever keep the sincerity and intemeratenesse of the fountain, whence they are derived. (114–15)

The connection between servants and letters lies in their status as forms of deputized speech: both letters and servants are at one remove from the author of their respective words. But unlike servants, who might speak irresponsibly or recklessly before others on Donne's behalf, letters contain his "intemerate" or undefiled voice. They remain true to their source regardless of the time and place they are read; they are a "permanent" testimony to his affection. Comparing letters to leaves on a tree, he concludes that wherever the leaves may fall, "this much information is in [them], that they can tell what the tree is, and these can tell you I am a friend, and an honest man" (115).

If one advantage of letters over conversations is their capacity to record the writer's words in a permanent and irrefutable manner, another advantage lies in their ability to engage the reader repeatedly. In a letter to the Countess of Montgomery written during his years as a preacher, he responds to her request for a copy of a sermon she has recently heard him deliver: "Madam, Of my ability to doe your Ladiship service, any thing spoken may be an embleme good enough; for as a word vanisheth, so doth any power in me to serve you; things that are written are fitter testimonies, because they remain and are permanent" (24). Donne compares his inability to serve so lofty a lady with the inability of spoken words to endure beyond the present moment—like words that vanish in the air, his service has no lasting consequences. The same cannot be said, however, of his written texts, which offer a more durable form of service: "they remain and are permanent."

As the letter continues, this quality of permanence is qualified: it does not inhere in the text itself, but depends upon its reader. "I know what dead carkasses things written are," he declares, "in respect of things spoken." Having just said that letters are permanent compared to words spoken, what can Donne possibly mean by this reversal? He means that left alone, the sermon or letter is a "dead carkass," equivalent to the body after the departure of the soul in death. But when texts are heard or read, "that soul that inanimates them, never departs from them": "The Spirit of God that dictates them in the speaker or writer, and is present in his tongue or hand, meets himself again (as we meet ourselves in a glass) in the eies and hearts of the hearers and readers" (25). What keeps the written text alive depends on a series of "inanimations." In the case of the sermon, God infuses his spirit into the preacher, who in turn inanimates his sermon; the sermon is then re-inanimated by its "hearers and readers." (In the case of letters, the role of divine inspiration would not ordinarily pertain, but the subsequent stages of both the writer's and the reader's inanimation apply.) Through her reading of the sermon, Lady Montgomery transforms the corpse into a living body in possession of a soul.

Petrarch remarks that in writing letters, the writer faces a double task: "to envisage the person he is writing to, and then the state of mind in which the recipient will read what he proposes to write" (20). Donne shares this concern with anticipating the letter's reception, but he raises the stakes considerably by imagining that the reader herself will supply at least part of the letter's content. He explains, for example, to Bridget White—a young gentlewoman twenty years his junior whom he seems to have met in 1610 and to whom he wrote a flurry of letters in the months after making her acquaintance—that his letter comes to her "like a bashfull servant, who, though he have an extreme desire to put himself in your presence, yet hath not much to say when he is come."[30] "Yet," he continues, the letter has "as much to say as you can think: because what degrees soever of honour, respect, and devotion you can imagine or believe to be in any, this letter tells you that all those are in me towards you. So that for this letter you are my Secretary" (6). The fantasy of the genteel Bridget White serving as Donne's secretary is filled with irony: unlike many of his wealthier contemporaries, he had no secretary, and wrote his letters in his own hand.[31] But what Donne means, of course, is not that Mistress White should actually transcribe his letter—this could be done by anyone, and involved manual, not spiritual labor. Instead, he wants a more serious engagement: he asks her to fill his letter with her own imagining of his "honour, respect, and devotion." Thus Donne becomes a reflection of Mistress White's ideal devotee, and the letter becomes his ultimate expression of praise. This is all envisioned, of course, almost without his having to say a word. The letter lacks the elaborate *complimenti* that we know Donne was capable of producing, and it remains for Mistress White to supply her own.

What, we might ask, is gained by this coy resistance to flattering this young lady with whom he was obviously quite taken? The most likely answer is that Donne wanted to create a particular form of intimacy between them, an intimacy that depended upon her complicity in authoring his praise. Mistress White is asked, in effect, to collude in Donne's adoration for her in a manner that Lord Kingsmill, whom she married later the same year, may have found somewhat discomfiting. A similar, if less flirtatious, request emerges at the end of the letter to Goodyer in which he compares letters to atoms that form bodies of friendship. This letter, which is uncharacteristically filled with news and gossip, comes to this abrupt conclusion:[32]

> Therefore give me leave to end this, in which if you did not finde the remembrance of my humblest services to my Lady *Bedford*, your love and faith ought to try all the experiments of pouders, and dryings, and waterings to discover some lines which appeared not; because it is impossible that a Letter should come from me, with such an ungrateful silence. (76–77)

Why could Donne not include a line or two of "remembrance" of his patroness at the end of this letter? The simple act of asking Goodyer to send his best wishes to Lady Bedford would certainly have taken less time and space if these were his concerns. But his aim here is clearly not to economize: he wants instead to test Goodyer's "faith and love." The idea that he might "discover some lines which appeared not" cleverly invokes the practice of invisible writing used by Catholic recusants. John Gerard, for example, explains in his *Autobiography of a Hunted Priest* that he prefers to write his secret messages in orange juice rather than lemon juice—writing in lemon juice may come out with both water and heat, he declares, but the writing disappears once it is dried; orange juice, by contrast, cannot be read with water, but once heat brings out its writing, it never evaporates again.[33] We do not have the original of this letter, so we cannot know if Donne actually experimented with lemons or oranges, but it seems fair to assume he did not. He does invoke, however, "the experiments of pouders, and dryings, and waterings" to suggest that the discovery of the letter's contents depends upon the active cooperation of a like-minded friend.

III

Letters for Donne are not only vehicles for conveying his soul. They are also vehicles for conveying his body. However unusual his depiction of the spiritual communication made possible by letters, perhaps his greatest innovation was his idea that letters reproduced certain aspects of the relationship between body and soul. Donne regarded the ideal letter, in short, as a form of animated matter. But what was the "matter" of Donne's letters? First and foremost, "matter" refers to the letter's content—what we would normally call its "news."[34] Earlier we saw that he dismissed the notion that his letters should be comparable to Pliny's or Cicero's in delivering knowledge. Indeed, he described his letters in a manner compatible with Fulwood's category of those letters written when "we have have no matter to write to our frend, & yet would gladly visit him."[35] At other times, however, Donne insists that his letters must possess some content or they risk not being letters at all. "You know that for aire we are sure we apprehend and enjoy it," he writes to Wotton, "but when this aire is rarified into fire, we begin to dispute whether it be an element, or no." The excessive "rarification" of letters into spirit without matter has the same effect: "When Letters have a convenient handsome body of news, they are Letters; but when they are spun out of nothing, they are nothing, or but apparitions, and ghosts, with such hollow sounds, as he that hears them, knows not what they said" (120–21). Letters that are "spun out of nothing" are mere shadows of what they ought to be: they are ghostly specters and not embodied souls. Far from conveying the author's own voice, the sounds of these letters are hollow.

The letter to Wotton continues by comparing the relationship between letters and news to that between spiritual love and the body. Just as love, he writes, "though it be directed upon the minde, doth inhere in the body, and find piety entertainment there," so the spirit of a letter requires matter for its realization.[36] This is a version of the sentiment he expresses in his lyric, "Aire and Angels":

But since my soule, whose child love is
Takes limmes of flesh, and else could nothing doe
      More subtile then the parent is
Love must not be, but take a body too. (7–10)

We need bodies in love, and news in letters, in order to substantiate our feelings—to make them, in the language of "Aire and Angels," less "subtile" (in the seventeenth century, "subtle" was regularly used to describe a substance of thin consistency). Letters, Donne argues, should be "seals and testimonies of mutuall affection," but the "materials and fuels" of such seals should be a "confident and mutual communicating of those things which we know" (121). The spiritual transmission of affection and love cannot occur without the ordinary stuff of letters—the so-called news of a letter, like the body in love, fulfills the spiritual ends that motivated the writer or lover in the first place. Hence the matter of the letter is the necessary embodiment of what is otherwise invisible.

"Matter" in Donne's letters does not only refer, however, to the letters' content. It also refers to their possession of his material body. Donne wants his letters both to perform the "mutual communicating" between souls that he described to Wotton, and to carry traces of his physical being. When he is ill, he not only writes about his poor health, but he expects that the form of his writing itself will embody his illness. A letter to Goodyer, for example, begins with the news that "for more than twenty days, I have been travelled [travailed] with a pain, in my right wrist, so like the Gout, as makes me unable to write." To this he adds: "the writing of this Letter will implore a commentary for that, that I cannot write legibly" (154).

Again and again, Donne draws attention to his "hand"—both his handwriting as well as his actual hand doing the writing—to insist upon the embodied nature of his letter. In letters to his close friends, he frequently refers to the "raggedness" of his writing, and excuses it as acceptable among intimates familiar with one another's "hand." A rushed letter to Wotton, for example, concludes: "Sir, you are used to my hand, and I think have leisure to spend some time in picking out sense, in ragges; else I had written less, and in longer time" (136–37). In letters to people whom he does not know well, he draws attention to the fact that he—not a secretary—is doing the writing. What is otherwise a social disadvantage is reframed as a source of potential intimacy: the recipient of the letter is given a special access to him through an acquaintance with his hand. "I present to your Lordship here a hand," Donne begins a letter in 1619 to Sir Dudley Carleton, then ambassador at The Hague, "which I thinke, you never saw, and a name, which

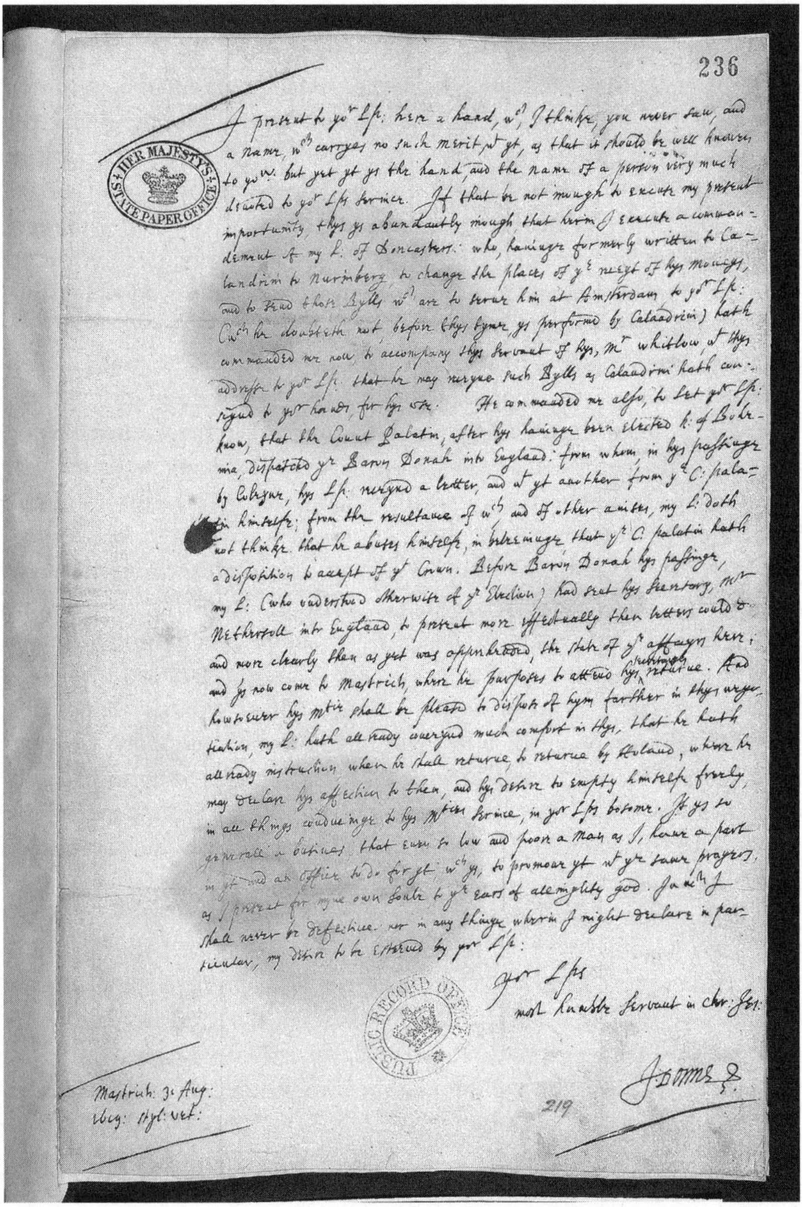

236

I present to yor Lp: here a hand, wch, I thinke, you never saw, and a name, wch carryes no such merit, as yt, as that it should be well knowne to yow. but yet yt ys the hand, and the name of a person very much devoted to yor Lps service. If that be not enough to excuse my present importunity, thys ys abundantly enough that herin I execute a commaundement of my L: of Doncaster: who, havinge formerly written to Calandrini to Nurimberg, to change the places of ye receyt of hys moneys, and to send those Bylls wch are to serve him at Amsterdam to yor Lp: (wch he doubteth not, before thys tyme ys performd by Calandrini) hath commanded me now, to accompany thys servant of hys, Mr Whitlow, wt thys addresse to yor Lp: that he may receyve such Bylls as Calandrini hath consignd to yor hands, for hys use. He commanded me also, to let yor Lp: know, that the Count Palatin, after hys havinge been elected K. of Bohemia, dispatched ye Baron Donah into England: from whom, in hys passinge by Colegne, hys Lp: receyvd a letter, and wt yt another from ye C: Palatin himselfe; from the resultance of wch and of other advises, my L: doth not thinke that he abuses himselfe, in beleevinge that ye C. Palatin hath a disposition to accept of ye Crown. Before Baron Donah hys passinge, my L: (who understood otherwise of ye Election) had sent hys Secretary, Mr Nethersole into England, to present more effectually then letters could, and more clearly then as yet was apprehended, the state of ye affayres here; and he ys now come to Mastrich, where he purposes to attend hys Maties returne. And howsoever hys Mtie shall be pleasd to dispose of hym farther in thys negotiation, my L: hath allready receyvd much comfort in thys, that he hath allready instruction, when he shall returne, to returne by Holland, where he may declare hys affection to them, and hys desire to empty himselfe freely in all things conducinge to hys Mties service, in yor Lps bosome. It ys so generall a business, that even so low and poore a man as I, have a part in yt, and an Office, to do for yt, wch ys, to promove yt wt ye same prayers as I present for myne own soule to ye ears of allmighty god. In wch I shall never be defective. nor in any thinge wherin I might declare in particular, my desire to be esteemed by yor Lp:

Yor Lps
most humble servant in Chr: Jes:

J. Donne

Mastrich: 31 Aug: 1619: Styl: vet:

219

Figure 1. Letter from Donne to Sir Dudley Carleton, August 31, 1619.

carryes no such merit in it, as that it should be well knowen to you" (figure 1).[37] Donne means, of course, to make his introduction to Carleton through the letter, and the "hand" serves as a synecdoche for his entire person. And yet, this letter—which survives in manuscript—also draws attention to the handiness, so to speak, of Donne's writing. It is written in perfectly straight lines of dark brown ink with characteristic flourishes across the top left and bottom right corners; it covers an entire piece of folio-size paper, with room at the end only for a signature; it includes a sizable ink splatter on the left-hand margin, a trace perhaps of Donne's having rested his hand while composing the lengthy epistle.

Letter writers commonly invoke the notion that the letter speaks in their voice or conveys the affections of their heart. But Donne attempts to literalize these conceits—he carries them to their limits. Before revealing a secret to Goodyer, he writes: "One thing more I must tell you; but so softly, that I am loath to hear my self: and so softly, that if that good Lady were in the room, with you and this Letter, she might not hear" (196). The repetition of "so softly" reinforces the sound of his voice rather than his writing: he wants Goodyer to feel as if he were standing beside him, whispering into his ear.

Donne claims on occasion not only to send his friend his love, but to include his actual heart. A letter to George Garrard's sister, Martha, ends with the remark: "since I cannot stay you here, I will come thither to you; which I do, by wrapping up in this paper, the heart of *Your most affection-ate servant J. Donne*" (41). Likewise, in an anonymous letter most likely addressed to Goodyer, he writes that "there is not a size of paper in the Palace, large enough to tell you how much I esteeme my selfe honoured in your remembrances; nor strong enough to wrap up a heart so ful of good affections towards you, as mine is."[38] Among the manuscript letters that survive, several consist of two sheets of paper—the first is the letter itself, the second wrapped the letter inside of it. This early modern envelope was folded identically to the letter, and includes on its outside the name and sometimes the address of the recipient.[39] When Donne describes "wrapping" his heart in his letter, it is tempting to think of the heart as the inner paper shielded by the skin of the second sheet.

IV

In addition to his prose letters, Donne also wrote letters in verse. Literary critics have largely focused on Donne's bids for patronage in these verse epistles, and the poems' concern with their own medium as a vehicle for exchanging bodies and souls has been surprisingly neglected. To the extent that the metaphysical concerns of the epistles have been addressed, they have for the most part been considered strategies for fulfilling the poems' deeper social purposes.[40] And, as is too often the case with Donne criticism, each category or genre is rigidly separated from one another, so that the similarities between his letters in verse and prose are almost entirely overlooked.[41] When we read the verse epistles in the context of their prose counterparts, however, strong continuities emerge. First, the circle of recipients is to a certain degree the same: Goodyer, Wotton, and the Countess of Bedford figure prominently in both groups, although there are more women among the addressees of the verse epistles. Second, both groups of letters dwell on the power of letters themselves as a constitutive force in friendship. Third, like the prose letters, the verse epistles are almost singularly preoccupied with the subject of body and soul and the relationship between the two.

Of the thirty-seven verse epistles that survive, twenty-two explicitly discuss the soul.[42] In certain cases, this discussion is limited to the soul alone; in others it includes the body as well. Some of these examples take the form of elaborate compliments: Donne praises Henry Wotton for having a soul like the purified spirit of a substance in an alchemical experiment; he flatters the sisters Lady Carey and Mrs. Essex Rich (daughters of Lord Rich and Penelope Devereux) that the "complexion[s]" of their souls are made up of pure "Vertue"; and he celebrates Lady Bedford for possessing a body made of either "better clay" or "Soules stuffe such as shall late decay, / Or such as needs small change at the last day."[43] (This last example, needless to say, is a bit double-edged: the reminder of the countess's eventual decay, notwithstanding the reassurances that it shall be "late" and slow, was probably not what she most hoped to hear).

More often, Donne invokes the soul not simply as a vehicle for delivering compliments, but to discuss one theory or another about its nature. In these letters, the discussion of the soul is neither central to, nor necessarily compatible with the purpose of the letter, and hence its inclusion is all the more surprising. Why, for example, in an epistle written to Sir Edward Herbert while he was fighting with the English army in the siege of Juliers, does Donne decide to mention the theory that "Soules (they say) by our first touch, take in / The poysonous tincture of Originall sinne" (19–20)? Similarly, why does he begin an epistle to the Countess of Huntingdon with the inauspicious suggestion that "Man to Gods image, Eve, to mans was made, / Nor finde wee that God breath'd a soule in her"? Surely the question of whether women had souls was not an obvious strategy to win the countess's favor—those readers who think these poems were written with the exclusive aims of flattery and self-advancement confront something of a challenge here. (Jonson, incidentally, strikes the more sympathetic note on the subject of women's souls in the *Masque of Beautie:* "Had those, that dwell in error foule / And hold that women have no soule / But seen these move; they would have, then, / Said *Women were the soules of men.*")[44] And why, moreover, does he rehearse the idea that "the noble Soule by age growes lustier, / Her appetite, and her digestion mend" in a verse letter to Goodyer that gently criticizes his friend for being "too indulgent" in his courtly pleasures?[45]

Donne's most extensive use of the verse letter to explore theories about the soul with seeming disregard to the occasion comes in an epistle to the Countess of Bedford. In this poem, which begins, "T'have written then, when you writ," Donne interrupts his extravagant praise of Lady Bedford's virtue—praise that he imagines is not to her liking—in order to take up a philosophical inquiry. "But since to you," he declares, "your praises discords bee, / Stoop, others ills to meditate with mee" (31–32). These "ills" involve the complexity of the soul's relationship to the flesh. Donne begins by lamenting that the soul ought to be guiding the movements and actions of the body, but has ceased to do so:

> As new Philosophy arrests the Sunne,
> And bids the passive earth about it runne,
> So wee have dull'd our minde, it hath no ends;
> Onely the bodie's busie, and pretends;
> As dead low earth ecclipses and controules
> The quick high Moone: so doth the body, Soules. (37–42)

These lines may seem to suggest that the body was culpable in its efforts to control the mind or soul, but in fact Donne makes clear that the body itself has little agency: the comparisons to "the passive earth" and the "dead low earth" make this powerlessness sufficiently clear.[46] (This letter was probably written three or so years before *The First Anniversarie,* and hence the famous description in that poem of "new philosophy" as responsible for the chaos in the world had already been rehearsed in this far less celebrated epistle.)

What Donne wants to convey is the damage inflicted on both parts of the self when the proper balance between them is not maintained. The soul, he contends, is just as responsible for the damage done to the body as the body is responsible for the corruption of the soul. Hence, on the one hand, he blames the body for contaminating the soul: "As men to'our prisons, new soules to us are sent, / Which learne vice there, and come in innocent" (59–60). On the other hand, he blames the soul for bringing sinfulness into the flesh. "What hate," he asks, "could hurt our bodies like our love? / Wee (but no forraigne tyrans could) remove / These not ingrav'd, but inborne dignities, / Caskets of soules; Temples, and Palaces" (53–56). Were we not to damage our own bodies, Donne declares, they would retain their "inborne dignities" and remain the glorious "caskets of soules" that they were designed to be.

Bodies and souls, Donne concludes to his genteel patroness, are finally not so different from one another as we might expect: "For, bodies shall from death redeemed bee, / Soules but preserv'd, not naturally free" (57–58). The idea that the soul was not naturally immortal was one that Donne generally embraced in his writings, as Helen Gardner rightly observed (although his position is not so absolute as she averred—in a 1622 sermon at St. Paul's, for example, he declares that the soul possesses "naturall immortality").[47] In the verse epistle to Lady Bedford, however, Donne adopts the idea of the soul's immortality through preservation not to affirm God's power as a creator, as he regularly does in his devotional prose. Instead, he adopts the belief that the soul was "but preserv'd, not naturally free" in order to refuse any privileging of the soul over the body in our posthumous fate. Whatever their earthly differences, he insists, both parts of the self depend upon God for their immortal life.

We will never know what Lady Bedford made of this letter, and whether she indeed preferred his metaphysical musings to his extravagant compliments. It is possible, of course, that she and Donne were engaged in an ongoing dialogue about the soul—of the seven surviving verse epistles to her, all but one include discussions of the soul, so this may well have been an interest that they shared. However, the frequency of references to the soul in the epistles as a whole suggests that he was not necessarily addressing his thoughts to the letter's addressee. It is much more likely that he expounded his different ideas about the soul without much thought for the letter's recipient. And his reasons for doing so, I would argue, lie in his deep association of letter writing with the exchange of souls. The subject of the soul, that is, seemed naturally to belong to the genre of letters.

As we see in the epistle to Lady Bedford, Donne was not only interested in souls. He was also interested in bodies. In his prose letters, we saw his repeated gestures of including his body inside the letter, of making the letter a conveyor of both his spiritual and physical self. In the verse epistles, he pursues a different capability of letters in relation to the body: he fantasizes that through both reading and writing letters, friends might be able to resurrect one another from the dead. In an epistolary sonnet written to Rowland Woodward, a friend Donne met as a student at Lincoln's Inn in the 1590s with whom he regularly exchanged verse letters,[48] he compares a poem he received from Woodward to a perfectly constructed body, "built of all th'elements as our bodyes are"—earth, fire, water, and air (line 2). The act of reading Woodward's poem has done nothing less, he claims, than bring him back from the dead. "Oh, I was dead," he concludes, "but since thy song new life did give, / I recreated, even by thy creature, live" (13–14).

The fantasy of being resurrected through the receipt of letters also explains a short epistle "To Mr. T.W.," whom Donne's editors have not positively identified, but is most likely Rowland's brother, Thomas Woodward. This poem begins by announcing what can only be described as a state of epistolary expectation:

> Pregnant again, with th'old twins Hope, and Feare,
> Oft have I askt for thee, both how and where
> Thou wert, and what my hopes of letters were;
>
> As in our streets sly beggers narrowly
> Watch motions of the givers hand and eye,
> And evermore conceive some hope thereby. (1–6)

Donne represents his condition of mingled hope and fear as a familiar one— he is "pregnant *again*" with his "*old* twins"—and his interest in T.W. seems equally divided between concern for his well-being and concern for whether he has written him letters. The ironic self-portrait as a "sly begger" who studies the "motions" of each passerby with keen anticipation suggests that letters are Donne's sustenance—they provide, like the beggar's coins, the means for him to survive. This suggestion becomes more explicit in the poem's next stanza:

> And now thine Almes is given, thy letter'is read
> The body risen againe, the which was dead,
> And thy poore starveling bountifully fed. (7–9)

The letter shifts quickly from serving merely as charitable "Almes" to effecting his resurrection. In writing, Donne claims, T.W. has done nothing short of returning him to life.

To receive letters is one source of rebirth; to compose them is another. I began by citing what Donne says to Wotton in the poem that begins, "Sir, more then kisses, letters mingle Soules." But in addition to mingling souls, letters also preserve the body:

Sir, more then kisses, letters mingle Soules;
For, thus friends absent speake. This ease controules
The tediousnesse of my life: But for these
I could ideate nothing, which could please,
But I should wither in one day, and passe
To'a bottle'of Hay, that am a locke of Grasse. (1–6)

Here Donne makes one of his strongest claims about the power of friendship,
and more specifically, about the power of friendship communicated through
letters: he claims that the letters of his friends enable him to "ideate." To
"ideate" is a neologism credited to Donne—in fact, the *Oxford English Dictionary* cites Donne's *Pseudo-Martyr* for the first two uses of this term, but
this verse epistle most likely preceded the 1610 prose work by at least a
decade. As I have already observed in the introduction, Donne very rarely
speaks of his own poetry making in anything but deprecating terms, but this
epistle to Wotton is an important exception. In these lines he connects the
writing of things that can please to his ability to stay alive—the difference
between ideating and not ideating is the difference between vital, green grass
and withered hay.

At moments like these, Donne understands his writing of letters as a
means to sustain his mortal life for as long as possible. But he also regards his
verse epistles as possessing the potential for a certain kind of afterlife. This
is not the same as his wishing, in a more traditional vein, that his name will
survive him through his poetry, bringing him fame long after he is deceased.
Instead, he imagines that his letters might somehow retain traces of his body
and soul after they have been separated by death. He gives full rein to this
fantasy in a verse epistle to Rowland Woodward, which begins:

If, as mine is, thy life a slumber be,
Seeme, when thou read'st these lines, to dreame of me,
Never did Morpheus nor his brother weare
Shapes soe like those Shapes, whom they would appeare,
As this my letter is like me, for it
Hath my name, words, hand, feet, heart, minde and wit;
It is my deed of gift of mee to thee,
It is my Will, my selfe the Legacie. (1–8)

Like Morpheus and his brother, who have the power to assume the shape of
men in dreams, Donne's letter has the power to simulate his self: it "hath

my name, words, hand, feet, heart, minde and wit."[49] The pentameter line of monosyllabic words moves from the conventional notion that poetry retains the author's "name" and "words" to the less conventional notion that it retains his or her physical and spiritual being. Of course, "hand" can refer simply to handwriting, and "feet" to the epistle's meter. But as the line proceeds to "heart, minde, and wit," with "heart" as the pendulum between the bodily and the spiritual parts, it becomes clearer that Donne means to conjure up his entire being—his actual hands and feet as well as his heart and mind. When he states to George Garrard that "our Letters are our selves," he means this to be taken as seriously as possible (240).

The most obvious advantage that Donne imagines in having letters replace his body is his belief that unlike his mortal self, his letters "remain and are permanent" (24). Given the nearly perfect condition of many of the surviving autograph letters, with their unfaded ink and smooth, untorn paper, we can credit Donne's perception with some truth. (When I hold the autograph letter that begins, "I present to your Lordship here a hand" at the National Archives in London, it is difficult not to feel the force of Donne's wish.) And yet, at the same time that he entertains the idea that his letters might retain his matter and spirit in a perfect union for all eternity, he also implicitly acknowledges the impossibility of this dream. The letters that survive in manuscript are vastly outnumbered by those letters that are lost. Donne himself took no steps to avoid this loss—as I have already observed, he neither collected his letters for publication nor made copies of them for himself.

Moreover, because Donne understood his letters as "mutual communicating" and depended upon his friends to "inanimate" and re-inanimate them, there was little chance of the letters' surviving in the fullest sense (and not becoming "dead carkasses") once his circle of friends was gone. And because he wanted his letters to convey his mortal body as well as his immortal spirit, he knew that their afterlife would at best be partial and incomplete. The poignancy of Donne's letters ultimately lies in their oscillation between soaring bids for immortality ("that which passes [in letters] is eternall, and out of the measure of time") and far more modest hopes for their endurance—that his soft, whispering voice might still be heard a year hence, that his grass might stay green and unwithered for at least another season, that the physical trace of his hand would linger in the letters on the page.

CHAPTER TWO

Songs and Sonnets

Donne has long been celebrated as one of the great love poets of the English language. But what is it that distinguishes his love poetry, and why do we keep coming back to it? Over the centuries, many different answers have been given, among them: the naturalism and colloquialism of his language; the brilliance of his metaphysical conceits; the mutuality of the love that he celebrates. In her mid-twentieth-century edition of these poems, Helen Gardner identified Donne's "bliss of union in love" as one of his preeminent accomplishments: on this subject, she affirms elsewhere, "he has no predecessors . . . and virtually no successors of any stature."[1] Gardner is right that at isolated moments in his poems, Donne celebrates a love that is mutually constituted. But what is missing from her account is an acknowledgment of Donne's obsession with the difficulty of sustaining such a union. Far from detracting from the poems' success, this obsession is what gives the lyrics their special urgency and force. What distinguishes Donne as a love poet is not his joyful assurance that his love will endure. What distinguishes him is at once the intensity of the pleasure he conveys in the moment of mutual love, and the ferocity with which he attempts to prolong that moment for as long as he can, knowing full well that its end may be near. "Stand still," he begs his beloved in "A Lecture upon the Shadow"—"stand still," he implores, so that this very second can be preserved, so that the love we share right now might miraculously evade the vicissitudes of time and place.

Why does Donne return so regularly to the death of the beloved, as we see in "The Dissolution," "A nocturnall upon S. Lucies Day," and "A Feaver"? Why does he like to begin from the imaginative position of the grave, as we find in "The Relique" and "The Funerall"? Why does he dwell so obsessively on imminent departures or journeys, as evinced in "Breake of Day,"

"Song: Sweetest love, I do not goe," "The Legacie," and "The Expiration"? Why, even, does he feel so threatened by his physical withdrawal in the aftermath of sex, as Christopher Ricks has convincingly argued about lyrics like "The Apparition"?[2] The best answer we can give is that these poems, however diverse in mood or tone, share a profound distaste for separation. In both its positive and negative formulations, Donne's poetics of love is a poetics of taking leave.

The subject of leave-taking was one that engaged love poets long before Donne. In the European literary tradition, there were at least two pronounced genres of valedictory poetry that influenced him: the *aubade*, a song of the lovers who part at dawn, and the *congé d'amour* lyric, written on the occasion of the male lover's departure for military service (typically for the Crusades).[3] In the *Songs and Sonnets*, Donne adopts some characteristics from both of these traditions, composing a straightforward *aubade*—for example, in "Breake of Day," which begins: "'Tis true, 'tis day; what though it be? / O wilt thou therefore rise from me?"—or leaving behind tokens of himself like the *congé d'amour* lover on a number of occasions, to which I will return. But, as Heather Dubrow has persuasively argued about his relationship to Petrarchanism, Donne was uneasy about practicing straightforward literary imitation, and he tends to distance himself from the very traditions that he seems to be working within.[4] In the *Songs and Sonnets* he takes up the project of writing valedictory poems, but in doing so, he brings to the surface all of the anxieties that surround the task of bidding farewell and ensuring reunion through the medium of verse.

The prospect of separation produces in Donne a wildly varied set of responses, but these responses are almost always marked by his desire to ensure the possibility of future reunion in the face of impending division. It is in response to the fear of lovers' parting that the *Songs and Sonnets* are often most vital and alive, just as it is in response to the fear of death—when body and soul must part—that his devotional verse becomes most animated. Indeed, Donne's attitude toward the bond between body and soul extends in crucial ways to his attitude toward the bond between two lovers. There are, of course, significant differences in his understanding of the two sets of relations, but in both cases, he feels the isolation of one party from the other as a potentially irreversible injury. Donne had little interest in solitude—his sensibility is a far cry, for example, from that of his younger contemporary Andrew Marvell, who declares in "The Garden" that "society is all but rude, / To this delicious solitude," and concludes: "Two Paradises 'twere in one / to live in Paradise alone."[5] For Donne, solitude is not a paradisal blessing but a curse. Thus in "The Extasie," he celebrates the union of the lovers' souls as conquering "defects of loneliness"; or, in the letter addressed "To all my friends: Sir H. Goodere," as we have seen, he confesses that he suffers from the ailment of "*Vae soli*" (Alas, alone). Whatever our life circumstances, Donne remarks, we are all governed by what he splendidly defines as the "common, and mutuall necessity of one another."

At the same time that Donne recognizes the "common and mutuall necessity of one another," he acknowledges the fragility of the dependence created by a bond between two ultimately separable creatures. Just as he regards his body and his soul as simultaneously connected to each other *and* as discrete beings, so he regards the individual lovers in their ideal state of union as essential to each other's existence *and* as inherently distinct. This frame of mind helps to explain, for example, the subtle shift in "The Good Morrow" from the idea that the couple's two loves were one to the idea that they were similar ("If our two loves be one, *or*, thou and I / Love so alike").[6] Once this twoness rather than oneness is recognized, the inevitability of the lovers' parting can neither be ignored nor denied. Donne's response to this inevitability is not to accept it, but to fight it as best he can. This combativeness surfaces again and again in the *Songs and Sonnets*, but is perhaps most succinctly captured in the final lines of "Song: Sweetest love, I do not goe": "They who one another keepe / Alive, ne'r parted bee." These lines can be read as a plea for the lovers to keep one another alive, to extend one another's life for as long as possible. But they are more pointedly a plea for the lovers to remain together, to sustain their love for as long as their lives will permit. They do not stay together to stay alive; they stay alive as long as they can to postpone separation.

I

The complexity of Donne's attitude toward valediction depends entirely upon his attitude toward love. Before we can understand why parting is so central a preoccupation in the *Songs and Sonnets*, it is crucial to understand the ways in which Donne imagines love to affect both the bodies and souls of the lovers. We will recall from the last chapter Donne's letter to Wotton in which he explains that love cannot be experienced exclusively in soul or body: "You (I think) and I am much of one sect in the Philosophy of love, which, though it be directed upon the minde, doth inhere in the body, and find piety entertainment there."[7] For love to flourish, two sets of relations need to be in place: both the bodies and souls of each lover need to be conjoined in the act of loving each other. Anything less than this, he suggests, cannot rightly qualify as love.

The *Songs and Sonnets* are filled with expressions of both skepticism and idealism about the possibilities for loving another person in body and soul. In "Loves Alchymie," Donne denounces as a hypocrite the bridegroom who claims his love is purely spiritual:

> That loving wretch that sweares,
> 'Tis not the bodies marry, but the mindes,
>   Which he in her Angelique findes,
>   Would sweare as justly, that he heares,
> In that dayes rude hoarse minstralsey, the spheares.
>   Hope not for minde in women . . . (18–23)

Just as the "rude hoarse minstralsey" of the wedding festivities bears no relation to heavenly music, so the mind of the bride bears no relation to the mind of an angel. Whatever the bridegroom ("that loving wretch") may claim to the contrary, Donne insists that "the bodies" form the basis of the union.

Donne is equally ruthless about the possibility that love might inhere exclusively in the body. In "Loves Usury," he begs Love to spare him so that he might enjoy the pleasures of the flesh unburdened by a spiritual attachment:

> For every houre that thou wilt spare mee now,
>   I will allow,
> Usurious God of Love, twenty to thee,
> When with my browne, my gray haires equall bee;
> Till then, Love, let my body raigne, and let
> Mee travell, sojourne, snatch, plot, have, forget,
> Resume my last yeares relict: thinke that yet
>   We'had never met. (1–8)

In a wonderful instance of his penchant for startling lists—"travell, sojourne, snatch, plot, have, forget, resume"—he imagines the myriad ways he can satisfy his carnal desires without falling into love's trap. These ways include the pleasures of having, forgetting, and resuming the conquest of last year's "raigne" without incurring any debt to Love.

Why does love need to involve both body and soul? In "Aire and Angels," as we saw in chapter 1, Donne explains love's double engagement as part of the history of human dualism. Love originates in the soul, he relates, and could perhaps have comfortably remained in the spiritual realm had not the soul itself descended into the flesh:

But since my soule, whose child love is,
Takes limmes of flesh, and else could nothing doe,
      More subtile then the parent is,
Love must not be, but take a body too. (7–10)

Love cannot be more "subtile"—which, we will recall, means primarily a substance that is refined or ethereal—than its parent. It must incarnate itself.

The most extensive treatment in the *Songs and Sonnets* of how love moves from the soul to the body is "The Extasie." In his *ABC of Reading*, Ezra Pound appended these shorthand notes to the poem: "Platonism believed . . . Absolute belief in the existence of an extra-corporeal soul, and its incarnation. Donne stating a thesis in precise and even technical terms."[8] This reading of "The Extasie" as the equivalent of a philosophical treatise with a clear, "even technical" thesis is de facto overturned by the fierce debates the poem has occasioned, debates that turn almost entirely on whether the spiritual love propounded by Platonism is in fact the desirable goal. As Arthur Marotti has convincingly shown, "The Extasie" was most likely written in response to Edward Herbert's "Ode Upon a Question Moved, Whether Love Should Continue For Ever." Marotti astutely observes, moreover, that Pound's description would be far better suited for Herbert's poem than for Donne's.[9] In Herbert's "Ode," the male lover seeks to convince his mistress that their love will transcend the realm of the earthly to become an immortal bond:

Let then no doubt, Celinda, touch
Much less your fairest mind invade:
Were not our souls immortal made
Our equal loves can make them such. (121–24)

Donne's poem, by contrast, follows exactly the opposite trajectory: it traces the movement of a harmonious love between two souls from their extracorporeal union to their resumption of the flesh.

"The Extasie" begins by staging the inability of the lovers to consummate their love through purely bodily mechanics:

Our hands were firmely cimented
      With a fast balme, which thence did spring,
Our eye-beames twisted, and did thred
      Our eyes, upon one double string;

So to'entergraft our hands, as yet
    Was all the meanes to make us one,
And pictures in our eyes to get
    Was all our propagation.
As 'twixt two equall Armies, Fate
    Suspends uncertaine victorie,
Our soules, (which to advance their state,
    Were gone out,) hung 'twixt her, and mee.
And whil'st our soules negotiate there,
    Wee like sepulchrall statues lay;
All day, the same our postures were,
    And wee said nothing, all the day. (5–20)

The immense physical efforts of the hands and eyes to join the lovers to-gether were futile, the poet tells us—however fiercely they pressed their hands, and however intensely they stared into each other's eyes, there was no yield of "oneness." Part of the humor of these opening lines is their failure to mention the obvious physical means to "make us one"—sexual intercourse—as if the lovers have not yet been informed that "propagation" does not come from lying side by side on a riverbank. But the point Donne wants to make is that bodies alone cannot achieve union in love. The fact that sex seems to have been overlooked as even an option reinforces one of the poem's central implications: that the act of full consummation requires the involvement of souls as well as bodies. Without their souls, the bodies are left with only inferior means of being together, and they spend their day frozen in their postures like funerary monuments.

If bodies without souls cannot achieve union in love, neither can souls stripped of their bodies. At first, the lovers' souls declare triumphantly that they have been merged into one creature:

This Extasie doth unperplex
    (We said) and tell us what we love,
Wee see by this, it was not sexe,
    Wee see, we saw not what did move:
But as all severall soules containe
    Mixture of things, they know not what,
Love, these mixt soules, doth mixe againe,
    And makes both one, each this and that . . .
When love, with one another so
    Interinanimates two soules,

That abler soule, which thence doth flow,
    Defects of lonelinesse controules. (29–36, 41–44)

The new creature the souls have formed emerges from what Donne calls—
coining yet another word—"interinanimat[ion]." Although some manuscript versions print the verb in line 42 as "interanimates," there is evidence
beyond its superior metrical claims that "interinanimates" is correct.[10] As I
have already observed, Donne invented the term "inanimation" to describe
the process by which spirit gets infused into a person; his neologism conveys a
sense of motion, a forward thrusting of soul into body in a manner that the ordinary term "animation" lacks. Interinanimation, then, doubles the pleasure
of inanimation—we can almost feel Donne's enthusiasm in adding the extra
prefix "inter" to his already supplementary prefix "in," transforming the act
of animation from something individual to something mutual. "Interinanimation" means both parties are giving life to each other, enabling them to form
from their purely spiritual exchange a new creature—"that abler soule."

Even the forging of a single, "abler soule" that rises above the implications of "sex" remains inadequate, however, to the task of making the two
lovers fully one. (The *OED* credits Donne with the first use of the noun
"sex" to indicate the distinction between male and female,[11] although the
editors ignore Donne's obvious associations of the term not simply with
sexual difference but with the sex act itself.) No sooner do the souls affirm their seamless union that knows no sex than they realize something
important has been left behind. They now ask with the force of a startling
Petrarchan *volta:*

But O alas, so long, so farre
    Our bodies why doe wee forbeare?
They are ours, though they are not wee, Wee are
    The intelligences, they the spheare. (49–52)

After nearly forty lines of absence, Donne reintroduces the bodies in the
poem, and he does so in a way that seems to emphasize their intrusion. The
word "bodies" seems to jump out of its line, supplying the deferred subject
of the preceding line ("But O, alas, so long, so farre") and, with its internal
rhythmic variation, demanding a different kind of attention.[12]

Why is it, the souls ask, that we "forbeare" our bodies? The souls may be
the "intelligences" that rule the "spheare" below, but without the spheres
they have no medium of expression. The souls recognize, in other words,
that they need their bodies to enjoy the full experience of love:

As our blood labours to beget
    Spirits, as like soules as it can,
Because such fingers need to knit
    That subtile knot, which makes us man:
So must pure lovers soules descend
    T'affections, and to faculties,
Which sense may reach and apprehend,
    Else a great Prince in prison lies. (61–68)

What connects body and soul are spirits, Donne contends, produced by the blood with the purpose of knitting together "that subtile knot, which makes us man."[13] (It is striking, but not unusual, that he describes spirits with "fingers"—as we shall see repeatedly in his writing, Donne has difficulty imagining disembodied agents.) Just as the soul needs spirits to connect it to the flesh, so love needs the "affections" and "faculties" of the body to connect it to the agency of sense. And it is only through our senses, Donne suggests, that love can be liberated—"Else a great Prince in prison lies." In a forceful reversal of the Platonic commonplace that the body is the prison house for the soul, what obstructs the love between these souls is their disembodiment.

T. S. Eliot remarked with palpable disapproval that the end of "The Extasie" posits "a distinction, a disjunction, between soul and body of which I think you will find no expression whatever in the *trecento*, and for which I do not think you will find much authority in Aquinas."[14] Grierson found himself equally troubled by what he took to be the poem's assertion of radical dualism. "There hangs about the poem," he declares,

> just a suspicion of the conventional and unreal Platonism of the seventeenth century. In attempting to state and vindicate the relation of soul and body [Donne] falls perhaps inevitably into the appearance, at any rate, of the dualism which he is trying to transcend. He places them over against each other as separate entities and the lower bulks unduly.[15]

Eliot and Grierson seem to share the conviction that Donne's desired end is hylomorphism—as we saw in the introduction, the Aristotelian idea that bodies and souls together make a compound of matter and form that cannot easily be divided. "It is not necessary to ask whether soul and body are one," Aristotle writes in *De Anima*. "We should not . . . inquire whether the soul and body are one thing, any more than whether the wax and its imprint are, or in general whether the matter of each thing is one with that of which it is the matter. For although unity and being are spoken of in a number of ways, it is of the actuality that they are most properly said."[16] Although Aristotle does not deny outright the possibility of separating body from soul, he deems it a question not worth pursuing. He insists, "Just as pupil and sight *are* the eye, so, in our case, soul and body *are* the animal." "It is quite clear then," Aristotle concludes, "that the soul is not separable from the body, or that some parts of it are not, if it is its nature to have parts" (ii 1, 413a2–6).

It is indisputable that in "The Extasie" Donne reifies the categories of body and soul. But the idea that, in doing so, he embraces a Platonism that debases the flesh seems entirely out of touch with the momentum of the poem, whose final lines celebrate the ultimate indistinguishability of spirit from flesh once the soul is reincarnated. On the surface of things, Donne may explain the souls' return to the flesh as a concession to "weake men" who require ocular proof before they can believe in love:

> To'our bodies turne wee then, that so
> > Weake men on love reveal'd may looke;
> Loves mysteries in soules doe grow,
> > But yet the body is his booke. (69–72)

It seems absolutely certain, however, that the exposition of love to weak men is not the purpose of their incarnation.[17] We turn to our bodies, Donne suggests, because we cannot love without them.

If Herbert's ode ends with the lovers looking upward toward the heavens, "The Extasie" concludes with the souls returning to their bodies on earth:

> And if some lover, such as wee,
> > Have heard this dialogue of one,
> Let him still marke us, he shall see
> > Small change, when we'are to bodies gone. (73–76)

The playful confusion in these lines of singulars and plurals subtly affirms the fulfillment of the poem's original goal: to discover the way to "make us one." And with a wink and a nod, this goal seems to be achieved. Gardner may protest that there is no "proposal" for seduction at the end of the poem,[18] and I think she is right to differentiate Donne's aims in "The Extasie" from those of Elegy 19 ("To his Mistris going to Bed") or "The Flea," two poems explicitly designed to lure his mistress to bed. But to deny that "The Extasie" leans toward a consummation of the couple's love through more than hand-holding is to deny the poem the consummation it has earned.

Donne's insistence on love as a bodily as well as spiritual experience differentiates him from the vast majority of early modern practitioners in the "philosophy of love." For Renaissance Neoplatonists, the body is at best a preliminary medium through which a deeper, more enduring connection to the soul is conducted; at worst, it is a harmful distraction, obstructing the lover from his or her true focus on heavenly, spiritual beauty. In his 1474 *Commentary on Plato's Symposium*, arguably the most influential and widely read treatment of love in the Renaissance, Marsilio Ficino describes "true love" as "nothing but a certain urge striving to fly up to the divine beauty, aroused by the sight of bodily beauty."[19] For Ficino, the body is no more than a passive instrument for the workings of the soul. "Everything that a man is said to do," he declares, "his soul does itself; the body merely suffers it to be done; wherefore man is soul alone, and the body of man must be its instrument" (157). This contrasts nicely with what Donne says in one his sermons: "All that the soule does, it does in, and with, and by the body" (4:358).

In his *Commentary on a Canzone of Benivieni*, written several years after Ficino's treatise, Pico della Mirandola condemns those who never ascend to anything higher than love of physical beauty. More perfect men, Pico writes,

> remember a more perfect beauty which their souls once saw, before being immersed in the body; then there arises in them an incredible desire to see it again, and in order to achieve this purpose, they free themselves as much as they can from the body, with the result that the soul returns to its original dignity, having become entirely superior to the body, and in no way subject to it.[20]

Bodily love reflects the unfortunate immersion of the soul in matter, Pico contends, and hence detracts from the goal of spiritual love. To transcend the physical is the only end worth pursuing.

There are certainly exceptions within Renaissance Neoplatonism to these deprecatory accounts of physical love. One striking example is Leone Ebreo's *Dialoghi d'amore*, which was published in Rome in 1535, and was almost certainly known to Donne.[21] The *Dialoghi* is remarkable for the frankness with which it affirms the role of sexual consummation in an ideal love. Leone's mouthpiece, Philo, reminds his beloved, Sophia: "I have been telling you that this act, far from dissolving perfect love, rather confirms and integrates it through the bodily activities of love." "Furthermore," he continues, "when two spirits are united in spiritual love, their bodies desire to enjoy such union as is possible, so that no distinction may persist, but the union be in all ways perfect; the more so as a corresponding physical union increases and perfects the spiritual love."[22]

In his 1525 *Libro di natura d'amore*, Mario Equicola, a court humanist who served as secretary to members of both the Este and Gonzaga families, reached a conclusion similar to Leone's. Drawing upon Aristotle's philosophy, Equicola declares: "To love truly is to love body and soul together, necessarily to love vigorously both the one and the other; and I affirm that in such love one may not be separated from the other. The lover seeks both sensual enjoyment, and to be loved in return."[23]

These treatises, however, represent significant deviations from the general consensus among Renaissance humanists that love should ultimately move, as Plato describes in the *Symposium*, from the physical to the spiritual as if ascending a staircase. "He should go from one to two and from two to all beautiful bodies," explains Socrates, quoting Diotima, "and from beautiful bodies to beautiful practices, and from practices to beautiful forms of learning."[24]

There is little doubt that Donne learned from Neoplatonism, and that he deployed it for his own purposes in the poems. Donne was not a Neoplatonist at heart, however, and he rejects the central Neoplatonic tenets that love should move both from particulars to generals and from bodies to souls. A. J. Smith made this point persuasively in his essay "The Dismissal of Love, or Was Donne a Neoplatonic Lover?" in which he concludes that there is no hint of a belief in transcendence anywhere in Donne's poems. In Donne's model of love, Smith remarks, "bodily desire isn't an impediment to love but may actually be essential to it."[25] If we were forced to identify Donne within a single philosophical school, it would almost certainly be Aristotelian—we might consider, for example, the close affinities between Donne's account of embodied love in "The Extasie" and Guido Cavalcanti's treatment of love in "Donna mi priegha," a poem that includes a more or less straightforward Aristotelian exposition of how love assumes a material form.[26] But strict philosophical affiliations are an unnecessary constraint upon a creative poet who did not understand himself as a philosopher. What matters is that Donne reacted against Neoplatonism in a way that energized his poems, and one consequence of this reaction was to exacerbate the problem of physical absence. Once Donne dismisses the possibility of a love that is entirely spiritual, the task of sustaining a love through physical separation naturally becomes more urgent.

II

In *Der Abschied: Theorie der Trauer*, the German literary theorist Karl Heinz Böhrer describes the ways in which literary conventions of saying good-bye (*Abschiednehmen*) can incorporate a *Wiedersehen*. The *Abschied* is not in these cases conclusive, he argues; instead, it demarcates the beginning of an eventual return. This sense of possible return is explicit in the German expression, *auf Wiedersehen*, which, like the French *au revoir*, anticipates a future meeting. It is missing from the English "good-bye," a contraction of "God be with ye," and "farewell," which neither suggest nor rule out the possibility of future encounters. It is also missing from Donne's crucial term "valediction."

In his expansive survey of Western literature, Böhrer draws a useful distinction between the *Abschied* as the precondition of a reunion (*die Voraussetzung einer Ruckkehr*) and the *Abschied* as a gesture of final parting. In the first category, the canonical example is Christ's promise in John 16:16: "A little while, and ye shall not see me: and again, a little while, and ye shall see me, because I go to the Father." Böhrer also includes in this category more ambiguous farewells that turn out to be final, but are not definitively recognized as such at the time of parting, such as that between Hector and Andromache in book 6 of *The Iliad*, or between Dido and Aeneas in book 6 of *The Aeneid*. In the second category of farewells—those that anticipate the finality and irreversibility of the separation—Böhrer cites, among other examples, Cassius and Brutus's exchange in Act 5 of *Julius Caesar*. On the eve of the battle of Philippi, Brutus says to Cassius, "But this same day / Must end that work the Ides of March begun / And whether we shall meet again I know not. / Therefore our everlasting farewell take: / For ever, and for ever, farewell, Cassius!" and Cassius replies: "For ever, and for ever, farewell, Brutus! / If we do meet again we'll smile indeed; / If not, 'tis true this parting was well made."[27] The two friends do admit, of course, the possibility that they might meet again. But the sense of doom that pervades the scene, a doom that sounds in the repetitions of "for ever" and "farewell," evocatively suggests that neither party holds out much hope for future conversations.

If we consider the distinction Böhrer draws between the two types of leave-taking—on the one hand, an *Abschied* that imagines a *Wiedersehen*, on the other hand, an *Abschied* that understands itself as final—we might provisionally observe that in his poems of valediction Donne hopes for the first kind but fears that he might actually be experiencing the second. He wants his act of leave-taking to incorporate a promise of meeting again, but he lacks any reassurance that such an outcome will come to pass. Donne is caught, in other words, between the two models that Böhrer describes, and it is the friction between the two that motivates the valedictory poems. For the project of these poems is to transform what might be a final good-bye into a temporary one.

There is no single formula in Donne's love poetry for transforming a final good-bye into a temporary one. But taken as a whole these lyrics reveal a poet who dwelt repeatedly on the problems raised by leave-taking, and who explored different strategies in his poems to lessen the blows of separation. One such strategy was to adopt the belief prevalent among medieval love poets as well as Neoplatonists: that love involved the exchange of hearts or souls. Within this understanding of love, the act of parting in body does not necessitate parting in soul, since each lover would already have incorporated the spirit of the beloved. Neoplatonists like Ficino or Pico did not imagine that any physical contact was required for the exchange of souls between lovers to occur. The transaction was purely spiritual, effected without engaging the senses, and especially without the base senses of taste or touch.[28] In the medieval courtly love tradition, by contrast, the surrender of the lover's heart or soul transpired through a kiss, and this kiss was typically exchanged at the moment of parting. These lines from a thirteenth-century German lyric illustrate the ways in which valediction, kissing, and the exchange of hearts were commonly intertwined: "'Min herze dir belibet hie.' / Si sprach 'so füere min herze hin.' / Der wehsel da mit kus ergie." ("'My heart remains here with you.' And she replied: 'Then let my heart go [with you].' The exchange [of hearts] took place with a kiss."}[29]

The site of convergence between the medieval courtly love tradition and Neoplatonism comes in Castiglione's *Book of the Courtier*, in which Pietro Bembo justifies kissing as a spiritual transaction so long as the love is "reasonable" rather than "sensuall." For the reasonable lover, Bembo explains, the kiss is

> the opening of an entry to the soules, which drawn with a coveting the one of the other, pour them selves by turn, the one into the other's body, and be so mingled together, that each of them hath two soules, and one alone so framed of them both ruleth (in a manner) two bodies. Whereupon a kisse may be said to be rather a cooplinge together of the soule, then of the bodye, because it hath suche force in her, that it draweth her unto it, and (as it were) seperateth her from the bodye. For this do all chast lovers covet a kisse, as a coopling of soules together.[30]

We will recall that Donne claims to esteem the letter over the kiss as a means
to "mingle soules," and we see now that this metaphor of "mingling" may
have come straight from Hoby's 1561 translation of Castiglione. We see as
well that in the *Songs and Sonnets* Donne eschews the idea of the kiss as a
meaningful site for spiritual exchange in the manner Castiglione describes.
The absence of the kiss is particularly conspicuous in "The Extasie," where we
might expect Donne to make use of the long history in Christian mysticism of
kissing as a means to release the soul into an ecstatic state.[31] In Donne's poem,
however, the souls leave the body without any "coopling" of their mouths.

When Donne does use the conceit of the soul-in-the-kiss directly in "The
Expiration," he deploys it for a negative purpose:

> So, so, breake off this last lamenting kisse,
>   Which sucks two soules, and vapors Both away,
> Turne thou ghost that way, and let mee turne this,
>   And let our selves benight our happiest day,
> We ask'd none leave to love; nor will we owe
>   Any, so cheape a death, as saying, Goe;
>
> Goe; and if that word have not quite kil'd thee,
>   Ease mee with death, by bidding mee goe too.
> Oh, if it have, let my word worke on mee,
>   And a just office on a murderer doe.
> Except it be too late, to kill me so,
>   Being double dead, going, and bidding, goe. (1–12)

In this poem, alternately entitled "Valediction" or "Valedictio Amoris" in
some of the extant manuscripts, the kiss serves as the agent of death.[32] Far
from safely implanting the souls in one another's breasts, it sucks both souls
away. Like Lucretius's account in *De rerum natura* of what happens to spiritual matter after death—the spirits leave the body, Lucretius tells us, and
"dispers[e] abroad like smoke"[33]—the souls in "The Expiration" are transformed into vapors, losing all of their individual properties as they fade into
the surrounding air. In the wake of this kiss, the lovers become ghosts: bodies without souls. Hence Donne reverses the courtly love tradition in which
kissing, by virtue of mingling two souls, shields the lovers from the harmful
consequences of parting. In "The Expiration," the kiss renders their parting
final.[34] There is no promise of a future encounter, nor is there any hope of
achieving what Donne would call the "interinanimation" that Castiglione
describes.

Elsewhere in the *Songs and Sonnets*, Donne does envision an exchange
of souls between the lovers that might sustain them during periods of absence, but the result is only to intensify, not lessen, their vulnerability to
each other. In "Song: Sweetest love, I do not goe," he counsels his beloved
against grieving while he is away:

> When thou sigh'st, thou sigh'st not winde,
>   But sigh'st my soule away,
> When thou weep'st, unkindly kinde,
>   My lifes blood doth decay.   .
>   It cannot bee
> That thou lov'st mee, as thou say'st,
> If in thine my life thou waste,
>   That art the best of mee. (25–32)

The simplest signs of sadness are freighted with metaphysical weight—for
his lover to sigh is to sigh away his soul, for her to weep is to deplete his
supply of blood. Far from protecting his spiritual self during his absence,
Donne's lover is dangerously porous, capable of "wasting" his life through
her outward expressions of grief.

This intensification of the lovers' fragility through their outward expressions of grief is the subject of "A Valediction: of weeping." In this poem,
Donne builds an elaborate conceit around the idea that in shedding tears, the
lovers threaten to drown each other in sorrow. He begins by comparing his
own tears to coins minted by his mistress's face and bearing her image:

> Let me powre forth
> My teares before thy face, whil'st I stay here,   .
> For thy face coines them, and thy stampe they beare,
> And by this Mintage they are something worth,
>   For thus they bee
>   Pregnant of thee;
> Fruits of much griefe they are, emblemes of more,
> When a teare falls, that thou falls which it bore,
> So thou and I are nothing then, when on a divers shore. (1–9)

Donne slows down the process of weeping in order to separate the eye's production of the tear from its dropping to the ground. The "worth" of the tear
is lost once that tear bearing her image ("that thou") falls and dissolves, just
as once the lovers are "on a divers shore," they too will lose their worth.[35]

There is nothing in the act of weeping, it would seem, to ward off the perils of separation.

In the next stanza Donne expands his metaphoric reach, likening his tears to "a globe, yea world":

> On a round ball
> A workeman that hath copies by, can lay
> An Europe, Afrique, and an Asia,
> And quickly make that, which was nothing, *All*,
>> So doth each teare,
>> Which thee doth weare,
> A globe, yea world by that impression grow,
> Till thy teares mixt with mine doe overflow
> This world, by waters sent from thee, my heaven dissolved so. (10–18)

The danger introduced in these lines does not lie, however, in the remarkable expansion of his tear's scope from containing a single image of his mistress to bearing a replica of the world. The danger comes with the introduction of his mistress's tears into the poem at line 17, tears that might drown the entire world by mingling with the world that his tears now contain.

By investing both his and his beloved's tears with supernatural powers, Donne transforms the simple act of weeping into a destructive force. Like the sea he is about to cross, their tears threaten to swallow him in their depths, and he begs his mistress to "forbeare / To teach the sea, what it may doe too soone." The poem retreats from its metaphysical excess only in its final couplet, which translates the idea of their mutual vulnerability into a more familiar idiom: "Since thou and I sigh one anothers breath, / Who e'r sighes most, is cruellest, and hasts the others death." We return to where we were at the end of "Song: Sweetest love": the threat raised by the lovers' parting is heightened, not diminished, by sighing each other's souls away.

Why is it that Donne takes so little solace in the prospect of sustaining his love through mingling parts of himself with his lover? One possible answer lies in his distaste for the idea of a shared soul. However intimate the relationship may be between himself and his beloved, he seems to find the notion of exchanging spiritual parts unsettling. We know from Donne's sermons that the posthumous mingling of bodies was repellent to him. This is expressed most vividly in his final sermon, *Deaths Duell*, where Donne rages against the violation of bodily integrity in the grave:

When those bodies that have beene the *children* of *royall parents*, and
the *parents* of *royall children*, must say with *Iob*, to corruption thou art
my father, and to *the Worme thou art my mother and my sister*. *Miser-*
able riddle, when the *same worme* must bee *my mother*, and *my sister*,
and *my selfe*. *Miserable incest*, when I must bee *married* to my *mother*
and my *sister*, and bee both *father* and *mother* to my *owne mother* and
sister. (10:238)

It is "the most inglorious and contemptible *vilification*," Donne concludes,
"the most deadly and peremptory *nullification* of man, that wee can consider . . . in this death of *incineration*, and dispersion of dust, we see *nothing*
that we call *that mans*" (10:239). The identity of "that man," which Donne
wants to preserve even posthumously, is entirely evacuated by the accidental and seemingly unavoidable mixing of his remains.

Less sensational but equally important was Donne's aversion to the idea
that people might share souls. In this context, we might recall Donne's letter
on the soul to Goodyer, in which he writes: "It is not perfectly true which a
very subtil, yet very deep wit Averroes says, that all mankinde hath but one
soul, which informes and rules us all, as one Intelligence doth the firmament
and all the Starres in it; as though a particular body were too little an organ
for a soul to play upon."[36] In language that subtly echoes Hamlet's famous
lines to Guildenstern—"there is much music, / excellent voice in this little
organ; yet cannot / you make it speak . . . Call me what / instrument you
will, though you can fret me, yet you / cannot play upon me" (3.2.355–60)—
Donne imagines the body as an "organ" (both a living organism and a musi-
cal instrument) that deserves a single soul as its possessor or player. As the
letter to Goodyer suggests, Donne's fear of sharing his soul connects to an
overarching desire to maintain his personal integrity, to keep the two parts
of himself together without outward interference or contribution. The idea
of exchanging souls with his lover may have appealed to him at particular,
isolated moments, but it also made him nervous. As he declares in "Lovers Infinitenesse," he wants to find a "way more liberall, / Then changing
hearts, to joyne them." Donne desired reciprocity in love, but not mutual
transformation.

Because Donne did not imagine parting to be surmountable through
"changing hearts," the challenge that arises is how to remain present to his
beloved without actually surrendering crucial parts of himself. One solution
that he experimented with was to leave tokens behind, or to obtain such
tokens from his beloved, in order to sustain each other during the period

of separation. We encounter one version of this in "A Valediction: of the booke"—arguably the least successful of the four Valedictions—in which Donne proposes to his mistress that while he is away she should "anger destiny, as she doth us" by transcribing the letters they have exchanged into a single book, which will become "our annals" of love. These letters are meant to occupy his mistress's time while he measures their love from afar:

> Thus vent thy thoughts; abroad I'll studie thee,
>   As he removes farre off, that great heights takes;
>   How great love is, presence best tryall makes,
> But absence tryes how long this love will bee; (55–58)

There is no hope in this poem of reunion, nor is there any real consolation given to his beloved. In the end, the letters become a source of information for "Loves clergy" rather than a compensatory presence during his time abroad.

A much more extreme—and more emotionally satisfying—formulation of leaving a token of the self behind during a period of absence comes in "The Relique." This poem begins with Donne's imagining himself in his grave, awaiting his beloved's return at the resurrection:

> When my grave is broke up againe
> Some second ghest to entertaine,
> (For graves have learn'd that woman-head
> To be to more then one a Bed)
>   And he that digs it, spies
> A bracelet of bright haire about the bone,
>   Will he not let'us alone,
> And thinke that there a loving couple lies,
> Who thought that this device might be some way
> To make their soules, at the last busie day,
> Meet at this grave, and make a little stay? (1–11)

The seeds of the anxiety Donne expresses so powerfully in *Deaths Duell* about the mixing of remains can be found in this poem, in which he begins with the horrible thought of his grave being reopened to accommodate a "second ghest." The piece of his beloved's hair serves as a guarantee that she will eventually return to him on "the last busie day," when souls search des-

perately to retrieve all missing parts of their scattered bodies. In the mean-
time—in the long period of absence between death and resurrection—he
imagines the physical remnants of bones and hair themselves as a "loving
couple," a synecdochal reminder of the intimacy they once had, and hope to
have, however briefly, again.

Donne's fullest exploration of the same hope—that leaving behind a *memento* of the self will both alleviate the experience of absence and hold out
the promise of a future encounter—arises in "A Valediction: of my name,
in the window." This poem begins with a deceptively simple premise: in
the face of his imminent departure, Donne has engraved his name in his
mistress's window, and expresses his wish that the "firmnesse" of the name
will serve as an embodiment of his constant love. The practice of engraving
names as well as verses in window glass was not uncommon at the time. According to John Foxe's *Acts and Monuments,* when Princess Elizabeth was at
Woodstock under house arrest, she "wrote with her diamond, in a glass window, 'Much suspected by me / Nothing proved can be. Quoth ELIZABETH,
Prisoner.'" Lady Jane Grey, Foxe reports, also engraved her window while she
was imprisoned in the Tower. The practice of engraving glass was certainly
not limited to prisoners: both Edmund Spenser and George Herbert refer in
their poems to windows scratched with words, and there is evidence that
jewelers at the time produced special "writing rings," designed with raised
diamonds so that they could be used for inscribing on glass.[37] In northern
Europe, moreover, one can still find examples of late seventeenth-century
homes with the inhabitant's name engraved in one of the windowpanes, as
if it were a means of registering possession.

Donne's decision to engrave his name in his mistress's glass emerges
from the desire to register a different form of possession. He wants his name
to become part of his lover's reflection—to be written, as it were, across her
face:

> My name engrav'd herein,
> Doth contribute my firmnesse to this glasse,
>   Which, ever since that charme, hath beene
>   As hard, as that which grav'd it, was;
> Thine eye will give it price enough, to mock
>   The diamonds of either rock.
>   'Tis much that Glasse should bee
> As all confessing, and through-shine as I,
>   'Tis more, that it shewes thee to thee,

And cleare reflects thee to thine eye.
But all such rules, loves magique can undoe,
　　Here you see mee, and I am you. (1–12)

These stanzas play with the Neoplatonic idea that the lover carries the image of his beloved engraved on his soul. "And so the soul of the lover," Ficino
writes, "becomes a mirror in which the image of the beloved is reflected."[38]
In Donne's "Valediction," his mistress does not find his image engraved on
her soul, but instead finds his name scratched in her glass. The name in
the window is at once an external substitution for the internal image that
Ficino describes, and a metonymic substitution for Donne's own presence.
For his purpose is not to create a spiritual bond, but a physical union. When
his mistress gazes in the glass, she not only sees his name, but receives his
name as part of herself: "Here you see mee, and I am you."

No sooner has such a solution for the two lovers to remain together been
proposed, however, than it is retracted. How, Donne asks, can his beloved
possibly accept a two-dimensional engraving in her glass as a viable surrogate for himself? His next move, surprisingly, is not to invent a new device
to retain some form of presence while he is away. Instead, he decides to shift
the intended purpose of his "scratch'd name":

　　Or, if too hard and deepe
This learning be, for a scratch'd name to teach,
　　It, as a given deaths head keepe,
　　Lovers mortalitie to preach,
Or thinke this ragged bony name to bee
　　My ruinous Anatomie. (19–24)

In a powerful metaphorical turn, the individual marks on the glass are transformed from robust and obdurate materials that can withstand "showers and
tempests" to a set of ragged bones representing the decay of his corpse.

Donne seems to have preferred this interpretation of his engraved
name—the name as "ruinous Anatomie"—to its role either as the mistress's
reflection or as a "deaths head" for her meditation, and in the poem's next
stanzas he expands this conceit so that his mistress becomes the agent of
his rebirth:

　　Then, as all my soules bee,
Emparadis'd in you, (in whom alone

I understand, and grow and see,)
    The rafters of my body, bone
Being still with you, the Muscle, Sinew, and Veine,
    Which tile this house, will come againe.

    Till my returne, repaire
And recompact my scattered body so.
    As all the vertuous powers which are
    Fix'd in the starres, are said to flow
Into such characters, as graved bee
    When these starres have supremacie.[39] (25–36)

Until now Donne has mentioned only his physical self—the self that is departing and that leaves as its surrogate the name engraved in the window. In
these two stanzas we learn that his spiritual self, composed of his threefold
(vegetable, sensitive, and intellectual) soul, has remained behind. Hence his
incorporation into his beloved is no longer limited to the surfaces of her
face—his very soul has been "emparadis'd" in her.

    Donne employs a similar conceit in "The Funerall," in which, as in "The
Relique," a strand of his mistress's hair is wrapped around the arm of his
shrouded corpse. This time, however, the purpose of the hair is not romantic—it is meant only to keep his bones intact during the dreaded interlude
between death and resurrection, and not to ensure a reunion:

Who ever comes to shroud me, do not harme
    Nor question much
That subtile wreath of haire, which crowns my arme;
The mystery, the signe you must not touch,
    For'tis my outward Soule,
Viceroy to that, which then to heaven being gone,
    Will leave this to controule,
And keepe these limbes, her Provinces, from dissolution. (1–8)

His mistress's hair becomes the temporary guardian of his corpse, a make-
shift solution for warding off the inevitable decay of the flesh. Donne does
not carry this conceit through in the rest of the poem—her lock of hair, it
turns out, was given in a spirit of cruelty ("she meant that I / By this should
know my pain" [14–15]) and by burying it with him Donne means to return
the favor. "As'twas humility," he concludes,

To afford to it all that a Soule can doe,
    So, 'tis some bravery,
That since you would save none of mee, I bury some of you. (21–24)

The "Valediction: of my name, in the window" is a much less bitter poem than "The Funerall," and the role of the mistress as "Viceroy" to his body is not compromised by misgivings about her motives. Not only does she enable Donne's eventual return to wholeness by maintaining the souls and bones that remain with her during his absence. She also draws as if by magnetic force those parts that have not remained—his "Muscle, Sinew, and Veine"—to "come againe." The language here is unmistakably sexual, and it corresponds to the initial description of the "firmnesse" of his name in the glass: Donne's mistress, he reminds her, has the power to bring him to life in more ways than one. In the subsequent command to "repaire / And recompact my scatter'd body," he moves from the sexual to the eschatological, employing language that will be reserved later in his career to describe the events of the last day. We might look forward, for example, to the opening quatrain of Holy Sonnet VII:

At the round earths imagin'd corners, blow
Your trumpets, Angells, and arise, arise
From death, you numberlesse infinities
Of soules, and to your scattred bodies goe. (1–4)

In the "Valediction: of my name, in the window," however, as in the Valedictions more broadly, Donne's register is entirely secular and earthly. The collection of scattered parts is the occasion not for divine resurrection, but for a double reunion: both with his beloved and with the missing parts of himself.

Donne's investment of his engraved name with a power he described in the second stanza as belonging to "loves magique" undergoes several further permutations before the end of the poem. "Trembling" and "alive," the name becomes the staunch defender of the jealous poet's honor, guarding against possible encroachments from rival lovers. "And when thy melted maid," he exclaims,

Corrupted by thy Lover's gold, and page,
    His letter at thy pillow'hath laid,
Disputed it, and tam'd thy rage,
And thou begin'st to thaw towards him, for this,
    May my name step in, and hide his. (49–54)

The comical battle between the now-animated name, on the one hand, and the love letter, on the other, comes to an abrupt halt, however, in the final stanza, when Donne seems to recognize that his conceit has gone too far. Not only does he cancel the domestic scene he was in the midst of describing. He also empties the engraving of all its accumulated significance:

> But glasse, and lines must bee,
> No meanes our firme substantiall love to keepe;
> Neere death inflicts this lethargie,
> And this I murmure in my sleepe;
> Impute this idle talke, to that I goe,
> For dying men talke often so. (61–66)

For John Carey, this stanza "returns us to reality and firm substantial love": "[t]he brusque recantation," he concludes, "surmounts fears."[40] This unflinching affirmation of the poem's triumph over the fears raised by absence entirely overlooks, however, the ways in which the original problem that the "Valediction" posed has in no way been resolved. We will recall that Donne not only wanted his love to endure, but that he described this endurance in distinctly corporeal terms: he wants his love to remain "firme" and "substantiall." Carey is certainly right that the poet disavows the effectiveness of his engraved name as a way to maintain their love during his absence. But he is mistaken if he believes this suggests a conquering of the poet's fears. If the "glass and lines" are finally deemed incapable of supplying these qualities, we are given no alternative. On the other side of the anthropomorphized name in the window that gives substance to a threatened love is a lover who cannot imagine anything that might reverse the hollowing out of his love once he has physically taken his leave.

The most obvious solution for avoiding the circumstances that arise at the end of this poem would be to have a love that needs no substantial embodiment, a love that can survive on a purely spiritual plane. This is what Donne attempts to convey in his most famous valedictory poem, "A Valediction: forbidding mourning," which begins where the "Valediction: of my name, in the window" leaves off—with the soft whispers of dying men:[41]

> As virtuous men passe mildly away,
> And whisper to their soules, to goe,
> Whilst some of their sad friends doe say,
> The breath goes now, and some say, no:

So let us melt, and make no noise,
    No teare-floods, nor sigh-tempests move,
T'were prophanation of our joyes
    To tell the layetie our love. (1–8)

Why does Donne compare the ideal parting between the two lovers to the separation of the virtuous man's soul from his body at the moment of death? Because like the good death, he wants the lovers' parting to be quiet, imperceptible, free of struggle. He wants it also to be willed and voluntary, despite the fact that it is inevitable. Above all, he wants to compare the two because in his mind parting is tantamount to dying—the separation of lovers is for him, as we have already seen, akin to the separation of body and soul. None of this means, however, that the division Donne describes in the poem is provoked by the threat of imminent death. This is a conclusion that readers often draw, and I believe it is in error.[42] The fear in this poem is not that death will make separation permanent. This is surely a fear that plagues Donne, and we have seen its expression on other occasions in the *Songs and Sonnets*, but it is not what preoccupies him here. What concerns him in "A Valediction: forbidding mourning" is what concerns him in nearly all of his valedictory lyrics: the challenge of securing future continuity in the face of present rupture.

In the first stanzas of this poem, Donne is preoccupied with the conditions of the rupture itself: he wants the actual moment of separation to be as easy and unremarkable as possible. "So let us melt, and make no noise," he urges, invoking an image at once straightforward and complex. To melt can simply mean, as Carey insists, to "disappear from the scene" (176). More common seventeenth-century (as well as modern) usage carries the sense of dissolving or liquefying, so that the image would suggest less the separation of two discrete bodies from each other than the breaking down of a single body. John Freccero connects the image of melting to the science of alchemy, a field that interested Donne and to which he refers regularly in his works. For alchemists, melting was a means not only to extract the philosopher's gold from the earthly gold, but also to extract spirit from body. "Once the melting of the gold begins," Freccero explains, "its 'spirit' is driven away uniformly and quietly precisely because it is so perfectly wedded to the body."[43] This process, moreover, is not final—the spirit "remain[s] in contact with [the body] from afar, refreshing it from time to time" (372). Within the context of alchemy, then, "So let us melt, and make no noise" is a call to imitate in love the alchemical process of separating, refining, and coming together again. It is a call to behave like gold.

The success of the lovers' valediction does not lie only in their smooth melting away from each other: it lies as well in the enduring power of what gets left behind. Unlike his other valedictory poems, Donne does not leave his beloved either a physical or spiritual piece of himself. Instead, he leaves her the power of his poetic making. What is meant to prevent her "mourning" is not her possession of his name or book or heart or soul. It is her possession of his metaphors, metaphors of their union that seem invulnerable to division. Thus Donne triumphantly declares their ability to overcome the obstacles normally posed by absence—or rather, he attempts to persuade his beloved, who is, we might imagine, on the verge of tears that the obstacles normally posed by absence do not pertain to them because they can imagine their love differently:

> Dull sublunary lovers love
> (Whose soule is sense) cannot admit
> Absence, because it doth remove
> Those things which elemented it.
>
> But we by a love, so much refin'd,
> That our selves know not what it is,
> Inter-assured of the mind,
> Care lesse, eyes, lips, and hands to misse.
>
> Our two soules therefore, which are one,
> Though I must goe, endure not yet
> A breach, but an expansion,
> Like gold to ayery thinnesse beate. (13–24)

Eliot criticized this last simile of the two souls "like gold to ayery thinnesse beate" on grounds similar to Dr. Johnson's famous complaints about metaphysical wit for the sheer sake of wit. "The figure does not make intelligible an idea," Eliot complains, "for there is properly no idea until you have the figure; the figure creates the idea—if gold can be beaten out thin, [Donne seems to ask] why should not a soul? He is not, and is never, stating a philosophical theory in which he believes" (132). Eliot's frustration with Donne as a philosopher assumes that Donne lacks a theory of the soul that drives his conceit—but this is mistaken on two different levels. First, the idea of comparing the growth of the soul to the beating out of gold can be traced to Donne's favorite church father, Tertullian, so there is good precedent for it—Donne's innovation is to double the souls, to make the gold leaf into an image not for the individual's soul, but for the lovers' souls combined. Second, and more importantly, Eliot fails to grasp that for Donne there were no rigid distinctions between the substance of the soul and body. Even when Donne describes the most incorporeal of substances, he never escapes the allure of matter. The gold leaf may, as Carey claims, "threaten to shade off into pure spirit," but to frame it this way is to confuse the order of things (186). The souls are meant to *be* spirit, and to compare them to gold is already to blur the lines, as Donne does repeatedly in his work, between the material and immaterial. Or rather, Donne does not like to think in terms of the spiritual alone—he likes to give the spirit body, even if that body is on the edge of slipping away into pure "ayery thinnesse."

Eliot's philosophical reservation about the image of the "gold to ayery thinnesse beate" seems all the same to connect to a poetic reservation Donne may himself have had about this simile as a way to describe the continuity between the lovers' souls, for in the poem's next quatrain he quickly replaces this image with another. He does not, however, venture further into the language of incorporeality. Despite its initial claims to the contrary, "A Valediction: forbidding mourning" never manages to depict metaphorically what a spiritual bond between the two lovers might look like. As the poem reaches its final climactic image, its language becomes increasingly corporeal. It also becomes increasingly dualistic. Instead of the single gold leaf, Donne offers the two legs of the compass:

> If they be two, they are two so
>   As stiffe twin compasses are two,
> Thy soule the fixt foot, makes no show
>   To move, but doth, if the'other doe.
>
> And though it in the center sit,
>   Yet when the other far doth rome,
> It leanes, and hearkens after it,
>   And growes erect, as that comes home. (25–32)

The compass, it seems, is exactly the right metaphor for both the oneness, and the twoness, of the lovers: like the legs of the compass, the lovers are parts of a single being, they are connected to each other whether near or far, they lean and straighten in response to each other's movements, and yet they are also distinct separate creatures. Donne's language of sexual excitation is nowhere more explicit than in this image of the compass's "grow[ing] erect"—and this insistence on the erotic anticipation of the lovers' reunion overwhelms all earlier invocations of a disembodied love.

Scholars are quick to point out that this metaphor of the compass—the single metaphor perhaps most deeply associated with Donne's poetry—was not in fact his invention. He most likely borrowed it from the fifteenth-century Italian poet Giovanni Battista Guarino, whose ninety-sixth madrigal includes these lines:

> I am ever with you,
> agitated, but fixed,
> and if I steal my lesser part from you, I leave my greater.
> I am like the compass,
> Fixing one foot in you as in my center:
> the other endures the circlings of fortune
> but can by no means fail to circle around you.[44]

There are many differences between Donne's use of the metaphor and Guarino's, but three stand out as particularly salient, and speak to what makes Donne's so extraordinarily effective. First, Guarino uses the two feet of the compass to describe himself; Donne uses the two feet of the compass to describe himself and his lover. Second, Guarino's arc of circling remains equidistant from his mistress—he circles continually around her. Donne's foot of the compass moves in harmony with his beloved's: as he moves from her, she leans towards him. Third, and perhaps most important, Guarino never mentions returning to the center, whereas Donne's distance from his beloved is only temporary. At the end of the quatrain, Donne's foot "comes home." "Home": this is the word, with its utter simplicity, which is missing from the other Valedictions and used but a handful of times in the entirety of the *Songs and Sonnets*.[45] "Home" is what lies on the other side of parting.

Marotti concludes that at the end of "A Valediction: forbidding mourning" the "spiritual relationship of lovers has its teleology not in the return following separation but in the resurrection following death" (176), and he concurs with Freccero that the poem reorients the speaker's attention towards God. I see nothing of God or resurrection in the final quatrain of this poem, a quatrain whose strength lies in its refusal to extend its reach beyond the simple goal of coming home:

> Such wilt thou be to mee, who must
>   Like th'other foot, obliquely runne;
> Thy firmnes makes my circle just,
>   And makes me end, where I begunne. (33–36)

At the end of "A Valediction: forbidding mourning," Donne does not ask for the lovers' immortality, nor does he ask for a vision of the divine. He asks only that his good-bye might include his return, that he might "end, where

I begunne." One of the most poignant features of Donne's poetry of valediction is that it never dares to imagine a real afterlife for love.

Donne's resistance to imagining an afterlife for love pervades both his
erotic and devotional writing. In his lyric "The Anniversarie," he invokes,
only to reject the possibility that the lovers' souls might dwell together in
heaven—"[t]hen wee shall be thoroughly blest," he allows, "But wee no
more, then all the rest / Here upon earth we'are Kings" (21–23). In place
of the dream of an eternal love between their souls, he prays instead for
more time on earth—he asks that they be allowed to "love nobly, and live,
and adde againe / Yeares and yeares unto yeares" (28–29). In "The Relique,"
Donne allows himself to imagine a reunion of the lovers after death, but, as
we have seen, this reunion is striking for its extreme brevity. We might hope
that the reward for the couple's horribly reduced form of loving as "a bracelet
of bright hair around the bone" will be their reunion for all eternity. Instead,
Donne tells us the purpose of this device—of their long wait as a "loving
couple" made up of hair and bone—is for their souls to "make a little stay,"
to share a moment of coming together before parting once again.

The modesty of Donne's hopes for a posthumous love are most fully
glimpsed in the stirring epitaph he composed for his wife, Anne (figure 2):

Faeminae lectissimae, dilectissimaeque;
Coniugi charissimae, castissimaeque;
Matri piissimae, Indulgentissimaeque; . . .
Immani febre correptae,
(Quod hoc saxum fari iussit
Ipse, prae dolore Infans)
Maritus (miserrimum dictu) olim charae charus
Cineribus cineres spondet suos
Novo matrimonio (annuat Deus) hoc loco sociandos

[A woman most choice or select, most beloved/well-read;
A spouse most dear, most chaste;
A mother most pious or dutiful, most indulgent . . .
By a ravishing fever carried off suddenly
Wherefore her husband ordered this stone tablet to speak,
Himself beyond grief made a speechless Infant,
Her husband, (most miserably uttered name or designation) once dear to
     the dear,
Pledges his ashes to these ashes
In a new marriage (may God assent) in this place joining together][46]

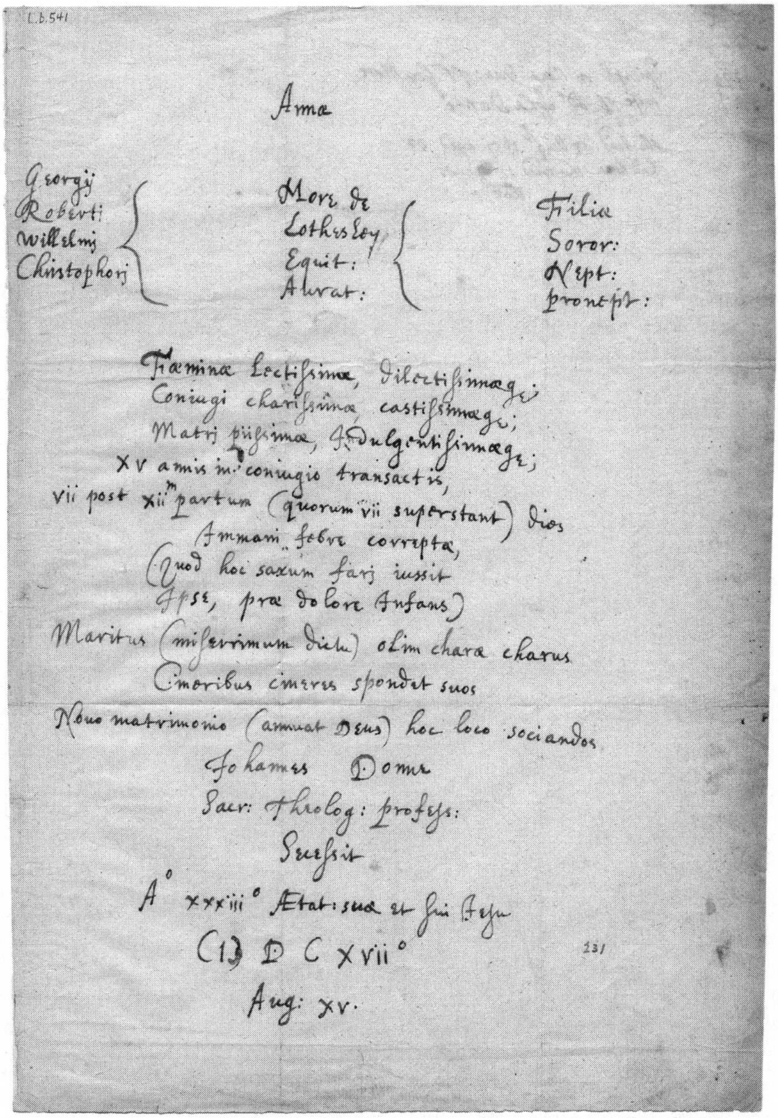
L.b.541

Anna

Georgij / Roberti / Willelmj / Christophorj — More de Lothesley, Equit: Aurat: — Filia / Soror: / Nept: / Pronept:

Fœminæ Lectissimæ, dilectissimæque;
Coniugi charissimæ, castissimæque;
Matri piissimæ, Indulgentissimæque;
XV annis in coniugio transactis,
vii post xii^m partum (quorum vii superstant) dies
Immani febre correpta,
(Quod hoc saxum farj iussit
Ipse, præ dolore Infans)
Maritus (miserrimum dictu) olim charæ charus
Cineribus cineres spondet suos
Nouo matrimonio (annuat Deus) hoc loco sociandos
Iohannes Donne
Sacr: Theolog: Profess:
Secessit
A^o xxxiii^o Ætat: suæ et sui Iesu
CIϽ DC xvii^o
Aug: xv.

231

Figure 2. Donne's epitaph for Anne Donne, August 15, 1617.
Reproduced by permission of the Folger Shakespeare Library.

The grieving husband asks God to allow him to be buried one day alongside his wife, to marry their ashes "*hoc loco,*" at the site of her grave. Missing from the epitaph, however, is the possibility of a new marriage forged from anything more than the mingling of their remains.

There can be no marriage in heaven, Donne will preach in his 1627 wedding sermon on Matthew 22:30: "For, in the resurrection, they neither marry nor are given in marriage, but are as the angels of God in heaven." "All that we can wish for," he declares to the newlyweds, is the possibility of "our *knowing,* or our *loving* of *one another* upon former knowledge in this world, in the next." "Christ does not say expressely we shall," he admits, "yet neither does he say, that we shall not, *know one another* there" (8.99). This is the most hopeful expression Donne gives us of a possible reunion between two earthly lovers, but his language is noticeably cautious and guarded. For the full realization of his deepest longing—the longing for an earthly union that will not only renew itself, but even strengthen its bond on the other side of this world—Donne turned, as we shall see, elsewhere.

CHAPTER THREE

The Anniversaries

In his *Apology for Raymond Sebond*, Michel de Montaigne dismisses Plato's reassurance that our souls will enjoy the rewards of the other life. "For by that reckoning," Montaigne declares, "it will no longer be man, nor consequently ourselves, whom this enjoyment will concern; for we are built of two principal essential parts, whose separation is the death and destruction of our beings."[1] Donne almost certainly knew Montaigne's great essay—he refers to Montaigne on multiple occasions in his writing—and it is even more likely that he agreed wholeheartedly with the sentiments Montaigne expresses here. For Donne, the parting of body and soul was nothing less than what Montaigne calls the "death and destruction of our beings"—and he anticipated this parting, compulsively, obsessively, with the deepest horror.

Although Donne celebrates the ascension of the soul to heaven on various occasions in his devotional writings, he never abandons his conviction that the separation of body and soul is an unnatural division of the self. To be sure, once the soul has left the body, he imagines its experience of heavenly joys will in certain ways exceed the pleasures of its earthly sojourn. Despite this expectation of future bliss, however, Donne regularly depicts the moment of parting between body and soul as one of mutual difficulty. This understanding of death as a difficult process for the soul as well as for the body was a conventional position among patristic and medieval theologians. Among many other examples, Augustine describes the soul's "natural appetite" for the body, and imagines that this appetite hinders the soul in its journey to the highest heaven, and St. Bernard, who generally regards the flesh as miserable and foul, still attests to the soul's longing to be reunited with its body.[2]

For English Protestants, however, the idea that the soul resisted its de-

parture from the flesh ran counter to some of the most fundamental as-
sumptions about death. According to the liturgy of the Church of England,
the soul should feel nothing but liberation at the moment of leaving the
body. This is made explicit in the Prayer Book's "Order for the Burial of the
Dead," in which the priest affirms that the "souls of them that be elected,
after they be delivered from the burden of the flesh, be in joy and felicity."[3]
Similar sentiments pervade the writings of the sixteenth-century Reformers
who shaped the church's official and unofficial doctrines. Thomas Becon,
chaplain to the archbishop of Canterbury, writes that we should rejoice at
our soul's departure from the body's "stinking filthiness of sin," whereby the
soul will pass on to "eternal life and pleasure without end"; Henry Bullinger,
minister of Zurich, affirms that "So truly the soul, being separated from
his earthly or slimy body, doth so little feel any discommodity, that, being
delivered from the trouble and burden of the body, it liveth more at liberty,
and worketh more effectually"; and Nicholas Ridley, bishop of London, declares that "death shall deliver us from this mortal body, which loaded and
beareth down the spirit, that it cannot so well perceive heavenly things; in
the which so long as we dwell, we are absent from God."[4]

When Donne preaches from his pulpit in St. Paul's that "naturally, the
soule and body are united, [and] when they are separated by Death, it is contrary to nature, which nature still affects this union; and consequently the
soule is the lesse perfect, for this separation" (4:358), he represents death in
a manner contrary to the standard position of his church. We will return in
chapter 6 to Donne's sermons about death and resurrection, but it is crucial to recognize that signs of his belief in the fundamental unnaturalness
of separating soul from body are not limited to his sermons alone. Indeed,
Donne's most daring depiction of the longing that soul and body feel for each
other at the moment of death comes neither in a sermon nor in a meditation. It comes in a long, commemorative poem. In *The Second Anniversarie*,
written in 1612 for the two-year anniversary of the death of Elizabeth Drury,
Donne stages in the most vivid terms the difficulty of convincing the soul to
leave the body behind. He also comes closer than anywhere else in his writings to explaining why the soul feels so strong an attachment to the flesh, an
explanation that turns on an unorthodox account of the soul's origins.

The notion that *The Second Anniversarie* is something other than a traditional celebration of the soul's passage to heaven will come as a surprise to
most readers. The bracingly unusual representation of the world as corpse in
The First Anniversarie has long been noted, and this poem's peculiar braiding together of an inquiry into the "new philosophy," on the one hand, and
a lament for the death of a girl whom Donne had never met, on the other

hand, has made it one of the most critically debated works in early modern literature. At the same time that the complexities of *The First Anniversarie* have been thoroughly considered, the radical nature of *The Second Anniversarie* has been almost entirely neglected. The title and subtitle of this poem declare a straightforward meditative work: *Of the Progresse of the Soule. Wherein, By occasion of the Religious death of Mistris Elizabeth Drury, the incommodities of the Soule in this life, and her exaltation in the next, are contemplated.* These claims—both to record the "incommodities" of the earthly and to celebrate the "exaltation" of the heavenly—have been accepted more or less at face value. Hence in a highly influential reading of the poem, Louis Martz declares it to retain its focus on a "true Progress" toward God's grace; in her seminal book-length study of the *Anniversaries*, Barbara Lewalski similarly concludes that the poem presents "a sequence of topics concerning the soul's benefit by death, ordered as a logical progression according to an ascending scale."[5] Other critics have overwhelmingly concurred. P. G. Stanwood describes *The Second Anniversarie* as bearing witness to the "life of grace made possible by God"; A. C. Partridge argues that Donne represents the death of the body as a "blessing, since it implies a release of the soul"; and Terry Sherwood declares that the poet presents a soul "yearning to be filled even further with Grace." Even Carey, who rarely takes Donne at his word, affirms that the poem "vigorously corroborate[s] . . . the traditional opposition of soul and body."[6]

The reasons behind this unusual critical willingness to accept a poem's description of itself are not accidental: they speak to the heart of Donne's method. For the heterodoxies of *The Second Anniversarie* are by no means clearly presented on its surface. Instead, the poem dramatizes the tension between the argument that readers expect from the promises of the title and the actual condition of the soul, a soul that remains attached to its own earthly flesh against its better theological interests. In representing the struggle of the soul to leave the body behind, Donne simultaneously rehearses and rejects the traditional wisdom of Western metaphysics about human dualism. In his Epistle to the Romans, St. Paul decries his imprisonment in his mortal flesh: "O wretched man that I am! Who shall deliver me from the body of this death?" (7:24). *The Second Anniversarie* borrows heavily from the Pauline notion of the body as the prison house for the soul, and yet the soul loves the body all the same. This is the disposition of the soul that Donne's poem records, a disposition so unexpected in its violation of normative Protestant belief that it has escaped our critical eye.[7]

Where do souls come from? Does the body contaminate the soul with original sin, or does the soul bring original sin into the body? Is the soul part

of the body, or is it generated separately? What is the relationship between
the body and soul? These are among the questions that Donne attempts to
address in *The Second Anniversarie;* they are also the questions that Augustine raised in a letter to Jerome, where he usefully if indecisively explores the
nature of the soul's creation. The issue that troubles Augustine is one that
has direct bearing upon Donne's consideration of the pristine soul of Elizabeth Drury in the *Anniversaries:* namely, how can we explain the presence
of sinfulness in otherwise innocent souls—in Augustine's case, the souls of
infants—unless we accept that souls are themselves generated in the body
and not made separately by God? "What kind of justice is it," Augustine
asks, "that so many thousands of souls should be damned because they departed from their bodies by death in infancy, without the grace of the Christian sacrament, if new souls, created separately by the will of the Creator,
are joined to separate bodies at birth, with no previous sin of their own?"[8]
If, however, the soul is formed in the body and not created independently
by God, Augustine's conundrum disappears. For, in this case, he concludes,
we can assume that sin is acquired in the flesh, and hence that God cannot
be blamed for implanting original sin in each new soul.

As we saw in the introduction, the theory that the soul is generated
inside the body is known as traducianism. Traducianism—also referred to
as *ex traduce*—stands in opposition to the theory that the soul is created
separately by God and then infused into the body before birth. In nearly all
respects, the infusion theory is more attractive to Augustine—it alone helps
to explain the immortality of the soul, for example, since the soul's origins
in this case have nothing to do with the mortal body. And yet, although
Augustine openly wishes it otherwise, he finds himself unable to embrace
the infusion theory wholeheartedly because of its implications of divine
responsibility for human sinfulness. "The opinion that all souls come from
the first soul [*ex traduce*] is one I do not wish to discuss," he concludes
to Jerome, "unless it should be necessary, and how I wish that the one we
are now debating [infusion by God] may be so well upheld by you that the
other may not require discussion!" (31). Despite the urgency of his plea for
help—he complains, in fact, that Jerome has sent him students "to learn the
very thing I have not yet learned myself" (14)—Augustine never received
an adequate reply.[9]

The difficulty of these questions about the origins of the soul continued
to plague theologians throughout the centuries, so that by the time Donne
attempted to tackle the problem himself in the early 1600s, he could rightly
declare a theological crux. As he succinctly put it in his *"De Anima"* letter
to Goodyer, both theories of the soul's origins are marked by "such infirmi-

ties as it is time to look for a better" (16). As we observed, no further thoughts on this subject appear in the letters that survive, nor does Donne ever attempt to write a treatise on the soul beyond his exposition to Goodyer. Once he assumes his position within the church, his pronouncements on the subject tend to uphold the establishment's preference for the infusion account. In a sermon from 1618, for example, he urges his listeners to consider that God took each of them from the "leavened lump of *Adam*," where they were "wrapped in damnation," and "himself created, and infused an immortal soul" into their bodies; in 1624, he describes "that soule, which was at first breath'd from God"; and many other examples can be adduced (1:273–74, 6:75).

Notwithstanding these signs of later conformity, the *ex traduce* position offered clear advantages for Donne's fundamental belief in the mutual dependence between body and soul. In the years preceding his ordination, he chose to explore these advantages most thoroughly not in prose but in poetry, a medium that afforded him an expressive and experimental space that his prose works did not seem to allow. In *The Second Anniversarie*'s portrayal of death as comparable to the reluctant parting of two lovers, Donne denies the soul's desire to be in heaven if such an "elevation" means leaving the body behind. The complexity of this representation of the soul is intensified by the explicit purpose of the poem: to honor the memory of a young girl whose soul is assumed to be safely lodged in heaven and whose parents—Donne's patrons—could hardly welcome any suggestions to the contrary. How, then, does Donne reconcile his depiction of the soul's longing for the body with the commemoration of Elizabeth Drury? And what form of comfort could such a poem ultimately offer?

⁓◈⁓

Donne first approaches the task of commemorating Elizabeth Drury in a poem known as "A Funerall Elegie," which has been printed with the two *Anniversaries* since their first joint edition.[10] Grierson speculates that "A Funerall Elegie" was written to complement the elaborate tomb the Drurys erected to their daughter's memory; the poem in this sense is dedicated to the corpse and not to the departed spirit.[11] This attention to the body is consistent with the elegiac tradition: as a poetics of mourning, elegy addresses loss rather than redemption, the death of the body and not the immortality of the soul.[12] Donne was a practitioner of this tradition, and in the years immediately surrounding Miss Drury's death, he had composed elegies for several close relatives and loved ones of his patroness, the Countess of Bedford—her brother, Lord Harrington; her first cousin Lady Markham; and her friend Cecilia Bulstrode—as well as for James I's son, Prince Henry. With the partial exception of his "Elegie on the Lady Marckham," however, in which he describes Lady Markham's grave as "her limbecke, which refines / The Diamonds, Rubies, Saphires, Pearles, and Mines / Of which this flesh was" (23–25), none of Donne's other elegies focuses so intensely as his elegy for Elizabeth Drury on the status of the corpse in the grave.

Given his interest in winning a new patron, Donne begins "A Funerall Elegie" with a risky dismissal of the expensive tomb purchased by the Drurys:

> 'Tis lost, to trust a Tombe with such a guest,
> Or to confine her in a marble chest.
> Alas, what's Marble, Jeat, or Porphyrie,
> Priz'd with the Chrysolite of either eye,
> Or with those Pearles, and Rubies, which she was?
> Joyne the two Indies in one Tombe, 'tis glasse;
> And so is all to her materials,
> Though every inch were ten Escurials,
> Yet she's demolish'd: can wee keepe her then
> In works of hands, or of the wits of men? (1–10)

Even the strongest and most durable of natural materials cannot compare, Donne contends, with the precious gems—chrysolite, pearls, and rubies—which constituted Elizabeth's body. (As we have just seen, he describes Lady Markham's flesh in similar terms, so the compliment was not reserved for Elizabeth alone.) The emphasis on Elizabeth's superior materiality heightens the devastation of her decay: "Yet she's demolish'd." The verb "demolish," from Latin *de* + *moliri* ("to build or erect a structure") corresponds to the reference in the preceding line to the Escorial, the palatial fortress constructed in granite for Philip II as both a home and a burial place for Spanish kings. The force of this passage is to conjure an almost unimaginable scale and solidity for the young woman's body in order to convey the enormity of the loss.

After establishing the futility of preserving the corpse, the challenge of preservation shifts from the tomb to the poem itself. "Can these memorials, ragges of paper," Donne asks, "give / Life to that name, by which name they must live?" (11–12). We return to the problem of dead matter that we found in Donne's letters: papers without souls are simply "ragges," material remnants stripped of their vitalizing force. "I know what dead carkasses things written are," Donne wrote to Lady Montgomery, "in respect of things spoken" (25). It was only through her reading of his sermon, he explained, that the text could be "inanimated," or resurrected from the dead. In a similar manner, Donne searches in "A Funerall Elegie" for a mutually animating principle between Elizabeth Drury and himself: both her corpse and his poem suffer from a lack of spirit that each seeks in the other. Just as letters without souls are "dead carkasses," so his poem risks becoming "carcasse verses": "Sickly, alas, short-liv'd, aborted bee / Those carcasse verses, whose soule is not shee" (13–14).

The challenge that Donne initially assigns himself is to overcome his medium's material limitations so that verses, unlike graves, might not be limited to corpses—they might also contain souls. In his letters, we saw that Donne described wrapping his own heart inside the rag of paper. "There is not a size of paper in the Palace," he effusively writes to Goodyer, "large enough to tell you how much I esteeme my selfe honoured in your remembrances; nor strong enough to wrap up a heart so ful of good affections towards you, as mine is" (254). Likewise in "A Funerall Elegie," he considers whether Elizabeth's soul would "stoop to be / In paper wrapt; or, when shee would not lie / In such a house, dwell in an Elegie" (16–18). The elegy assumes a more durable materiality than the paper upon which it is written—it promises a longevity that exceeds its strictly physical qualities.

No sooner, however, does Donne attempt to secure immortality for his verse than he dismisses this as a worthwhile goal. In response to the question of where Elizabeth's soul should be housed, he replies: "But 'tis no matter; wee may well allow / Verse to live so long as the world will now" (19–20). Given the poem's preoccupation with the nature of materiality, it would be hard not to see "'tis no matter" as a pun. Donne does not simply dismiss the problem of housing Elizabeth's soul as outside of his concern: he also declares that the soul is "no matter," and hence that the larger project of enveloping or capturing it within his earthly verse needs to be laid aside. This question of the soul's materiality is not settled by any means in these lines—it returns as a concern in the *Anniversaries*—but in the elegy Donne does not attempt to interrogate this further. Instead, by connecting the life span of verse to the life span of this world alone, he means to deny himself the possibility of achieving immortality in verse.

In cordoning off the prospect of writing immortal poetry, Donne defines himself as a poet of this world and not the next. His task in "A Funerall Elegie" is focused on mourning Elizabeth's death rather than celebrating her rebirth:

But must wee say she's dead? . . .
May't not be said, that her grave shall restore
Her, greater, purer, firmer, then before?
Heaven may say this, and joy in't; but can wee
Who live, and lacke her, here this vantage see?
What is't to us, alas, if there have beene
An Angell made a Throne, or Cherubin? (37, 45–50)

To the living, to the grieving Drurys and their loved ones, Donne declares that no "vantage" lies in the notion of Elizabeth's triumphant arrival in heaven. This is an unorthodox sentiment, and Donne rarely voices it so explicitly—the only other instance we can adduce is his 1624 memorial poem, "An hymne to the Saints, and to Marquesse Hamylton," in which he declares:

What ever order grow
Greater by him in Heaven, wee doe not so.
One of your orders growes by his accesse;
But, by his losse grow all our *orders* lesse;
The name of *Father, Master, Friend,* the name
Of *Subject* and of *Prince,* in one are lame. (7–12)

The poet registers no pleasure from the idea that Lord Hamilton's death increases the numbers of a heavenly "order"—he registers only the diminishment of the earthly categories of father, master, friend, subject, and prince.

In "A Funerall Elegie," Donne responds to his at once comic and despairing question about the logistics of heavenly promotions—"What is't to us, alas, if there have beene / An Angell made a Throne, or Cherubin?"—with a simple assertion of loss: "Wee lose by't" (49–51). The poignancy of this response—the deeply human sense that whatever transpires in heaven does nothing to lessen the grief of those left behind—is intensified by the repetition of "wee" in this stanza, which expands the circle of mourners from the Drurys to Donne and his readers. Although he did not know Elizabeth Drury, this gesture is not a sign of his insincerity—a charge that has been repeatedly leveled against him since the *Anniversaries'* first publication. Instead, Donne suggests that Elizabeth's death affects all who survive in a manner comparable to the experience he describes in the celebrated lines from the *Devotions:* "Any mans *death* diminishes *me,* because I am involved in *Mankinde;* And therefore never send to know for whom the *bell* tolls; It tolls for *thee*" (87).

Donne's elegy for Elizabeth Drury represents the consequences of her death as affecting those people who survive her, but there is no suggestion that this single event will take its toll on the physical world at large. The more or less conventional representation of the scale of loss that we find in "A Funerall Elegie" is radically reconceived in *The First Anniversarie*, in which Miss Drury's death is the precipitating cause for nothing less than the death of the world. Readers as early as Ben Jonson have complained about the extravagance of Donne's conceit, and critiqued what they saw as the poem's indecent hyperbole. As Jonson famously put it, *The First Anniversarie* was "profane and full of Blasphemies." "If it had been written of ye Virgin Marie," he declared, "it had been something," to which Donne is said to have replied that he described "the Idea of a Woman and not as she was."[13] This is not the occasion to rehearse the many responses to either Jonson's charge or Donne's retort, which have generated a significant body of literary criticism on their own.[14] I want only to add that Donne's decision to imagine Miss Drury as the soul of a place is not unique to *The First Anniversarie*, nor is his idea that the entire world may die as the result of a single person's death. In his love poem "A Feaver," he describes his beloved as the "worlds soule" and begs her not to die:

> But yet thou canst not die, I know;
> To leave this world behinde, is death,
> But when thou from this world wilt goe,
> The whole world vapors with thy breath.
> Or if, when thou, the worlds soule, goest,
> It stay, tis but thy carkasse then. (5–10)

Similarly, in a letter to Bridget White, probably written several years before *The First Anniversarie*, Donne laments Mistress White's departure from town, and observes that her "going away hath made *London* a dead carkasse." "A Tearm and a Court do a little spice and embalme it," he explains, "and keep it from putrefaction, but the soul went away in you" (1). Whether we find the conceit extravagant or not, it is important to realize that it was merely expanded, rather than invented, for Donne's commemoration of Elizabeth Drury.

In *The First Anniversarie*, Donne laments the state of the world once Elizabeth's soul has departed—his focus is firmly placed on the corpse left behind, which he proposes to "anatomize." In *The Second Anniversarie*, he shifts his focus from the earthly to the heavenly, from the body to the soul. It is here, we imagine, that consolation will finally be delivered: by addressing the soul's joyful ascent to heaven and not the pitiful state of the world as corpse, this poem promises a hopeful vision of Elizabeth's posthumous life. In both its sweeping indictment of mortal existence and its affirmation of heavenly pleasures unattainable on earth, *The Second Anniversarie* does seem at first glance to be, as Martz and others have argued, a series of *contemptus mundi* meditations designed to prepare the soul for heaven.[15] But although such readings are certainly available—and in isolated passages convincing—they overlook the profound idiosyncrasies of Donne's poem. For those familiar with the meditative traditions that Donne inherited, what is altogether startling about *The Second Anniversarie* is its representation of the great difficulty of releasing the soul from its earthly attachments. Given the wretched condition of the world so vigorously evoked in *The First Anniversarie,* we have no reason to expect such resistance from the soul. Despite the promises of its title, however, *The Second Anniversarie,* or *Of the Progresse of the Soule,* does not ultimately celebrate the soul's ascension. Instead, the poem portrays the unnaturalness of separating the two parts of the self.

The Second Anniversarie represents the most sustained, and most imaginative, exploration of the disposition of the soul and its feelings toward the body in all of Donne's writings. Much to the surprise of first-time readers, Donne places his own soul at the center of the poem: it is the hypothetical "progresse" of his soul that he proposes to chart and not the soul of Elizabeth Drury, which he assumes has already completed its journey to its resting place in heaven. The decision to focus on himself may derive from his desire to produce an extensive and probing exploration of a soul—the spiritual equivalent of the earthly "anatomie" in *The First Anniversarie*—a task that would be difficult to perform on even an intimate friend, let alone on someone he had never met. The decision may also be explained in terms of the highly unconventional treatment of the soul that he provides, one that surely would not have pleased Robert Drury should it have been applied to the soul of his beloved daughter. For in striking contrast to a traditional Protestant narrative that celebrates the soul's "liberation" at the moment of death, *The Second Anniversarie* describes an entirely unhappy and begrudging parting between soul and body.

Donne begins *The Second Anniversarie* by expressing a kind of sympathy for the body when it loses the soul. From the opening lines, we observe a significant difference in tone from *The First Anniversarie,* where Donne describes with clinical detachment the death of the body once the soul has departed:

But though it be too late to succour thee,
Sicke World, yea, dead, yea putrified, since shee
Thy'intrinsique balme, and thy preservative,
Can never be renew'd, thou never live,
I (since no man can make thee live) will try,
What wee may gaine by thy Anatomy. (55–60)

Far from pitying the suffering of the corpse, Donne assumes the role of a cool, dispassionate anatomist.

In *The Second Anniversarie*, by contrast, the poet begins with a nuanced account of the strange, lingering impression of the body's vitality in the moments following death:

But as a ship which hath strooke saile, doth runne
By force of that force which before, it wonne:
Or as sometimes in a beheaded man,
Though at those two Red seas, which freely ranne,
One from the Trunke, another from the Head,
His soule be sail'd, to her eternall bed,
His eyes will twinckle, and his tongue will roll,
As though he beckned, and cal'd backe his soule,
He graspes his hands, and he pulls up his feet,
And seemes to reach, and to step forth to meet
His soule. (7–17)

In his edition of the poems, Grierson traces the simile of the beheaded man to a passage in Lucretius's *De rerum natura* in which the Roman poet describes the slaying of a soldier: "Even the head shorn off from the hot and living trunk retains on the ground the look of life and its open eyes, until it has rendered up all that is left of the spirit."[16]

If Grierson is right that Donne relied on this description in composing his own—and there is ample evidence in Donne's work that he knew Lucretius's poem[17]—it becomes all the more striking that Donne emphasizes the corpse's gestures of longing. Lucretius's corpse is without attachment or affect: the process of giving up the soul is purely reflexive. In Donne's hands, by contrast, the grotesque and macabre figure of the beheaded man becomes a spectacle of pathos, a pathos no doubt heightened by the likelihood that Donne witnessed several such executions and would have observed the effects on the corpse.[18] Even if we know not to believe it rationally, he suggests, the body gives the impression of bidding a reluctant farewell to its spirit—"as though he beckned, and cal'd backe his soule." This impression is compounded by the image that follows of a last, desperate attempt, in which the body "seemes to reach, and to step forth" into a final encounter with the soul so recently lost. The involuntary nature of these motions—evocatively likened to the cracking of ice after a thaw, or the sounds produced by a lute when its strings begin to break—merely intensifies the force of the body's desire.[19]

This early passage in the poem establishes the cravings of the body to stay connected to the soul. For the rest of the poem, Donne shifts his attention to the more surprising depiction of the soul's comparable cravings to remain with the body. The soul's attachment to the body is the real, if undeclared subject of *The Second Anniversarie*; that attachment also represents one of Donne's least recognized, but most important, contributions to early modern poetry. For Donne shows us a soul that we rarely, if ever, encounter in this body of literature—a soul that clings desperately to its flesh despite repeated assurances of its freedom. Compare, for example, the soul in Andrew Marvell's "On a Drop of Dew," which, "remembr'ring still its former height / Shuns the swart leaves and blossoms green" that constitute its earthly home. "How loose and easy hence to go," Marvell exclaims, "How girt and ready to ascend" (22–23; 33–34). Or compare the same poet's "Dialogue Between the Soul and Body," which begins with the soul's plaintive cry:

> O, who shall, from this dungeon, raise
> A soul inslaved so many ways?
> With bolts of bones, that fettered stands
> In feet; and manacled in hands.
> Here blinded with an eye; and there
> Deaf with the drumming of an ear.
> A soul hung up, as 'twere, in chains
> Of nerves, and arteries, and veins.
> Tortured, besides each other part,
> In a vain head, and double heart. (1–10)

"Inslaved," "fettered," "manacled," "blinded," "hung up," "tortured": this is the language Donne might use to characterize what he dismissively refers to in *The First Anniversarie* as a mere "In-mate soule" (6), one who lodges only temporarily in the body and is desperate to escape.[20] If Marvell's soul begs in the traditional idiom of Christian metaphysics to be freed from the "dungeon" of mortal flesh, Donne's soul in *The Second Anniversarie* reveals a great unwillingness to leave its mortal home.

The idea of the reluctant soul is introduced early in *The Second Anniversarie,* where Donne instructs his soul to thirst for the day when human hymns shall be overwhelmed by God's own:

> These Hymnes thy issue, may encrease so long,
> As till Gods great *Venite* change the song.
> Thirst for that time, O my insatiate soule,
> And serve thy thirst, with Gods safe-sealing Bowle.
> Be thirstie still, and drinke still till thou goe
> To th'only Health, to be Hydroptique so.
> Forget this rotten world. (43–49)

What does it mean that Donne needs to command his soul to thirst? At first glance, it might seem that his soul lacks thirst altogether, and hence needs its desires to be stimulated. On reflection, however, it becomes clear that the possession of thirst per se is not the problem. Instead, it is the object of the soul's thirst that needs to be corrected. For the problem is not that Donne has a lackluster soul: his soul is thirsty, even "insatiate," but its thirst does not naturally incline toward the drink placed before it.[21] Donne has chosen, in other words, to represent a soul that does not want "God's safe-sealing Bowle," a soul that leans, as it were, in the wrong direction.

The challenge that arises is one of redirecting the soul's desire: Donne wants to orient the soul's "hydroptique" drive toward heavenly and not earthly ends.[22] To argue—as nearly all commentators on these lines have done—that the soul already yearns for this spiritual drink, and that Donne describes, in the words of one critic, only further "fulfillment of the soul's thirst in joy," is to miss not only the central project of the poem, but one of Donne's central preoccupations throughout his writings: to comfort the soul as well as the body in the face of their separation.[23] The soul of *The Second Anniversarie* is not naturally filled with the desire for its union with God. It is a soul stuck in attachments that it has been taught by Protestant doctrine to relinquish, a soul that bemoans rather than celebrates its imminent "freedom" from earthly matter.

Donne's efforts to convince the soul to leave the earth begin with arguments that he rehearsed in *The First Anniversarie* about the world's corruption. In that poem, he characterized the world's "generall sickenesse" not to lie "In any humour, or one certaine part; / But as thou sawest it rotten at the heart" (240–42). In *The Second Anniversarie,* he is less interested in the status of the world as corpse than in the soul's parasitic relationship to this carcass. "The world is but a carkasse," he declaims,

> thou art fed
> By it, but as a worme, that carkasse bred;
> And why should'st thou, poore worme, consider more,
> When this world will grow better then before,
> Then those thy fellow wormes doe thinke upon
> That carkasses last resurrection. (55–60)

The shock of these lines lies in their unprecedented address of the soul as "poore worme." No longer the source of the body's animation, the soul becomes the equivalent of a maggot feeding off death. Donne suggests, moreover, that the soul's lingering presence on earth threatens to confuse the division between material and spiritual beings. This confusion is intensified by the caesura in line 55—"the world is but a carkasse; thou art fed"—which creates an uncomfortable closeness between "carkasse" and "thou" (the soul). Some lines later, Donne returns to Elizabeth's death as further proof of the world's worthlessness:

> Shee, shee is gone; she is gone; when thou knowest this,
> What fragmentary rubbidge this world is
> Thou knowest, and that it is not worth a thought;
> He honors it too much that thinkes it nought. (81–84)

These arguments do nothing, however, either to propel the soul forward or to sever its attachments to a world that it has been instructed to despise. If Donne means to represent the "incommodities of the soule in this life," why does he depict his soul as so reluctant to depart?

The most compelling answer to this question lies in Donne's account of the soul's origins. In *The Second Anniversarie,* Donne experiments with the idea that the soul is not a strictly divine creation. Instead, he imagines that the soul is made in the body. We might gauge the unusualness of Donne's depiction of the soul's relation to the body by comparing it with John Davies's 1599 poem, *Nosce teipsum,* a meditation on the immortality of the soul that explicitly rejects traducianism:

> But as Gods handmayde, Nature doth create
> Bodies in time distinct, and order due,
> So God gives soules the like successive date,

Which him selfe makes in bodies formed new:
Which him selfe makes of no materiall thing . . .
For though from bodies [Nature] can bodies bring,
Yet could she never soules from soules traduce,
As fire from fire, or light from light doth spring.[24]

For Davies, souls are created not from any "materiall thing": they are made from "substance of the heaven" (620). Nature may create bodies, that is, but it cannot create souls. To traduce the soul—to generate spiritual substance from bodily procreation—is also to traduce the soul in the pejorative sense. It is to suggest an ungodly origin for the immortal part of the self.

If Davies's poem represents, in the words of its twentieth-century editor, "the average Christian philosophy at the end of the Renaissance," Donne's poem surely does not.[25] This is not to claim that traducianism was unique to Donne. In the English Protestant tradition, he could look to the work of the Elizabethan divine John Woolton, for example, who argued in his 1576 *Treatise of the Immortalitie of the Soule* that "mans Soule commeth *ex traduce*, and hath his origin together with the body." "For as the soule is not before the body," Woolton concludes, "so in the beginning of manne the body is not before the soule. They have both one beginning."[26] Later in the seventeenth century, both Thomas Browne, in *Religio Medici*, and Milton, in *De Doctrina Christiana*, would embrace this position. Browne remarks that he "cannot but wonder at the multitude of heads that do deny traduction," and, leaning on rather odd evidence, explains his own certainty as a result of observing those "equivocal and monstrous productions in the copulation of man with beast." "For if the soul be not transmitted and transfused in the seed of the parents," he asks, "why are not these productions merely beasts, but have also a tincture and impression of reason?"[27] Milton frames the problem in more conventional, Augustinian terms, arguing that the infusion theory suggests unequivocally that God contaminates souls with original sin. "My answer," he declares, "is that to create pure souls which lack original righteousness, and then to put them into contaminated and vicious bodies, to surrender them to the body as to an enemy, imprisoned, innocent and unarmed . . . to do all this would argue injustice just as much as to have created them impure would argue impurity."[28]

Unique to *The Second Anniversarie* is not its advocacy of traducianism per se, but its deployment of this belief as a means to explain the soul's attachment to the body. To convey the absurdity of this attachment, Donne paradoxically affirms the soul's tainted, bodily origins. Hence he instructs his soul to meditate on its creation in the flesh: "Thinke further on thy selfe, my Soule," he commands, "and thinke / How thou at first wast made but in a sinke" (157–58). Nothing could be further, of course, from a pristine creation in heaven than this image of the stomach or womb as a "sinke"—a term used in the period only to describe sewers, cesspools, or other receptacles for waste.[29] Donne's choice of the word "sinke" in relation to the soul's birth is further sharpened if we contrast it with these lines from a verse epistle to Goodyer: "Our soule, whose country'is heaven, and God her father, / Into this world, corruptions sinke, is sent."[30] Here, Donne imagines the soul's descent from its native "country" in the heavens to the corrupting "sinke" of this world.

In the subsequent lines of *The Second Anniversarie*, Donne intensifies our impression of the utterly dirty conditions in which the soul is made. "Thinke but how poore thou wast, how obnoxious," Donne continues,

> Whom a small lumpe of flesh could poyson thus.
> This curded milke, this poore unlittered whelpe
> My body, could, beyond escape or helpe,
> Infect thee with Originall sinne, and thou
> Couldst neither then refuse, nor leave it now. (164–68)

In chastising the soul for its excessive vulnerability (or "obnoxious[ness]")—here suggesting frailty or liability to illness—to the hardly threatening "curded milke" or "lumpe of flesh" that is the human body, Donne implies that a purer soul could certainly have withstood the infection of original sin. And yet, one of the central questions raised in *The First Anniversarie* is whether even the purest of creatures, Elizabeth Drury, can resist contamination.

In *The First Anniversarie*, Donne describes Elizabeth as the world's "intrinsique balme, and thy preservative" (57), as if she alone could protect the world from the corruption that ensues upon her death. It is worth pausing to consider what Donne means by this metaphor of the "balme," as it has important consequences for his depiction of the soul in *The Second Anniversarie*. Donne's use of the metaphor can be traced to the sixteenth-century German physician known as Paracelsus, who maintained that every living creature contained its own balsam that protects its body from decay. Although at times Donne is skeptical of Paracelsus, whose collected works he owned and seems to have read with attention, he was clearly attracted to the idea of a human balm and employed it on several occasions as a vehicle for praise.[31] Hence in a verse epistle to Lady Bedford, he imagines the favor of his patroness replacing his own balm as a means for his self-preservation: "That thankfullnesse your favours have begot / In mee, embalmes mee, that I doe not rot."[32] A second epistle to Lady Bedford likewise extols her exquisite preservation in Paracelsian terms:

> In every thing there naturally growes
> A *Balsamum* to keepe it fresh, and new,
> If 'twere not injur'd by extrinsique blowes;
> Your birth and beauty are this Balme in you.[33]

The only threat Donne imagines to the countess's beauty originates from outside her body, in "extrinsique blowes."

In the verse epistles to Lady Bedford, Donne imagines the balm as a corporeal equivalent to the soul: both perform the crucial task of keeping the body from becoming a corpse. The exclusively corporeal nature of the human balm will later prove troubling to Donne, however, for it suggests that the body can somehow itself overcome the spiritual ills of the soul. "Every thing hath in it," he preaches in a Whitsunday sermon, "as Physitians use to call it, *Naturale Balsamum*, A naturall Balsamum, which, if any wound or hurt which that creature hath received, be kept clean from extrinsique putrefaction, will heale of it self." And yet, he continues, we also have a "naturall poyson in us, Originall sin" (6:116). One solution to this problem is to imagine that the soul possesses the equivalent of the body's balsam, her "*Nardus*" or "spikenard, a perfume, a fragrancy" that ought to have a "naturall disposition to Morall goodnesse, as the body hath to health."[34] But the soul's disadvantage is this: whereas the body's illnesses are caused by "extrinsique offences of the Ayre, and putrefaction from thence," the "causes in the wounds of the soule, are intrinsique, so as no other man can apply physick to them" (5:348–49). They are not only intrinsic, Donne concludes in this sermon, "they are hereditary, and there was no time early inough for our selves to apply any thing by way of prevention, for the wounds were as soone as we were, and sooner; Here was a new soule, but an old sore; a yong childe, but an inveterate disease" (5:349).

In *The First Anniversarie*, Donne adapts his critique of the Paracelsian balm to explain why Elizabeth Drury, the balm of the world, was ultimately incapable of saving the world from decay. The reasons for this lie in the pervasive nature of earthly corruption, a corruption that spreads unsparingly to the protective balm itself. "Her death hath taught us dearely," Donne remarks to the corpse of the world lying on his dissection table, "that thou art / Corrupt and mortall in thy purest part" (61–62).[35] It is not altogether

clear what Donne means by the earth's "purest part"—presumably he does
not refer to Elizabeth's soul, which might be corrupted by original sin, but
which he would not characterize as "mortall." More likely, he refers to the
combination of Elizabeth's body and soul, which together came closest to,
but could not finally possess the level of purity required to withstand the
corroding forces of decay.

Donne's interest in determining the purity of the earth's "purest part"
corresponds to one of the crucial tasks in *The First Anniversarie:* to identify any form of corporeality that might be invulnerable to corruption. In a
strange passage that follows shortly upon the lines describing the penetrative
power of the disease's corruption, he conjures up the world that remains after
Elizabeth's death, a "new world; and new creatures" whose very bodies are
composed out of Elizabeth's virtue:

> And though to be thus elemented, arme
> These creatures, from home-borne intrinsique harme,
> (For all assum'd unto this dignitie,
> So many weedlesse Paradises bee,
> Which of themselves produce no venemous sinne,
> Except some forraine Serpent bring it in)
> Yet, because outward stormes the strongest breake,
> And strength it selfe by confidence growes weake,
> This new world may be safer, being told
> The dangers and diseases of the old. (79–88)

These new creatures are vulnerable, Donne tells us, only to what he describes
in his sermon as "extrinsique offences" (5:348)—like Lady Bedford, whom,
we will recall, was said to be vulnerable only to "extrinsique blowes"—and
not to the "home-borne intrinsique harme" that afflicted human beings up
to this point. Hence to be immune to the corrosive forces of earthly decay,
one must also be exempt from original sin. There is no possibility of maintaining material integrity while suffering from spiritual corruption.

However close Elizabeth came to perfection, then, her death ultimately
reflects her inclusion among the race of humans whose sinfulness is innate
and not foreign. As Donne remarks in his "Elegie on the Lady Marckham":

> Of what small spots pure white complaines! Alas,
> How little poyson cracks a christall glasse!
> She sinn'd, but just enough to let us see
> That God's word must be true, All, sinners be. (41–44)

Although he is not nearly so frank about the inevitable sinfulness of Eliza-beth Drury's soul, the implication is clear: like Lady Markham, Elizabeth was as close to perfection as human beings can come, but still could not be exempted from the general curse of original sin.

In *The Second Anniversarie*, Donne connects the question of original sin to the question of the soul's origins. Just as Augustine could not reconcile the tension between the theory that the soul was infused into the body and the presence of original sin in each soul, so Donne struggles with the idea that something forged by God outside of the body could be susceptible to corporeal infection. Donne explains his problems with the infusion theory in the *Devotions*, where, as we have seen, he writes that it is "hard, to charge the *soule* with the guiltiness of *Originall* sinne, if the *soule* were infused into a *body*, in which it must necessarily grow *foule*, and contract *originall sinne*, whether it *will* or *no*" (91). The clarity of this exposition is not trans-ferable to *The Second Anniversarie*, however, and the pleasure of the poem lies to no small degree in its complex depiction of a soul that is not making a theologically sound decision. However, if we return to the question posed earlier—why does Donne simultaneously declare the soul's earthly life to be full of "incommodities" and represent its attachment to the body as so deep?—we can provisionally conclude that the complicity between body and soul emerges out of the soul's status as a bodily creation.

After stressing the foul conditions of the soul's birth, Donne returns to the task of imagining the soul's liberation from the body in death. "This to thy Soule allow," he instructs,

> Thinke thy shell broke, thinke thy Soule hatch'd but now.
> And think this slow-pac'd soule, which late did cleave
> To'a body, and went but by the bodies leave,
> Twenty, perchance, or thirty mile a day,
> Dispatches in a minute all the way
> Twixt heaven, and earth. (184–89)

To advance the soul's contemplation of this "long-short Progresse" to heaven (219), Donne reintroduces Elizabeth Drury after a nearly eighty-line absence. In lines that have been praised by readers over the centuries—already by 1829 Anna Jameson observes that the lines "have been quoted *ad infini-tum*"[36]—Donne bids his soul to remember Elizabeth's example:

> remember then, that shee,
> Shee, whose faire body no such prison was,

But that a Soule might well be pleas'd to passe
An age in her; she whose rich beauty lent
Mintage to other beauties, for they went
But for so much as they were like to her;
Shee, in whose body (if we dare preferre
This low world, to so high a marke as shee,)
The Westerne treasure, Easterne spicerie,
Europe, and Afrique, and the unknowne rest
Were easily found, or what in them was best . . .
She, of whose soule, if wee may say, 'twas Gold,
Her body was th'Electrum, and did hold
Many degrees of that; wee understood
Her by her sight; her pure, and eloquent blood
Spoke in her cheekes, and so distinctly wrought,
That one might almost say, her body thought. (220–30; 241–46)

The elaborate accumulation of dependent clauses describing the unique nature of Elizabeth's flesh culminates in perhaps the finest compliment any
metaphysician could give to the body: "one might almost say, her body
thought." Donne seems here at once to anticipate and to rebut Descartes'
cogito, the supreme isolation of mind as the exclusive sphere of thinking. Of
course, the *"almost"* in "one might almost say" gently retreats from affirming the radical possibility that the body itself does the thinking, and hence
that there is really no distinction between corporeal and mental faculties.
But the suggestion is certainly there, and it corresponds to Donne's larger interest in blurring the lines between material and spiritual, body and soul.

     This reluctance on Donne's part to recognize or reify the distinctions
between the two parts of the self first surfaced in *The First Anniversarie,*
where he describes a world so plagued by the "generall sickenesse" that not
even its "subtilst immateriall parts" are immune: "For the worlds subtilst
immateriall parts / Feele this consuming wound, and ages darts" (247–48).
What he means by the "subtilst immateriall parts" is not immediately clear.
As we saw in chapter 1, in the seventeenth century "subtle" was regularly
used to describe a substance of thin consistency. (It is clearly this meaning
that Donne has in mind, for example, when he describes in "The Funerall" his mistress's "subtile wreath of haire" [3] wrapped around his bone.)
As Donne knew from Aristotle and Aquinas, among others, substances are
either material or immaterial, but while there are varying degrees of materiality, there are not comparable categories for immateriality. The parts can

be immaterial or they could be subtly material, but they cannot be "subtle" and immaterial at the same time.

Donne was not a metaphysician by trade, however, and what was impossible for Aristotle or Aquinas was imaginatively suggestive for the poet. In *The First Anniversarie*, as on other occasions, Donne reveals his interest in testing the boundaries between materiality and immateriality, in locating those substances that belonged precisely on the borders between the two states of being.[37] When he mentions the "worlds subtilst immateriall parts" in *The First Anniversarie* (247), he does so as a gesture of approximating but never reaching the point where matter, however fine or pure, becomes spirit. In *The Second Anniversarie*, his compliment to Elizabeth—"one might *almost* say, her body thought"—similarly attempts to define what it would mean for a body to be indistinguishable from a mind.

Donne began the long compliment in *The Second Anniversarie* with the instruction to remember: "remember then, that shee, / Shee, whose faire body no such prison was . . ." Following the nearly thirty-line deferral of his main verb, over the course of which he describes in extravagant terms how extraordinary Elizabeth's body was, we might expect the climax of the sentence to be something like: "Shee, ev'n shee, chose to shed her mortal flesh." But the conclusion we anticipate—that unlike Donne's soul, which cannot part from the inferior home of Donne's flesh, Elizabeth's soul willingly left the most intelligent, alluring, and pure of bodies—is denied us. Instead, Donne records her soul's departure as neither voluntary nor resistant but simply as fact. The passage ends with a declaration of loss more appropriate to "A Funerall Elegie" than to a poem meant to celebrate the ascension of Elizabeth's soul: "Shee, shee, thus richly and largely hous'd, is gone" (247).

Why is this conclusion so surprising? Because there is no assertion whatsoever of her soul's eagerness to leave the body behind; because the challenge that the poem has posed for itself—to persuade the soul to relinquish its mortal trappings—is left entirely unresolved. Granted, Donne does allow that once it has severed itself from the body and found its way to heaven, Elizabeth's soul chastises those who remain on this earth. He describes her soul in the subsequent lines as "chid[ing] us slow-pac'd snailes who crawle upon / Our prisons prison, earth, nor thinke us well, / Longer, then whil'st wee beare our brittle shell" (248–50). But given both the paucity of evidence provided for the superior life after death and the devastating poetic effect of concluding this final line with the iambic foot "is gone"—and not, for example, with something suggestively positive like "arose"—it would be difficult not to feel that the loss of "Shee, shee, thus richly and largely hous'd"

exceeds any joy over her ascension. There is no gratitude for the soul's liberation. Instead, there is an overwhelming sense of the tragedy in the soul's
loss of the body.

The tragedy for the soul of separating from the body has so far been explained as a result of the soul's corporeal origins. A second, related explanation turns on the soul's inadequate self-knowledge. Donne suggests, in fact,
that the inability to understand itself is a fundamental feature of the soul
and that this feature intensifies the soul's unwillingness to leave the body
behind. "Thou know'st thy selfe so little," Donne exclaims,

> as thou know'st not,
> How thou didst die, nor how thou wast begot.
> Thou neither know'st, how thou at first cam'st in,
> Nor how thou took'st the poyson of mans sinne.
> Nor dost thou, (though thou know'st, that thou art so)
> By what way thou art made immortall, know. (255–60)

Earlier in the poem Donne expounded to the soul its *ex traduce* creation and
contamination in the flesh. In these lines, he suggests that the soul's ignorance not only about its birth, but also about its immortality, is responsible
for its misguided attraction to the flesh. If only, Donne wryly suggests, the
soul could intuitively understand what philosophers have been debating for
thousands of years, it would no doubt be able to make a sound decision and
abandon its earthly home.

The skepticism that underlies this passage about the soul's ability to
understand itself extends as well to its ability to understand the body that it
inhabits. "Knowst thou but how the stone doth enter in," Donne asks,

> The bladders cave, and never breake the skinne?
> Know'st thou how blood, which to the heart doth flow,
> Doth from one ventricle to th'other goe?
> And for the putrid stuffe, which thou dost spit,
> Know'st thou how thy lungs have attracted it?
> There are no passages, so that there is
> (For ought thou know'st) piercing of substances.
> And of those many opinions which men raise
> Of Nailes and Haires, dost thou know which to praise?
> What hope have wee to know our selves, when wee
> Know not the least things, which for our use be? (269–80)

Donne moves from detailed questions about how the body works—the inquiries about kidney stones, the circulation of the blood, the production of phlegm, the growth of hair and nails even after death—to a more general assault on our self-knowledge. As others have remarked, the passage strongly echoes Montaigne's *Apology*, an essay that, as we have seen, shares Donne's fundamental belief in the horrible rift between body and soul wrought by death, and raises nearly identical questions about the soul's capacity for knowledge.[38] Indeed, Donne's choice of reference to kidney stones may be a quiet homage to Montaigne's well-documented sufferings with the same. "Now it is likely that if the soul knew anything," Montaigne writes, "It would first of all know itself; and if it knew anything outside of itself, that would be its body and shell before anything else. If we see even to this day the gods of medicine disputing about our anatomy, 'Vulcan against, Apollo for Troy stood' (Ovid), when do we expect them to agree? . . . If man does not know himself, how does he know his functions and powers?" (421). Montaigne remains focused in this essay on the variability and instability of earthly knowledge. Donne, by contrast, denounces human knowledge to imagine a heavenly position from which our self-understanding would be vastly improved. Hence he moves from attacking the soul's ignorance—"In this low forme, poore soule, what wilt thou doe? / When wilt thou shake off this Pedantery, / Of being taught by sense, and Fantasie?" (290–92)—to offering the promise of enlightenment:

> Thou look'st through spectacles; small things seeme great
> Below; But up unto the watch-towre get,
> And see all things despoyl'd of fallacies:
> Thou shalt not peepe through lattices of eyes,
> Nor heare through Labyrinths of eares, nor learne
> By circuit, or collections to discerne.
> In heaven thou straight know'st all, concerning it,
> And what concernes it not, shalt straight forget. (293–300)

Edward Tayler concludes in his study of this poem that Donne regards the "watch-towre" not as a heavenly place, but as a symbol for the intellect once it is divorced from sense perception.[39] This reading depends upon the assumption of a transition between lines 298–99, as if "heaven" represents an alternative to the watchtower, a place where knowledge can even more easily be acquired. My preference is to read these lines as a single, continuous description of how knowledge is acquired once the soul has left the body behind. Wherever the watchtower may be, however, it is clear that learning will no longer be a somatic experience: it will not involve the bodily instruments of eyes or ears, which are likened to the media of lattices and labyrinths. Although "labyrinth" was already used at the time to describe part of the inner ear, and "lattice" conjures up the retina of the eye, Donne puns on the obfuscating rather than enabling implications of both terms: seeing and hearing are at once facilitated and hindered by our anatomical structure. In heaven, by contrast, apprehension becomes entirely unmediated—it is something we experience "straight" without any need for our senses.

Even the promise of unmediated knowledge about both body and soul seems inadequate, however, as a means to sever the soul's attachment to the flesh. Once again, it is striking that Donne does not end his long description of heavenly knowledge by affirming the soul's newfound readiness to shed its mortal home. Instead, the soul persists in its inclinations downward. As if he feels his soul turning slowly but decisively away from the glorious offerings of the heavens, he implores it to stay put: "Returne not, my Soule, from this extasie, / And meditation of what thou shalt bee, / To earthly thoughts . . ." (321–23). Donne's fascination with ecstasy—literally, a standing beside or outside of oneself—pervades his writings. And yet, as we witness in "The Extasie," the ecstatic departure of the soul is ultimately valued for enhancing, not diminishing, the sensation of embodiment. Despite the warning to "returne not," the description of this experience as an "extasie" has as a precondition the resumption of the flesh.

If we compare these intimations in *The Second Anniversarie* of the soul's indifference to the proffered visions of heavenly bliss with, for example, Spenser's account of a similar moment in book 1 of *The Faerie Queene,* the peculiarity of Donne's depiction becomes even more pronounced. Having glimpsed the New Jerusalem, the Redcrosse Knight expresses his reluctance to return to his earthly life: "O let me not (quoth he) then turne againe / Backe to the world, whose joyes so fruitlesse are; / But let me here for aye in peace remaine."[40] In *The Second Anniversarie,* by contrast, Donne's soul finds the visions or arguments presented insufficiently compelling to lure it up to heaven. "Up, up, my drowsie Soule," Donne wearily beseeches yet again, "where thy new eare / Shall in the Angels songs no discord heare" (339–40).

After more than three hundred lines of witnessing the refusal of Donne's soul to depart from its corrupted mortal home, we are now in a position to answer the central question: why is a poem entitled "Of the Progresse of the Soule" so incapable of leaving the body behind? The simplest conclusion is that the poem somehow slipped from Donne's control—that he meant but somehow failed to represent a willing soul's ascent to heaven. But the careful representations of the soul's inability to sustain its meditation on heavenly prospects, the deliberate refusal to portray the soul's eagerness to depart at the time of death, the syntactically delayed sentences that do not deliver the conclusions we expect—each of these features suggests simultaneously a poet very much in control of his material and one whose ostensible purpose masks what he actually wants to represent.

Despite the poem's saturation in *contemptus mundi* and *vanitas* traditions, despite its piling of negative attributes upon everything earthly, Donne chooses not to represent the soul as joyfully anticipating its liberation from the flesh. This is the central paradox of *The Second Anniversarie,* a paradox that readers have so long ignored perhaps because it violates traditional notions of the relationship between soul and body in English Protestantism, or perhaps because, more simply, it seems to negate the success of the poem. Yet the act of representing the difficulty of divorcing soul from body cannot be adduced as evidence of *The Second Anniversarie*'s failure. On the contrary, it is an achievement unparalleled in English poetry. It is also Donne's most significant challenge to a philosophical and theological dualism that unequivocally privileges the spiritual over the material self.

Toward the end of the poem, Donne ventures a final argument for the benefits of heaven over earth. Even the "accidentall" joys of heaven, he tells his soul, surpass our "essentiall" earthly pleasures, and he observes "how poore and lame, must then our casuall [joys] bee" (473). He does not describe in any detail, however, the nature of these heavenly joys. Instead, he simply affirms that what differentiates heavenly joys from earthly joys is their duration:

> Only in Heaven joyes strength is never spent;
> And accidentall things are permanent.
> Joy of a soules arrivall ne'r decaies;
> For that soule ever joyes and ever staies. (487–90)

The use of the verb "decaies" in this last couplet echoes the language of *The First Anniversarie* and speaks to what Donne seems to value above all as a characteristic of heavenly life: its permanence. This quality of constancy does not only apply to the soul, moreover, but also speaks to Donne's fantasy about the body. Hence he describes the joy that "approaches in the resurrection; / When earthly bodies more celestiall / Shall be, then Angels were, for they could fall" (492–94). Unlike the angels who were capable of falling, resurrected man is not susceptible to further degradation or sin.

The perfection of the flesh depends upon its reunion with the soul, and at the end of *The Second Anniversarie*, Donne turns to the prospect of this reunion. If in "A Funerall Elegie" Donne denies his readers the "vantage" of the body and soul's heavenly reunion while we still live our mortal lives, at the end of *The Second Anniversarie* he seems poised to assume such a visionary position. The very last lines of the poem affirm Donne's role as *vates:* "Thou art the Proclamation; and I am / The Trumpet, at whose voyce the people came" (527–28). This is the prophecy he wants to proclaim—the day described in 1 Corinthians, when "the trumpet shall sound, and the dead shall be raised incorruptible" (15:52). For Donne to imagine himself as God's trumpet—the embodied instrument of a heavenly spirit—is his most exalted vision of what it means to be a poet.[41]

The climactic vision of a heavenly reunion between body and soul at the end of *The Second Anniversarie* is not only the moment for Donne's affirmation of himself as a poet. It is also where the Drurys might find an unexpected but compelling form of consolation. As someone who had experienced the death of children, Donne may have felt a certain inadequacy in assuring the Drurys that the soul of their beloved daughter was in heaven while her mortal remains, however elaborate the tombstone, lay buried in the cold ground. He may have imagined that although Protestant liturgy and theology told the Drurys to celebrate the ascension of the soul, real comfort lay elsewhere. It lay in the prospect of future continuity—a day when body and soul were forever united—and not in the confirmation of rupture.

In his "Elegie on Mistress Boulstred," Donne boldly declares: "Death gets 'twixt soules and bodies such a place / As sinne insinuates 'twixt just men and grace / Both worke a separation, no divorce" (43–45). As he reassures his readers or listeners on multiple occasions, there may be a temporary parting between body and soul, but—unlike what happens to earthly lovers—there will be no permanent division. For "as farre as man is immortal," he preaches, in his 1626 funeral sermon for Sir William Cokayne,

> man is a married man still, still in possession of a soule, and a body too; And man is for ever immortall in both; Immortall in his soule by Preservation, and immortall in his body by Reparation in the Resurrection. For, though they be separated *a Thoro & Mensa*, from Bed and Board, they are not divorced; Though the soule be at the *Table of the Lambe,* in Glory, and the body but at the table of *the Serpent, in dust;* Though the soule be *in lecto florido,* in that bed which is alwayes green, in an everlasting

spring, in *Abrahams bosome;* And the body but in that green-bed, whose covering is but a yard and a halfe of Turfe, and a Rugge of grasse, and the sheet but a winding sheet, yet they are not divorced; they shall returne to one another againe, in an inseparable re-union in the Resurrection. (7:257–58)

However far the soul and body may be from each other, however glorious the meal of one, and wretched the meal of the other, however verdant the home of one, and vermicular the home of the other, Donne envisions their return to each other in an "inseparable reunion." The marriage between body and soul is not a mortal arrangement, in the words of the Prayer Book service for matrimony, binding two parties until "death us depart."[42] It is a marriage that ultimately transcends the limits of the grave. This is why the soul cannot bear to leave the body in *The Second Anniversarie,* and this is why Donne ultimately forgives its resistance.

CHAPTER FOUR

Holy Sonnets

Donne struggled throughout his life with the fear of death. In *The Second Anniversarie*, this fear manifests itself as a fear of separating the soul from the body. There is little doubt in that poem about either the fate of the soul—its passage to heaven seems secure—or the eventual fate of the body. In the *Holy Sonnets*, by contrast, Donne's fears fall squarely on his hopes for salvation. It is here that he confronts the flawed nature of his physical and spiritual being. It is here that he questions what will become of him not in the grave, but in the aftermath of his resurrection. It is here that he demands immediate attention from God.

The *Holy Sonnets* represent Donne's earliest imaginings of the consequences of divine judgment. We will find more extensive imaginings of this sort later in his career, both in the *Devotions* and in the sermons, and we will also find in these texts more coherent expressions of Donne's eschatological beliefs. But although the *Holy Sonnets* are riddled with theological inconsistencies, they nonetheless reveal many of Donne's most fundamental preoccupations about his posthumous fate. On the one hand, the sonnets include the famous challenge to death issued in "Death be not proud," which affirms with great bravado the ultimate defeat of death through eternal life. In this poem, Donne triumphantly declares the sting of death to be only temporary: "One short sleepe past, wee wake eternally, / And death shall be no more; death, thou shalt die." On the other hand, in many of the other *Holy Sonnets* Donne grapples directly with the anxieties that "Death be not proud" overlooks. Our sleep will not necessarily be short, and we will not necessarily awaken to a triumphant victory. Death itself may indeed be finite, but greater horrors may lie in our eternal life.

Because Donne's primary concern in the *Holy Sonnets* lies in gauging his chances for salvation, he attends more to the state of the soul than to the state of the body. In this respect, these poems are less immediately interested in the relationship between the two parts of the self than many of his other works. Yet, Donne's concerns about his spiritual condition are always entangled with his concerns about his physical condition. The *Holy Sonnets* are suffused with the language of bodily decay, and their urgent pleas for repair are with equal frequency directed at the mortal flesh as at the immortal soul. In sonnet after sonnet Donne asks, why did God make me, and what are his obligations toward me? Who is responsible for my decay and sinfulness? How can I understand the apparent absence or neglect of my maker? Will God save me from damnation at the final judgment? The answers Donne gives depend heavily upon the form of the poem in which the questions are posed.

It is no coincidence that when Donne chooses to address his anxieties about his salvation, he turns to the highly controlled form of the sonnet. For the sonnet's complexity enables Donne to manage or control the existential extremity of the situations he imagines. The sonnet is not, in other words, a transparent vehicle for Donne's devotional exercises—it is not the case that the sentiments of these poems happen to come in the form of sonnets, but could just as easily be conveyed in sestinas or in prose. With its built-in mechanisms for posing and answering its own questions, the sonnet allows Donne to unleash and then rein in his imaginative reach, to create hypothetical and counterfactual scenarios that can be poetically if not devotionally resolved.

Unlike his near contemporary George Herbert, Donne never claims in his poems to have heard God's voice. He is also fundamentally uncertain about whether he is one of God's chosen creatures. The result of these qualities is the particular content and particular form of the sonnets he chooses to write, sonnets that at once attest to his being divinely made and affirm his own ability as a maker. The *Holy Sonnets* are Donne's fullest poetic effort to anticipate, and negotiate, the shape of God's judgment. More than any of his other lyrics, they embody most clearly what might be called a poetics of brinksmanship: Donne positions himself on the threshold between one world and the next in order to imagine—and attempt to control—what awaits him on the other side.

I

One surprising feature of the posthumously entitled *Songs and Sonnets* is that it includes no sonnets whatsoever. Indeed, with the exception of a handful of verse epistles written in the form of sonnets, Donne turned to the sonnet exclusively as a medium for devotional expression. His first venture into the religious sonnet—the seven poems collectively titled *La Corona*, composed around 1608—employs the sonnet to transform Catholic rosary devotions to Mary into a celebration of the life of Christ. Aside from the sonnet entitled "Resurrection," in which Donne implores God to enroll his name in "thy little booke," *La Corona* is largely impersonal in tone, and is not primarily concerned with the poet's spiritual life. As Annabel Patterson has persuasively argued, the poems move our attention away from the devotional preoccupations of Donne himself to focus on Christ alone.[1]

In the *Holy Sonnets*, Donne embarks on an entirely different kind of poetic enterprise. These poems reflect their author's struggle to come to terms with his own history of sinfulness, his inconstant and unreliable faith, his anxiety about his salvation. Far from offering paradigmatic models of praise in the manner of *La Corona*, the *Holy Sonnets* are idiosyncratic and personal. Although they circulated in manuscript, they show no signs of having been intended for broad readership, and the date of their composition is unknown. The only clear reference to an event in Donne's life surfaces in the sonnet that begins, "Since she whom I lov'd hath payd her last debt," which seems to recount the death of his wife, Anne, in 1617, following the birth of their twelfth child. This sonnet, along with two others, was found only in the 1890s with the discovery of the so-called Westmoreland manuscript, and hence was not included in the series of sonnets printed in seventeenth-century editions of Donne's verse. Although there is no conclusive view as to how to reconcile the date of the sonnet to Anne with less concrete evidence pointing to a much earlier composition for the rest of the poems, critical consensus for the last fifty or so years holds that the sixteen sonnets published in the 1630s were composed sometime between 1608 and 1610, and certainly before Donne's ordination in 1615.[2]

Unlike the devotional sonnets of Donne's contemporaries, such as Barnabe Barnes's *A divine centurie of spirituall sonnets*, or Henry Lok's *Sundry Christian Passions, contained in two hundred sonnets*, Donne's *Holy Sonnets* do not make up a continuous spiritual narrative. Of the sixteen sonnets published in the first two editions of Donne's poems, there is no definitive ordering. Twelve *Holy Sonnets* were published in the first edition of Donne's poetry in 1633, and to these four were added in the second edition of 1635. The differences in the ordering of the poems in these first two editions reflect the differences in the two central groups of surviving seventeenth-century manuscripts. Nearly all modern editors have simply kept the order of the sixteen poems from 1635—which I will, for ease of reference, adopt in this chapter—and have made few claims for any unfolding drama or *telos*.

The one significant exception to this general rule is Helen Gardner, who, in her 1952 edition of the *Divine Poems*, makes a persuasive case for returning to the 1633 ordering of the poems, basing her argument upon what she perceives to be a thematic coherence in the twelve poems included therein.[3] She shows that the first six poems cohere around the subject of the Last Things, while the next six address the subject of divine love. This division between the two groups of poems is strained in many respects—the sonnet that begins, "What if this present were the worlds last night?" for example, certainly belongs equally to the category of death and judgment as it does to that of love—and there are shortcomings to her textual argument, as the recent *Variorum* edition of the *Holy Sonnets* has convincingly shown (the *Variorum* in fact eschews any ordering of the poems, organizing them simply in the alphabetical order of their first lines). But notwithstanding these criticisms, Gardner's insistence on the 1633 ordering forces us to attend to the thematic preoccupation with eschatology in these poems, and raises the crucial question as to why the sonnet seemed an appropriate form for the poet to contemplate death and salvation.

In his highly influential 1954 study, *The Poetry of Meditation*, Louis Martz answered this question by arguing that Donne understood the sonnet as the poetic equivalent to a Jesuit spiritual exercise, and hence that the sonnet was for Donne a straightforward devotional tool. Because the sonnet can be formally divided into three parts—two quatrains and a sestet—Martz argues that Donne would have found it inherently well suited for the Jesuit meditations that Ignatius prescribes, which also entail three crucial phases. First, the penitent conjures up the scene of the meditation before him. Second, he is instructed to analyze the scene he has visualized, seeking to glean, and then embrace, whatever truths or "verities" it may contain. Finally, after composing and analyzing his subject, he is ready either to address God in a form of petition, or to resign himself to the divine will that the meditation revealed.

Given Donne's family connections to the Jesuit order—his uncle Jasper Heywood became head of the Jesuit mission in 1581 after the arrest of Edmund Campion—his familiarity with Ignatius's *Spiritual Exercises* can reasonably be assumed. And because Donne's sonnets regularly position their speaker on the brink of final judgment, they can easily be compared to the meditations on Last Things that Ignatius and his followers recommend. Despite these surface affinities, however, there is something reductive about reading the poems this way, something that corresponds to Martz's implicit aim to strip Donne of his originality as a poet, to normalize and conventionalize what strike most readers as deeply unconventional poems. Donne uses the formal constraints of the sonnet, to be sure, but not to create a clean tripartite meditation of the sort Martz describes. If an Ignatian exercise follows a regular pattern, building a ladder, as it were, by which the worshiper climbs his way closer and closer to resolution, Donne's sonnets seem built upon ruptures, breaks, turns. Hence in Donne's sonnets, we typically find multiple turns or *volte*, unlike the single *volta* in line 9 that characterizes the standard Petrarchan sonnet. Moreover, the *Holy Sonnets* may conjure up scenes of imminent death, but the purpose of such an exercise is not always to heighten Donne's awareness of his own sinfulness or to intensify his devotional focus. The purpose is more often for Donne to provide himself with the kind of reassurance that would otherwise come from God.

"Thou hast made me," Donne asks, "And shall thy worke decay?" This is the opening line of Holy Sonnet I, and it raises three of the central concerns in these poems as a whole. First, it declares Donne's interest in asserting his status as a divine creature. Second, it acknowledges that he is in a state of deterioration. Third, it suggests, with the implicit tone of a reprimand, that God has failed to fulfill his obligations to his own "worke." This failure on God's part takes on real urgency in the lines that follow:

> Repaire me now, for now mine end doth haste,
> I runne to death, and death meets me as fast,
> And all my pleasures are like yesterday. (2–4)

God's role in the speaker's decay is in fact ambiguous: "thy worke" in line 1 can be either the subject or object of the verb "decay" (hence either God's creature is decaying on his own or God is intentionally causing him to decay). It is altogether unambiguous, however, that the work of "repaire" demanded in line 2 can be done only by God. To repair is to return something to its original condition, to restore and hence compensate for a prior deterioration or loss.[4] God's task, Donne insists, is to "repaire me now," to reverse the rapidly consuming decay that will otherwise lead straight toward death.

"I runne to death": around the time that Donne wrote this sonnet, he also wrote a treatise on suicide, *Biathanatos,* in which he defends under certain circumstances the taking of one's own life. In the preface to this text, composed in 1608, Donne confesses his own temptation to suicide, and explains that "whensoever my affliction assayles me, me thinks I have the keyes of my prison in myne own hand, and no remedy presents it selfe so soone to my heart, as mine owne sword."[5] The emphasis here on his own agency—"myne own hand," "mine owne sword"—helps to explain his attraction to the subject: as he makes clear throughout his writings, Donne loathed the idea of a passive death, and longed either to combat death as well as he could, or, should this prove impossible, to meet it with open arms.[6] The open embrace of death that Donne sometimes longs for is best captured for him by Christ's yielding of his soul on the cross "before his Naturall tyme."[7] In a conclusion that earned Donne the admiration of Jorge Luis Borges some 300 years later as a truly radical thinker, Donne describes Christ's death as the paradigmatic act of self-slaughter.[8] It "is a brave death," Donne declares, "which is accepted unconstraynd. And . . . it is an Heroique act of fortitude, if a Man when an urgent occasion is presented, expose himself to a certayne and assured Death, as he did."[9]

The willful embrace of death dangled before us in the opening lines of Holy Sonnet I, "Thou hast made me, And shall thy worke decay?" bears no relation, however, to what Donne admires in just acts of suicide: the impulse to initiate one's death so long as it better serves the glory of God than one's life. For there is nothing glorious in the sacrifice that the sonnet proposes, and the meeting with death is quickly transformed from something Donne welcomes to an event he anticipates with "despaire" and "terrour." Behind the threat of death in the first quatrain of this poem lies the far graver threat of damnation. This threat surfaces with the figure of the devil, "our old subtle foe," whose temptations Donne can hardly withstand:

> I dare not move my dimme eyes any way,
> Despaire behind, and death before doth cast
> Such terrour, and my feeble flesh doth waste
> By sinne in it, which it t'wards hell doth weigh;
> Onely thou art above, and when towards thee
> By thy leave I can looke, I rise againe;
> But our old subtle foe so tempteth me,
> That not one houre my selfe I can sustaine;
> Thy Grace may wing me to prevent his art,
> And thou like Adamant draw mine iron heart. (5–14)

The condition of helplessness that Donne describes stems from his fear of abandonment by God. The only solution he can imagine to the terror weighing down his "feeble flesh" is a direct intervention from the divine, proposed in the final couplet: "Thy Grace may wing me to prevent his art, / And thou like Adamant draw mine iron heart" (13–14). The sonnet tellingly does not conclude with any intimation of a divine response—God neither answers the question of whether he shall allow his creature to decay, nor does he offer any assistance in saving him from the devil. We are left merely with Donne's own suggestion to God as to what he "may" do, a suggestion that provides the poem with formal, but not theological closure.

Donne's fear of being abandoned by God pervades his devotional writings. We see it in the *Essayes in Divinitie*, a prose meditation on the opening verses of Genesis and Exodus written around 1614, in which he dwells on whether God would allow his creatures to be returned to nothingness. We see it most spectacularly in the sermons, in which Donne conjures up what it would feel like to fall out of God's hands. "*Horrendum est*," Donne preaches before the Earl of Carlisle and his company in an undated sermon, "when Gods hand is bent to strike, *it is a fearefull thing, to fall into the hands of the living God.*"[10] "But to fall out of the hands of the living God," he continues, "is a horror beyond our expression, beyond our imagination." In the conclusion to this sermon, Donne ventures to imagine the unimaginable: what it would feel like to be permanently forgotten by God. The passage itself is long, but I quote it here in its entirety to convey at least some of the rhetorical force it must have had when it was spoken aloud before a group of worshippers:

> That God should let my soule fall out of his hand into a bottomlesse pit, and roll an unremoveable stone upon it, and leave it to that which it finds there, (and it shall finde that there, which it never imagined, till it came thither) and never thinke more of that soule, never have more to doe with it. That of that providence of God, that studies the life and preservation of every weed, and worme, and ant, and spider, and toad, and viper, there should never, never any beame flow out upon me, that that God, who looked upon me, when I was nothing, and called me when I was not, as though I had been, out of the womb and depth of darknesse, will not looke upon me now, when, though a miserable, and a banished, and a damned creature, yet I am his creature still, and contribute something to his glory, even in my damnation; that that God, who hath often looked upon me in my foulest uncleannesse, and when I had shut out the eye of the day, the Sunne, and the eye of the night, the Taper, and the eyes of all the world, with curtaines and windowes and doores, did yet see me, and see me in mercy, by making me see that he saw me, and sometimes brought me to a present remorse, and (for that time) to a forbearing of that sinne, should so turne himselfe from me, to his glorious Saints and Angels, as that no Saint nor Angel, nor Christ Jesus himselfe, should ever pray him to looke towards me, never remember him, that such a soule there is; that that God, who hath so often said to my soule, *Quare mori-*

eris? Why wilt thou die? and so often sworne to my soule, *Vivit Dominus,*
as the Lord liveth, I would not have thee dye, but live, will neither let me
dye, nor let me live, but dye an everlasting life, and live an everlasting
death; that that God, who, when he could not get into me, by standing,
and knocking, by his ordinary meanes of entring, by his Word, his mer-
cies, hath applied his judgements, and hath shaked the house, this body,
with agues and palsies, and set this house on fire, with fevers and calen-
tures, and frighted the Master of the house, my soule, with horrors, and
heavy apprehensions, and so made an entrance into me; That that God
should loose and frustrate all his owne purposes and practices upon me,
and leave me, and cast me away, as though I had cost him nothing, that
this God at last, should let this soule goe away, as a smoake, as a vapour,
as a bubble, and that then this soule cannot be a smoake, nor a vapour,
nor a bubble, but must lie in darknesse, as long as the Lord of light is light
it selfe, and never a sparke of that light reach to my soule; What Tophet
is not Paradise, what Brimstone is not Amber, what gnashing is not a
comfort, what gnawing of the worme is not a tickling, what torment is
not a marriage bed to this damnation, to be secluded eternally, eternally,
eternally from the sight of God? (5:266–67)

There are many remarkable things in this passage, beginning with the extraordinary transformation of the soul itself into a body, positioned under the
tombstone of human burial. Unlike so many of his sermons, which struggle
with the prospect of the body's putrefaction, Donne casts aside the bodily
experience of death. It is the fate of the soul that preoccupies him—the soul
that God so generously created *ex nihilo;* that God continued to nurture even
in its state of extreme sinfulness; that God spoke to in its illnesses, and encouraged to live. Donne struggles palpably to reconcile God's generosity in
creating him with his subsequent rejection: as the examples of God's love
for him accumulate, Donne's outrage at his abandonment grows stronger
and stronger, culminating in the ambiguous counterfactual declaration: "as
though I had cost him nothing." The dissonance Donne experiences here is
the central tension in the passage, and the explanation for its tone: how, he
asks, can God behave as if he had meant nothing to him, when Donne has
ample evidence to the contrary? It is at this point in the sermon that Donne
makes the subtle, but shocking, transition from indirection to direction,
from distance to presence: after a lengthy series of addresses to "*that* God,"
he shifts now to "*this* God."

For Donne, damnation is not the flames and tortures of hell. It is to be denied God's light. When he was in his "foulest uncleannesse," when he pulled

the curtains on the rest of the world, and hid inside his own chamber, God came to him then, he claims, and "ma[de] me see that he saw me." When he could not heed God's "ordinary meanes of entring," when he was untouched by his "standing, and knocking," God shook his body with illness, and "set this house on fire," to enter his soul. But now, Donne laments, assuming fully the imaginative position of one dead and damned, God denies ever to see him again, and leaves him in perpetual darkness. Donne's soul cannot simply disappear, it cannot take the form of a "smoake, nor a vapour, nor a bubble," but instead must remain forever materialized, and forever without light. None of the traditional horrors of hell compare to the horror of being "secluded eternally, eternally, eternally from the sight of God."

The full power and horror of this passage from the sermons never makes itself felt in the *Holy Sonnets*, which, for reasons of scale alone, could not accommodate the incantatory force of this seemingly limitless prose. But these poems are, in an important sense, an early symptom of the fear that the sermon captures, and their response to the seeds of this fear is to affirm repeatedly, even obsessively, Donne's claims as God's creature, to imagine that the sheer fact of his divine origins obliges God to offer regular maintenance and care. Divine creation is not treated in these poems as an act completed at birth. Instead, it carries with it the necessity of further remaking.

Donne's self-conception as a divine "worke" that needs immediate attention lies at the heart of Holy Sonnet V, "I am a little world made cunningly." Critical readings of this poem have dwelt on what it means for Donne to define himself as a "little world." But little attention has been paid to what it means for him to assert that he is made. He asserts not simply that he is made, moreover, but that he is made "cunningly":

> I am a little world made cunningly
> Of Elements, and an Angelike spright,
> But black sinne hath betraid to endlesse night
> My worlds both parts, and (oh) both parts must die. (1–4)

The elemental and the spiritual, the body and the soul: the excellence of God's design lies in the fact of human dualism. Unlike the angels who have only "spright," humankind is blessed with bodies as well. As Donne declares in a 1621 sermon we looked at in the introduction, "The Kingdome of Heaven hath not all that it must have to a consummate perfection, till it have bodies too." It was for this reason, he argues, that God made a "materiall world, a corporeall world": "There must be bodies, Men, and able bodies, able men. . . . They are glorified bodies that make up the kingdome of Heaven" (4:47).

Donne's emphasis on the dualism of his "little world" in "I am a little world made cunningly" resonates with what may well be the single most consistent principle in his metaphysics: that no aspect of our devotional experience belongs exclusively to body or soul. In the poem's subsequent lines, he bemoans his undoing as an affliction that besets both parts of the self: "But black sinne hath betraid to endlesse night / My worlds both parts, and (oh) both parts must die." The repetition in line 4 of "both parts" stresses, on the one hand, the dualism of the self and, on the other hand, the apparent impossibility of splitting that self in two. This impossibility is in turn responsible for the heretical suggestion that the soul as well as the body shall perish at the moment of death.

When Donne wrote the *Holy Sonnets*, the idea of mortalism—that both soul and body are subject to death—seems to have held out real interest to him. A variant on the same idea arises in the most common manuscript version of Holy Sonnet VI, "This is my playes last scene," in which he declares:

And gluttonous Death will instantly unjoynt
My body and my soule, and I shall sleepe a space,
Or presently (I knowe not) see that face. (5–7)

In these lines, Donne entertains two possibilities: either his "unjoynt[ed]" body and soul shall sleep together following death, or he shall, in body and soul, immediately receive his *visio Dei*. The alternative version of these lines, which Gardner believes reflects a revised version of the poem, strips them of their heretical charge. In place of "Or presently (I knowe not) see that face" is "But my ever-waking part shall see that face," an exact reversal of the suggestion that the soul shall sleep along with the body.[11] One weakness of this theory, quite apart from questions of manuscript authority, is that it makes the "I" in line 6—"I shall sleepe a space"—signify only the body. In the standard text for the poem that I have quoted, Donne's "I" is made up of both body and soul, and this composite "I" either sleeps or sees God as a united self.

As we have already observed, Donne does not ever seriously endorse the idea of mortalism. In *The Second Anniversarie*, he takes as his governing premise that the soul will ascend to heaven long before it is rejoined by its earthly flesh, and later in his career as a preacher, he rejects mortalism

outright for both blessed and damned souls. Despite these disavowals, however, mortalism was attractive to him: it meant that body and soul stuck
together, as it were, through death as well as life. At the time that the *Holy
Sonnets* were composed, a time when Donne was free from any obligation to
maintain the orthodox positions of the church, he allowed himself to entertain the idea as an alternative to the horrific specter of separation. In "I am
a little world," Donne combats this prospect of death for both body and soul
by imagining a series of at once physical and spiritual purifications:

> You which beyond that heaven which was most high
> Have found new sphears, and of new lands can write,
> Powre new seas in mine eyes, that so I might
> Drowne my world with my weeping earnestly,
> Or wash it, if it must be drown'd no more:
> But oh it must be burnt! alas the fire
> Of lust and envie have burnt it heretofore,
> And made it fouler. (5–12)

Donne wants his "little world" to be alternately drowned, washed, or burnt,
and we might reasonably assume that he makes these demands of God, who
made him in the first place. But the association of his addressee ("You") with
"new sphears" and "new lands" makes clear that he means to invoke scien-
tists like Galileo and navigators like Magellan, rather than God, who lives
not "beyond" but within "that heaven which was most high."

The arch tone of these lines already suggests that the proposed gestures
of cleansing will be doomed to failure, but this failure finds confirmation
with the mention of a second kind of burning—this time with divine and
not human flames: "Let their flames retire," he pleads, "And burne me ô
Lord, with a fiery zeale / Of thee and thy house, which doth in eating heale"
(12–14). This invocation of God is the first mention of him in the poem so
far: the poem's first line, "I am a little world made cunningly," is a passive
construction, and hence strikingly elides any acknowledgement of who did
the making. Donne's evasion of God's role is not driven by an implicit claim
to an alternative account of creation—it is not comparable, for example, to
Satan's challenging the basis of his createdness in book 5 of *Paradise Lost*
("Remember'st thou / Thy making," Satan asks his fellow angels, "while
the Maker gave thee being?").[12] Instead, it is Donne's way of making God's
entrance into the poem assume the force of a revelation. For the very strain
under which the suppression of the divine must labor throughout the first
twelve lines intensifies the feeling of release afforded by the final couplet.

The challenge that the poem poses for itself is not to secure God's promise of redemption, a promise that Donne does not imagine himself likely to receive. The challenge seems simply to bring himself to the point of speaking directly to God, and to acknowledge that God alone can reform him.

In "I am a little world made cunningly," Donne traces the process through which he recognizes his dependence on God. The occasion for his alarm, as in so many of the sonnets, is the apparent imminence of his death. In Holy Sonnet VII, "At the round earths imagin'd corners," he pursues a similar goal of reaching out toward God, but he does so by staging an apocalyptic scene from which Donne is, at least initially, absent. This sonnet begins with the voice of an anonymous heavenly agent who initiates the chain of events on the last day:

> At the round earths imagin'd corners, blow
> Your trumpets, Angells, and arise, arise
> From death, you numberlesse infinities
> Of soules, and to your scattred bodies goe. (1–4)

The irony of the opening line—the begrudging acknowledgment that he knows, of course, that the earth is round at the same time that he wants to hold on at least to imagined corners—is typical of Donne's sensibility: he simultaneously acknowledged the Copernican revolution and resented it for its decentering of humankind. Once again, we glimpse the mortalism that we encountered in "I am a little world": the repetition of the command to the souls to "arise" in line 2—"arise, arise"—and the specification that they are rising "from death" allows for no ambiguity. Like the bodies, these souls are dead, Donne tells us, and they require resurrection. The central advantage of mortalism—that the soul and body stick together in death—does not, however, pertain to this poem, in which the risen souls are instructed to begin the search for their bodies. The difficulty of this search lies in the fact that the bodies are not only decayed but also "scattred," which can mean both that the bodies are spread throughout the earth, and that individual parts of individual bodies are themselves dispersed. Donne conjures up, in effect, a scene of apocalyptic chaos in which each soul seeks out its missing limbs.

The challenge of collecting one's missing parts in order to be fully resurrected preoccupied Donne throughout his writing. We encountered it in "A Valediction: of my name, in the window," in which he playfully directs his beloved, as the caretaker of his soul, to "repaire / And recompact my scattered body," and we saw it as well in "The Relique," in which he describes tying a bracelet of his lover's hair around his arm to ensure that she will come to his grave to retrieve her missing part on the last day. We see it regularly in his sermons, as in this example from the 1620 sermon on Job 19:26 discussed in the introduction, in which he reassures his congregation that God will bring all of their missing pieces together, however remote they may be:

> Shall I imagine a difficulty in my body, because I have lost an Arme in the East, and a leg in the West? because I have left some bloud in the North, and some bones in the South? Doe but remember, with what ease you have sate in the chaire, casting an account, and made a shilling on one hand, a pound on the other, or five shillings below, ten above, because all these lay easily within your reach. Consider how much lesse, all this earth is to him, that sits in heaven, and spans all this world, and reunites in an instant armes, and legs, bloud, and bones, in what corners so ever they be scattered. (3:109)

The language of "At the round earths imagin'd corners" reverberates throughout this passage—we are back to the "corners" of the earth and the "scattered" parts of the body. For Donne the preacher, however, it is God who is responsible for the collecting, and not—as we see in the sonnet—the souls themselves.

"At the round earths imagin'd corners" moves in its second quatrain from the eschatological scene of the last day to an explanation of the manifold ways in which death was visited upon the numberless souls:

> All whom the flood did, and fire shall o'erthrow,
> All whom warre, dearth, age, agues, tyrannies,
> Despaire, law, chance, hath slaine, and you whose eyes,
> Shall behold God, and never tast deaths woe. (5–8)

The last group mentioned—those who were still alive on the last day and, according to St. Paul, shall die and be reborn in an instant—Donne particularly envies, since mortalism or not, they will not experience any long-term division of their two parts. In an early sermon on Psalm 89:48, "What man is he that liveth, and shal not see death?" Donne questions whether any man will in fact escape the "taste" of death. "It may be," he allows, "that those Men, whom Christ shal find upon the earth alive, at his return to Judge the World, shall dye then, and it may be they shall but be changed and not dye" (2:204). But whether their transformation is instantaneous or requires

a quick passage through death, these lucky men are still spared the horrors
of the grave. These are the only souls whom Donne addresses in the second
person—"you whose eyes, / Shall behold God, and never tast deaths woe."

Having conjured up a biblical scene in the sonnet's first quatrain and
then provided an analysis in its second, "At the round earths imagin'd corners" seems so far to conform to the Jesuit model of meditation that Martz
describes. In the third phase of the meditation, as Ignatius describes it, the
worshiper inserts himself or herself into the scene described. What we should
expect in the sestet is an account of Donne's own inclusion among the resurrected selves rushing to Judgment. What happens, however, is something
like the opposite:

> But let them sleepe, Lord, and mee mourne a space,
> For, if above all these, my sinnes abound,
> 'Tis late to aske abundance of thy grace,
> When wee are there; here on this lowly ground,
> Teach mee how to repent; for that's as good
> As if thou'hadst seal'd my pardon, with thy blood. (9–14)

Ushered in by an abrupt and contrastive "But" at the point of the Petrarchan
volta in line 9, Donne introduces himself into the poem as a "mee" whose
identity turns on its difference from "them." Having just asked the angels
to blow their trumpets and begin the resurrection of the flesh, he now can-
cels the scene, asking God instead for delay. The caesura in line 12 between
"there" and "here," heaven and earth, speaks to the central urgency of the
poem. "Here," not "there," is the time and place for repentance. "Here," not
"there," is where God might "teach mee how to repent." Visualizing the last
day propels Donne to imagine himself as a would-be penitent rather than an
indifferent stage manager, and he begs God to help him begin the process.

What Donne finally desires is to be taken in, regarded, addressed by God,
while there is still time on this earth—"let them sleepe," but "teach mee."
To be taught directly by God is described as the equivalent of not simply
inheriting but experiencing firsthand the original sacrifice: the pardoning of
mankind with Christ's blood. Indeed, Donne pushes the desire for unmediated contact with God so far as to suggest that whatever benefits Christ's
sacrifice may have for humankind generally, they do not pertain to him.
We could say that the pardon of Christ's blood is, in effect, too abstract and
detached to be of use in his current crisis—he needs a personal intervention
from God. We might also see a more radical suggestion in the final line of
the sonnet: that Christ has not sealed Donne's pardon, and therefore that he

has been excluded from the general dispensation of Christian souls. Such an exclusion is implicit in the force of the counterfactual "as if": it is as if his pardon had been personally sealed, but it has not; it is as if God had treated him as one of the elect, but in fact he remains dangerously outside the purview of his grace.[13]

Donne offers no corrective inside of the poem to this radical suggestion—unlike what we might expect from one of Herbert's lyrics, for example, there is no scolding but loving reminder from God that Christ's blood has already been shed on his behalf (in *The Temple* this reminder would come in the form of God completing Herbert's poem with a perfect rhyme). Instead, Donne represents himself in a state of unnecessary, extravagant dependence: he needs immediate contact with God to be reassured of his fundamental rights as his creature. This desire for immediate contact is also a desire for unmediated contact—even the gift of Christ's blood stands in the way of Donne's access to God. Here as elsewhere in the *Holy Sonnets* it is God and not Christ whom Donne longs for—the intimacy he craves is not with his savior but with his maker.

The craving for personal renewal from God reaches its climactic expression in Holy Sonnet XIV, "Batter my heart, three person'd God." The intertwining of erotic and sacred metaphor in this sonnet has over the centuries produced a predictably wide array of responses. Some readers find the physicality of the verse "detestable"; others defend it as an entirely appropriate and unremarkable form of sacred metaphor; still others claim the power of the poem lies precisely in the tension produced by petitioning God in a manner so explicitly sexual.[14] My own inclination is toward the last of these readings, although I do not regard this poem as striking a note fundamentally different from the other *Holy Sonnets*. "Batter my heart" is a more physically demanding expression of what we have seen elsewhere in these poems: the idea of the self, in body and soul, as a broken artifact.

"Batter my heart" begins with Donne's refusal of all responsibility for his stated condition of decay. Assuming a position of complete passivity, even inertia, he imagines himself as matter that God must repair. This stance of total passivity contrasts powerfully with the forcefulness of his voice—the first quatrain of this sonnet bombards its reader with no fewer than fourteen verbs, beginning with the imperative trochee "Batter":

Batter my heart, three person'd God; for, you
As yet but knocke, breathe, shine, and seeke to mend;
That I may rise, and stand, o'erthrow mee,'and bend
Your force, to breake, blowe, burn and make me new. (1–4)

In the seventeenth century, the primary uses of "batter" were "to strike with repeated blows of an instrument or weapon" and "to operate against (walls, fortifications, etc.) with artillery" in order to break them down.[15] In this quatrain, the verb can be read in either sense: Donne demands either that God as blacksmith or God as military vanquisher strike his heart in order not simply to mend him, but to "make me new."[16]

Donne's petition to "make me new" hovers on the edge of something that on the whole horrified him throughout his life: the possibility of personal annihilation. He speaks out against this possibility on multiple occasions, and perhaps most notably in the *Essayes in Divinitie*, in which he insists that humankind was not created *ex nihilo*. Instead, humankind was made out of preexistent matter.[17] "When *Paul* says himself to be *Nothing*," Donne writes, "it is but a diminution and Extenuation (not of himself, for he says there, *I am not inferior to the very chief of the Apostles*, but) of Mankind. Where it is said to Man [Isaiah 41:24], *Your making is of Nothing*, it is but a respective, and comparative undervaluing; as in a lower descent then that before, *All Nations before God are less then Nothing*."[18] "Nothing," Donne insists, cannot really mean nothing—it must surely be a lesser something, a "respective and comparative undervaluing," but not nothing whatsoever. Behind the anxiety over *ex nihilo* creation lies the far deeper anxiety that our creation could be undone. So horrible is this prospect, Donne continues, "so deep a curse, and high degree of punishment, that Hell and the prisoners there, not only have it not, but cannot wish so great a loss to themselves, nor such a frustrating of Gods purposes" (30).

"Hell and the prisoners there, not only have it not, but cannot wish so great a loss to themselves": this is an extraordinary sentiment, and one that suggests an entirely new hierarchy to the punishments doled out to the fallen. "Even in Hell," he continues,

> where if our mind could contract and gather together all the old perse-
> cutions of the first Church, where men were tormented with exquisite
> deaths, and oftentimes more, by being denied that; And all the inhuman-
> ities of the Inquisition, where repentance encreaseth the torture. In Hell,
> I say, to escape which, some have prayed to have *hils fall upon them*, and
> many horrours shadowed in the Scriptures and Fathers, none is ever said
> to have wished himself Nothing.

However ghastly the horrors of hell, none can produce the desire to be un-made. "As reposedly, and at home within himself no man is an Atheist, however he pretend it," Donne observes, "so it is impossible that any man

should wish himself Nothing" (31). The impulse to cancel out one's own existence, like the desire to deny God's existence, is finally inconceivable—one
might recklessly declare such a thing aloud but would not actually maintain
it "at home within himself."

In "Batter my heart," Donne does not desire annihilation, even if it were
followed by rebirth. Instead, he desires the repair of what already exists.
Donne wants his imperfect flesh to be perfected. And he wants God to inter-
vene not at the last day, but now. The first quatrain of this sonnet reveals an
unprecedented dissatisfaction with God, who has not "as yet" done enough
for him. The replacement of "knocke, breathe, shine" with "breake, blowe,
burn" reflects a longing for God to intensify his actions. This first set of verbs
draws upon scriptural descriptions of gentle moments of divine intervention:
"knocke" recalls Revelations 3:20, "Behold, I stand at the door and knock";
"breathe" can be traced to Genesis 2:7, "And the Lord God . . . breathed into
his nostrils the breath of life"; and "shine" has multiple sources, including
Psalm 31:16, "Make thy face to shine upon thy servant." These actions are
supplanted by the violent trinity of "breake, blowe, burn," which draws
upon decidedly less positive moments in scripture: Psalm 2:9, "Thou shalt
break them with a rod of iron"; Isaiah 40:7, "The grass withereth, the flower
fadeth: because the spirit of the Lord bloweth upon it"; Luke 3:17, "The chaff
he will burn with fire unquenchable."[19] The violence of this second cluster
of verbs is heightened by the sheer power of the alliterated *b*'s echoing the
opening command. Batter me, break me, blow on me, burn me—up to now,
God has been merely tinkering.

In the second quatrain of this sonnet, Donne describes his "usurpation"
by a foreign, hostile force, and despairs over his seemingly involuntary be-
trothal to this enemy:

> I, like an usurpt towne, to'another due,
> Labour to'admit you, but Oh, to no end,
> Reason your viceroy in mee, mee should defend,
> But is captiv'd, and proves weake or untrue. (5–8)

One of the great puzzles for readers of this poem is its radical shift in metaphors from one quatrain to the next. To explain this, critics have attempted
to impose upon the poem a Trinitarian logic: Donne invokes God as "three
person'd" in the opening lines, and each of the predominant metaphors describes a desired intervention from, respectively, God the Father, the Son,
and the Holy Ghost. To separate out the petitions as directed to three different persons of God, however, is to diminish the force of the poem's accumu-

lative power. In these lines, the metaphors move from military to erotic—or rather, the initially military images take on erotic resonance once the erotic is introduced. It is difficult, in other words, to read the description of "labour[ing] to admit you" without conjuring up a sexual as well as strategic dilemma, and the idea of sexual violation serves to intensify the impression we already have of profound physical dissolution.

The climax of the poem ratchets up its intensity by resuming the imperative voice with which Donne began:

> Yet dearely'I love you,'and would be loved faine,
> But am betroth'd unto your enemie:
> Divorce mee,'untie, or breake that knot againe,
> Take mee to you, imprison mee, for I
> Except you'enthrall mee, never shall be free,
> Nor ever chast, except you ravish mee. (9–14)

In their relentless physicality, Donne seems to insist that we read his requests literally and not metaphorically. Stripped of all similes, these lines demand a physical intimacy that cannot readily be excused as spiritual longing. But however extreme the formulation, it is crucial to recognize that the achievement of physical intimacy is not the ultimate goal of the poem. It is a vehicle for a different goal. The sonnet does not build toward union with God, either bodily or spiritually. Instead, it builds toward personal regeneration. The demands to be taken, conquered, imprisoned, enthralled, and ravished are ultimately expressions of the fundamental desire that pulsates throughout these poems as a whole. And this is Donne's desire to be given in body and soul a *volta* of his own.

II

I have so far considered sonnets in which Donne affirms his claims as a divine creature in order to demand repair from God. In these poems, Donne represents himself as an instrument that needs to be regularly tuned, or, more simply, as matter in process. Because he never describes the experience of hearing back from God, his pleas for divine remaking go unanswered. Donne's response to this silence is twofold. On the one hand, he uses the space of the sonnet to provoke God's response. On the other hand, he explores the idea that the sonnet itself might provide a means to resolve his fears about his salvation. Thus if some of the *Holy Sonnets* reveal an extreme dependence upon God as creator, others seem designed to avoid the necessity of divine intervention—and even to propose alternative solutions that lie within the form of the sonnet. In these poems, Donne's deft manipulation of the sonnet form seems to shift the task of resolution from divine hands to his own. As Donne experiments in transforming his own role from creature to creator, the sonnet itself supplies what is lacking in his desire for reassurance from God.

Donne's use of the sonnet as a space to create and resolve devotional crises without divine intervention underlies Holy Sonnet VI, "This is my playes last scene." Here Donne does not conjure up the moment of death to beg God for forgiveness, as we have seen in other sonnets. Instead, he conjures up the moment of death to attempt to determine his own posthumous fate. To conceive of life as a play is a commonplace—examples of this sentiment have been traced to the third century BC, when Bion the Borysthenite wrote, "Chance like a poet makes all sorts of roles: the role of a ship-wrecked, of a beggar, of a famous or an infamous man"—and Donne may himself have heard Jaques utter, "All the world's a stage," in *As You Like It*.[20] What Donne does with this metaphor is to personalize and possess it: "This is *my* playes last scene," he declares, as if to suggest that he is not merely a player in a larger drama, but the author of a drama that belongs to him alone.

By declaring his own "last scene," Donne seems to want to provoke his own death, and the sonnet performs the urgency of this final moment—the moment just before dying—almost viscerally. The octave is remarkable for the sheer breathlessness of its pace, effected by a series of increasingly short syntactical units that finally give way to an unbroken line, and an early *volta*, introduced in line 7 by the traditional "But":

> This is my playes last scene, here heavens appoint
> My pilgrimages last mile; and my race
> Idly, yet quickly runne, hath this last pace,
> My spans last inch, my minutes latest point,
> And gluttonous death, will instantly unjoynt
> My body, and soule, and I shall sleepe a space,
> But my'ever-waking part shall see that face,
> Whose feare already shakes my every joynt. (1–8)

The frequent repetitions of "last" ("last scene," "last mile," "last pace," "last inch") and the rush not only to his final minute, but to that minute's "latest point" convey Donne's impatience for the moment of death when he imagines his "ever-waking part" shall encounter God.

At the same time, however, that Donne displays this hurried impatience to arrive at his absolute end, he also suspends the moment, piling image upon image as if the poetic accumulation might somehow dilate the instant before he "sees that face," an instant that he anticipates with fear, not pleasure. This fear in itself may not be a troubling sign: the tradition of fearing God (*timor dei*) is entirely consistent with Christian theology and has its own devotional efficacy, as Donne will discuss in *Devotions*, and in Holy Sonnet XIX he concludes that "Those are my best dayes, when I shake with feare" (14).[21] But what follows in Holy Sonnet VI, by contrast, suggests an unsalutary fear, a fear that prevents, rather than encourages, the devotional resolution Donne desires.

Hence the tension in this sonnet between rushing desperately to the moment of meeting God and delaying the moment's arrival through a kind of poetic dilation spills over into the sestet, in which the desire for evasion, not encounter, ultimately seems to hold sway. These lines hover over the instant of death, as Donne chronicles his desperate preparations for his final reckoning:

> Then, as my soule, to'heaven her first seate, takes flight,
> And earth-borne body, in the earth shall dwell,
> So, fall my sinnes, that all may have their right,
> To where they'are bred, and would presse me, to hell.
> Impute me righteous, thus purg'd of evill,
> For thus I leave the world, the flesh, the devill. (9–14)

The gesture of dividing himself into three parts rather than two—body, soul, and sin—reflects Donne's desire to isolate that part of the self that he expects will not fare well at the Last Judgment. It also reflects his fantasy of reconceiving himself as someone not limited by the ordinary conditions of human dualism, someone whose sinfulness does not afflict the constitution of either his body or soul.

It is only in the final couplet that Donne speaks to God, but even this remains implicit. For the imperative "Impute me righteous" does not indicate its addressee. Although contextually we can assume this command is intended for God, Donne does not name God here or elsewhere in the sonnet—the synecdoche, "that face" in line 7, is the only other invocation of the divine, and it is comparably elusive. "Impute me righteous" also suggests a second type of avoidance: he avoids recognizing Christ as an agent in his salvation. By demanding that he be imputed righteous, Donne attempts to claim for his own soul what Christians believe belongs to Christ alone.

As Gardner describes it, even a purged soul is not righteous, but carries the imputed guilt of Adam: "it can only be 'imputed righteous,'" she argues, "by the merit of Christ."[22] Hence Donne attempts to create for himself the conditions of a righteous soul and, in so doing, to cancel his dependence on the sacrifice of God's son. "Impute me righteous" is perhaps unspecified in its address because unspecificity allows the demand to be answered within the terms of the sonnet itself. Donne's poem, in other words, has constituted the conditions in which the speaker might be regarded as righteous: it has performed its own process of redemption. Shorn of God's answer, the sonnet ends with the poet's self-instantiation as a blessed creature.

The most powerful example of Donne's staging and resolving devotional crises within the space of the sonnet is Holy Sonnet XIII, "What if this present were the worlds last night?" The power of the hypothetical or counterfactual envisioning of his demise, introduced with the "what if," embodies Donne's brinkmanship: he suspends himself on the boundary between life and death, dilating the moment before he learns his posthumous fate. This poem begins with the imaginative fulfillment of what we have seen to be one of Donne's deepest fantasies—he finds himself alive on the eve of the last day:

> What if this present were the worlds last night?
> Marke in my heart, O Soule, where thou dost dwell,
> The picture of Christ crucified, and tell
> Whether that countenance can thee affright,
> Teares in his eyes quench the amasing light,
> Blood fills his frownes, which from his pierc'd head fell.
> And can that tongue adjudge thee unto hell,
> Which pray'd forgiveness for his foes fierce spight? (1–8)

In a certain respect, Donne's practice in this poem seems consistent with early modern Protestant ideas about preparing for divine judgment. English Protestants were regularly encouraged to prepare for the Second Coming by treating every moment as if it were the last, and hence to assume a level of devotional vigilance in daily life that might otherwise be reserved for the deathbed. The early reformer Hugh Latimer explains, for example, that if we should know the exact time or day when Christ would come, we would enjoy the pleasures of this world for as long as possible, and defer thinking about salvation until the last possible minute. "And therefore," he warns, "lest we should be made careless, this day is hidden from us: for the angels of God themselves know not the hour or moment of this great and fearful day."[23] Edwin Sandys, the archbishop of York, similarly preaches at St. Paul's Cross in the 1570s that God keeps knowledge of the Second Coming from men for two reasons. First, he fears that any foreknowledge might paralyze us with fear—"it should terrify and amaze us"—and hence make us careless in providing for ourselves and others. Second, our state of ignorance forces us to "make ready and prepare for it, seeing it might happen at any time, even at any instant."[24]

When Donne begins Holy Sonnet XIII by imagining this night to be the world's last, he is at one level performing the kind of exercise that English divines recommended to their parishioners. What he proceeds to do in this exercise, however, represents an important departure. Instead of turning to God in a state of heightened repentance, Donne withdraws to analyze the current state of his soul. Far from jolting himself to prayer and begging God for mercy, he attempts to gauge what will await him at heaven's gate by reading the image of Christ within. He decides that the degree to which his soul is frightened by what it sees will represent God's final disposition toward him. He also hedges his bets, as it were, by reminding himself that even if the image turns out to be frightful, the fact that Christ showed loving forgiveness toward his enemies guarantees him some degree of sympathy.

In the sonnet's sestet, Donne registers with relief the beauty of the picture he has found lodged in his heart, and concludes that its beauty signals Christ's "pitious" intentions:

No, no; but as in my idolatrie
I said to all my profane mistresses,
Beauty, of pitty, foulnesse onely is
A signe of rigour: so I say to thee,   ·
To wicked spirits are horrid shapes assign'd,
This beauteous forme assures a pitious minde. (9–14)

The syntax in these lines is complicated, but makes best sense if we read it as follows: just as Donne flattered his mistress by assuring her that her "pity" corresponded to her beauty, whereas her unyielding rigor would only be a sign of her ugliness, so he reassures his soul that the beauty of Christ's image suggests his compassion. Implicit in this analogy is that Christ, like Donne's earthly lover, can be persuaded or seduced into merciful behavior because such behavior will render him beautiful. Donne's slyness here is further heightened by the fact that he is not speaking to Christ—the address, "so I say to thee," is ostensibly to his soul.[25]

The difficulties raised by the question of the addressee in line 12—"so I say to thee"—are ultimately mooted, however, by the resolution of the final line. For Donne is not awaiting a transformation of Christ's image from ugly to beautiful—he has already determined the image to be beautiful, and hence feels "assured" of his own salvation. (In the 1633 edition, the last line reads: "this beauteous forme *assumes* a pitious minde," but this version is not supported by any of the extant manuscripts.[26]) Readers have long been discomfited by Donne's claim for the beauty of the image itself. Identifying this sonnet as exemplary of the fourth type of ambiguity—when the poet's "feelings were painfully mixed"—William Empson asks with open distaste whether "a man in the last stages of torture" can be found beautiful, "even if blood hides his frowns."[27] In a similar spirit, R. V. Young compares the image to a graphic baroque painting, concluding that the most natural response would not be one of aesthetic appreciation.[28] These critics are presumably immune to the pleasures of European portraits of Christ on the cross—the vast collection of paintings and sculptures whose aesthetic power has moved viewers over the centuries. But notwithstanding our responses to what the poem describes, it is important to remember that Donne claims for himself the power of reading the signs—there is no evidence presented for predicting his fate outside of his willful decision that the bloody, tearful picture he describes is to be regarded as beautiful.

One last possibility remains for the meaning of this "beauteous forme," and this possibility raises the larger question of what it means not only for Donne to be made—to be a creature made by the divine—but also what it means for him to be a maker. Because the sonnet depends entirely upon the poet's own processes of rationalization, the "beauteous forme" that "assures a pitious minde" might be the sonnet itself. I share this opinion with Stanley Fish, although he draws very different conclusions from it. According to Fish, Donne is as usual acting in bad faith:

> It is the poem's verbal felicity and nothing else that is doing either the assuring (which thus is no more than whistling in the dark) or the assuming (which as a word at least has the grace to name the weakness of the action it performs). The poem ends in the bravado that marks some of the other sonnets (e.g., "Death be not proud"), but the triumph of the rhetorical flourish . . . only calls attention to its insubstantiality.[29]

Fish's profound distrust of Donne's intentions overwhelms all other critical impulses in reading this poem, and his claim for the "insubstantiality" of the rhetorical "triumph" overlooks the significance of what stands plainly before us: a beautifully executed poem. The perfect shape Donne's thoughts have taken on what may turn out to be the world's last night is perhaps the strongest evidence he can imagine of his status among God's elect—as if to be able to create a sonnet under the pressure of contemplating final judgment reflects a sign of grace.[30]

Donne never explicitly connected his own abilities as a poetic maker to his hopes for salvation. But in *The Essayes in Divinitie*, he implicitly draws this connection. After completing his exposition of divine creation, he petitions God to bless him with his own creative powers:

> Though this soul of mine, by which I partake thee, begin not now, yet let this minute, O God, this happy minute of thy visitation, be the beginning of her conversion, and shaking away confusion, darknesse, and barrennesse; and let her now produce Creatures, thoughts, words, and deeds agreeable to thee. And let her not produce them, O God, out of any contemplation, or (I cannot say, *Idæa*, but) *Chimera* of my worthinesse, either because I am a man and no worme, and within the pale of thy Church, and not in the wild forrest, and enlightned with some glimerings of Naturall knowledge; but meerely out of Nothing: Nothing prexistent in her selfe, but by power of thy Divine will and word. (37)

Let my soul begin its conversion, he begs, by freeing itself from its "barrennesse," and let it produce "thoughts, words, and deeds, agreeable to thee." Let me produce these Creatures not from any sense of my own worthiness—not "because I am a man and no worme," and not because I am a Christian and no savage in the "wild forrest"—but because I am blessed with the force of God's "will and word." Let me understand my own madeness, he implores, by making things of my own. Let me recognize myself as your creature by becoming a creator. Nearly all of the *Holy Sonnets* were written before the *Essayes*, and hence they cannot reflect the direct answer to this prayer. But they are perhaps Donne's first exploration of a lifelong hope, the hope that through the act of writing he might gain a form of divine reassurance. When Holy Sonnet V begins, "I am a little world made cunningly," it is not only the voice of the poet that speaks. In an elegant turn of prosopopoeia, Donne also gives voice to the poem.

CHAPTER FIVE

Devotions

Despite its physical hardships, illness held a certain appeal for Donne. In a letter written toward the end of his life to his friend Mrs. Cokayne, Donne describes the symptoms he was experiencing from his current sickness. "I have neither good temper," he begins, "nor good pulse, nor good appetite, nor good sleep, . . . I [have] been more affected with Coughs in vehemence, more with deafeness, more with toothach, more with the vurbah, then heretofore." Donne's attitude toward these ailments, however, is neither one of bitterness nor of quiet resignation. Instead, he regards his infirmities as a means of preparing his body for its death and eventual rebirth. "All this mellows me for heaven," he concludes, "and so ferments me in this world, as I shall need no long concoction in the grave, but hasten to the resurrection" (317).

Donne's idea of proleptic putrefaction—that through physical deterioration now, he might reduce his time as a corpse later—belongs to his peculiar obsession with shortening his time in the grave, an obsession that surfaces repeatedly in his sermons. But in this letter Donne's interest lies in understanding his illness as a sign of God's love. "I am not alive," he writes, "because I have not had enough upon me to kill me, but because it pleases God to passe me through many infirmities" (317). The notion of illness as a time in which God simultaneously visits and tests his creatures takes us to the heart of the *Devotions*, a prose narrative written after Donne's recovery from what was probably typhoid fever during the autumn of 1623. Throughout this work, Donne struggles both to accept his sickness as a message from God, and to effect a return to health in soul as well as in body. With the exception of his physicians, Donne seems to be entirely alone throughout the illness he recounts, and his only sustained dialogue is with God.

In English literature, there is no precedent for the *Devotions*. Part spiritual exercise, part medical journal, the text is divided into twenty-three "stations" charting the individual days of his illness. Each station, or Devotion, is further divided into a Meditation in which Donne ponders earthly topics and the condition of mankind; an Expostulation, in which he addresses the realm of the spirit, and directs at once desperate and challenging questions to God; and a Prayer in which he provisionally achieves some form of resolution. Donne made the decision during his convalescence to chronicle his weeks of sickness, presumably using notes he took during the active stage of the disease. In transforming his sickbed musings into the rich, often baroque prose of the *Devotions*, he relives each phase of the illness: all of the stations are written in the present tense, and there is no foreshadowing of his recovery.

The sheer act of reading this text is surprisingly difficult: the three sections of each Devotion do not always follow logically upon one another, and although Donne moves through the days of illness chronologically, the narrative lacks an obvious forward thrust. Due no doubt to a combination of the difficulty of reading this text and its idiosyncratic position within English literary history, most of the critical literature has dwelled on how we can best classify the *Devotions* generically. (The assumption seems to be that if we can figure out what the *Devotions* is, we might discern how to read it most profitably.) The particular question that has preoccupied critics is whether the *Devotions* should be regarded as a meditative manual, and if so, whether it is Catholic or Protestant in nature.[1] In light of the tripartite structure of each Devotion, some readers have sought to explain this text through the model that they also apply to the *Holy Sonnets:* namely, the spiritual exercises recommended by St. Ignatius.[2] When we compare the structure of these spiritual exercises to the structure of the *Devotions*, we see that both conclude with a divine prayer, but otherwise they are rather different in character. Ignatius's cycle of composition of place, analysis, and colloquy, depends upon an initial act of visual conjuring followed by a sustained and focused meditative practice. Donne's Meditation, Expostulation, and Prayer, by contrast, move from an often wild and irascible contemplation of the human condition to combative "debatements with God" and then finally to a becalmed petition.

Those who dispute the Jesuit frame of the *Devotions*, advocating instead a Protestant model of meditation on scripture, dwell on the Expostulations, where Donne engages directly with biblical texts. But to consider the *Devotions* in this manner is to ignore the overall interest and energy of the work, which is certainly more preoccupied with the realities of Donne's world than with contemplation of scriptural passages. Indeed, the points of reference in the *Devotions* most often derive from what transpires either outside Donne's window or inside his body. The *Devotions* is a personal narrative, engaged with a particular experience of illness and recuperation.

Instead of regarding the *Devotions* in terms of meditation, a practice that depends upon conditions of calm and stasis, we might be better served by reading it in terms of crisis. This is a text that confronts sudden illness and imminent death, a text that responds, as Donne puts it in the subtitle, to "emergent occasions." The full title reads *Devotions upon Emergent Occasions, and severall steps in my Sicknes,* and the emphasis on "sicknes" as its primary subject cannot be overlooked. The occasion for writing was a crisis in body and soul—an illness that, as Donne quickly discovers, has penetrated both parts of the self. And this illness poses new opportunities to reflect upon the relationship between his physical and spiritual condition. On the one hand, Donne is suffering from typhus or spotted fever. On the other hand, he is suffering from the sinfulness of his soul. Although these two conditions are in many ways discrete and require different treatments, they are for Donne deeply intertwined.

As we have repeatedly seen, Donne was preoccupied with the relationship between his body and soul throughout nearly all of his writings. But nowhere is the subject so overtly interrogated as in the *Devotions.* Here the questions surrounding the origins of disease, the relationship between physical and spiritual suffering, the means by which God speaks to body and soul are all framed as matters of urgent metaphysical inquiry. When we consider Donne's lifelong commitment to understanding his body and soul through their "interinanimation," the project of the *Devotions* becomes increasingly coherent and compelling.

I have already said that illness held a certain appeal for Donne. In addition to granting proximity to God, it also provided an unusual, perhaps unique occasion in which the body and soul might share nearly identical states of being. Consistent with the Protestant doctrine of original sin, Donne understood the soul to be in a more or less constant state of sinfulness. Whereas periods of bodily health often disguise spiritual disease, physical sickness creates a sudden, unanticipated opportunity, as it were, for the physical and the spiritual to be as one. At the same time, however, that sickness creates a greater symmetry between the conditions of body and soul, the prospect of dying continually threatens to separate the two parts of the self. The crisis of Donne's illness allows him to practice the brinksmanship that we have seen to be central to his metaphysics: he approaches, and then retreats from, the threshold between life and death; he rehearses the experience of resurrection. The act of writing the *Devotions* was an attempt to possess or control what is otherwise outside of Donne's control. It was an effort to contain within his own script the otherwise terrifying uncertainty that surrounds the cycle of health, illness, and possible recovery.

I

Early modern Protestant culture was divided between medical and spiritual understandings of disease. For devout Protestants, as for many Catholics before them, sickness was generally regarded as a visitation from God. Catholic doctrine, however, held that physical suffering on earth could reduce future suffering after death; one's term in purgatory, for example, could be shortened if one endured certain pains or punishments during one's mortal life. Protestants, by contrast, rejected the whole concept of purgatorial suffering, and hence did not imagine the period of sickness to have any bearing on the duration of one's posthumous pain. (When Donne writes to Mrs. Cokayne that his illness may help him "hasten to the resurrection," he is striking a highly unorthodox, Catholic note.) The divine "visit" was largely understood in two distinct but related ways. First, it was a means of testing the sufferer's faith through the temptations of illness—impatience, fear of death, despair. Second, it was a warning intended to alert individual sinners to repent before their end was to come. Hence illness was for Protestants simultaneously a trial and a blessing: to be touched by God's rod with sickness was to be given a further chance to receive his grace. As Thomas Becon describes in the "Prayer for Them that are Sick" from his 1551 *Flower of Godly Prayers*, "Some that thus ungodly behave themselves thou sufferest to go forth still in their beast-like manners, without correction or punishment," whereas others, whose salvation God intends, receive "the loving rod of thy correction."[3]

Because illness was understood as a message from God, it is not surprising that Protestant literature on the subject disregards the body in favor of treating the soul. The most orthodox of such accounts can be found in the Book of Common Prayer, whose "Order for the Visitation of the Sick" outlines the procedures that the minister should follow when visiting his ill parishioners. Designed to be used domestically, the Prayer Book service alternates between addressing God, whose mercy is petitioned on behalf of the sufferer, and comforting the ill, whose patience and understanding are repeatedly invoked. The minister exhorts the sick man or woman to remember that "whatsoever your sickness is, know you certainly, that it is God's visitation," and proceeds to explain the proper frame of mind for understanding the illness's purpose. "And for what cause soever this sickness is sent unto you," the minister continues, "whether it be to try your patience for the example of other, and that your faith may be found in the day of the Lord laudable, glorious, and honourable, to the increase of glory and endless felicity, or else it be sent unto you to correct and amend in you whatsoever doth offend the eyes of our heavenly Father . . . it shall turn to your profit."[4] According to the church's official liturgy, then, sickness provides the ill with an opportunity for spiritual conversion.

Although contemporary manuals on illness and death do not strictly reproduce the kinds of texts printed in the Book of Common Prayer, their treatment of illness as a beneficial visitation from God persists as a common theme.[5] In Becon's *Sick Man's Salve*—the first major Protestant *ars moriendi* in English, which was first published in 1561 and had reached its twentieth edition by the mid-1600s—the ailing Epaphroditus is told by his wise friend Philemon not to lament his poor condition.[6] In response to Epaphroditus's complaint that "this sickness hath utterly marred me," Philemon replies, "Say not so neighbour Epaphroditus; yea, rather think that this your sickness is the loving visitation of God, and bringeth (although to the body weakness and trouble) yet to the soul valiance and consolation."[7] This division of body and soul is entirely typical of this literature more broadly: illness might bring pain to the body, but it affords "valiance and consolation" to the soul. According to Philemon, who serves as Becon's mouthpiece, his sick friend should be grateful to God for bestowing such a favor upon him. "You, neighbour Epaphroditus," Philemon explains, "have a great occasion to thank the Lord our God, that it hath pleased him to remember you with this his loving visitation, and through this sickness to declare his good and fatherly will toward you. For by laying this cross upon you he proveth you, whether you be constant in your faith and profession or not; and whether you will patiently and thankfully bear this his working in you, which is unto your everlasting salvation, or not" (96). The idea that God "proveth"—that is, tests—the individual's faith through the burden of sickness is an interesting example of how untenable predestination actually was as an operating principle in the Protestant church. Although Article 17 of the Church of England's *Thirty-Nine Articles* published in 1571 states that each individual's salvation was determined "before the foundations of the world were laid,"[8] in reality English Protestants imagined salvation to be somewhat negotiable. As Becon describes in the *Sick Man's Salve*, sickness provides an opportunity to show God one's mettle. The result of this test could not have greater consequences: it is "unto your everlasting salvation, or not."

The seemingly paradoxical recasting of illness as a blessing depends on the idea that the sick are granted an unusual opportunity both to recognize their sinfulness and to beg God for forgiveness during their mortal lives. In his *Manual of Directions for the Sick*, Donne's contemporary Lancelot Andrewes advises the ill man to be thankful for his disease "as for a wholesome medicine."[9] The notion that the illness itself is "medicine" nicely captures the chasm that falls between medical and devotional treatments during this period. Far from treating the physical symptoms per se, the symptoms are themselves regarded as a divine gift. God "could & would have suddenly taken you away with a quick destruction," Andrewes continues, "and not have given you this time to bethink yourself, and to seek and sue to Him for grace" (182). Hence at the same time that one's fate is said to have already been sealed, there is room for adjustment: the ill man has time to "bethink" himself and to petition God accordingly. Once the mind is "illuminated by God" through illness, it can discover "those sins you never knew" (183).

Because of this emphasis on illness as an occasion for reckoning with the soul, the body is at best ignored, and at worst mistrusted. In Andrewes's *Manual*, the body seems to be regarded primarily as an obstacle in the path to spiritual health. When he interrogates the ill person's beliefs, his series of inquiries begins with whether he or she believes the Creed, the Confession of Holy Faith, and so forth, and is followed by the questions: "If your sense fail you, or if the pain of your disease, or weakness otherwise, so work with you, as it shall happen you with your tongue to speak aught otherwise than this your faith or religion would; Do you renounce all such words as none of yours? and is it your will we account of them as not spoken by you?" (185). The right answers, of course, are yes, yes: I recognize that physical pain and weakness distort my consciousness, and I renounce the words that emerge from my body but do not reflect my rational will. What Donne will term "expostulations" or "debatements with God" are framed here as perversions wrought by the body, whose suffering obstructs the otherwise faithful pronouncements of the believer's spirit. For the words issued forth from the mouth are not only treated as accidental or nonvolitional. Andrewes imagines them as somehow foreign to the individual's self, as if the body is an entirely separate and hostile being. This is the force of the final question—"is it your will we account of them as not spoken by you?"—a startling articulation of an agonistic division between soul and body that Donne strives in his illness to resist.

In his *Rule and Exercise of Holy Dying* (1651), Jeremy Taylor offers a different account of physical pain in illness, although he is equally indifferent to treating the sufferings of the body. Pain, Taylor argues, focuses our attention on the spiritual realm by rendering the material world less appealing. "Sicknesse is a messenger of God," he explains, "sent with purposes of abstraction and separation, with a secret power and a proper efficacie to draw us off from unprofitable and useless sorrows: and this is effected partly by reason that it represents the uselessnesse of the things of this world."[10] "Abstraction and separation" become mental gifts—akin, we might imagine, to certain meditative practices—which somehow elude the healthy man preoccupied with the "useless . . . things of this world." Paramount among these useless things is the body, whose appetites and senses only prevent us from our appropriate longing for the next world.

In a section straightforwardly (and, to our eyes, surprisingly) entitled "Advantages of sicknesse," Taylor describes the ways in which the soul begins in sickness "to dresse her self for immortality." The flesh is now finally—and to Taylor's mind—rightly dismissed: "it sits . . . uneasily and dwells in sorrow" (86). Only then does the spirit find itself completely at ease, "freed from the petulant sollicitations of those passions which in health were as buisie and as restlesse as atomes in the sun, always dancing and always busie and never sitting down till a sad night of grief and un-easinesse draws the vail, and lets them dye alone in secret dishonour" (86). Although ostensibly intended to celebrate the freedom of the soul, Taylor's language to a certain degree betrays its designated purpose by creating an image of our bodily passions so poetically alluring and rich—"as restlesse as atomes in the sun, always dancing"—as to invite their lingering presence. The vision of the body dying alone "in secret dishonour" seems somewhat belatedly to undo the sympathy Taylor has himself just expressed toward the body's plight: the night, he tells us, is filled with sadness and grief; the veil is drawn not with confidence, but with "unease." Perhaps the ambivalence here is unintended—Taylor's aim in *Holy Dying* is to encourage the sick to look toward God, not to dwell on the body. To this end, the only "medicine" that he acknowledges is the "medicinal" rod with which God strikes us. God "strikes us that he may spare us," he exclaims, echoing Hebrews 12:6: "For whom the Lord loveth He chasteneth; and scourgeth every son whom He receiveth."[11] But what undermines Taylor's insistence that we should desire to die "in all things but *faith* and *its blessed consequents*" is his quiet acknowledgment of the pulls of our attachment to the flesh (93).

Taylor might unwittingly acknowledge the claims that the body makes on us. But neither he nor his fellow devotional writers seem interested in treating illness as a physical condition that deserves attention as such. There were, needless to say, a few voices of protest from English ministers concerning this division between treating the body and soul. The Puritan divine Richard Greenham, for example, attempts to bridge the divide in this passage from a work published in 1605:

If a man troubled in conscience come to a minister it may be he will look all to the soul and nothing to the body: if he come to a physician, he only considereth of the body and neglecteth the soul. For my part, I would never have the physician's council severed, nor the minister's labour neglected: because the soul and body dwelling together, it is convenient, that as the soul should be cured by the word, by prayer, by fasting, by threatening or by comforting, so the body also should be brought into some temperature [health] by physic, by purging, by diet, by restoring, by music, and by such means; providing always that it be done so in fear of God.[12]

It seems unlikely that so reasonable a position would have been resisted by even the most committed physicians or ministers. But it is remarkable how infrequently such opinions are articulated in the period's Protestant literature, a literature that, as we have seen, latently suggests that attempts to palliate or cure the body are potentially impious evasions of God's will. In seventeenth-century England, disease seems to be consigned to a dualistic model in which the respective health of body and soul bear little relation to each other.

II

In addressing at once the physical and spiritual diseases that plague its author, the *Devotions* stands apart from the standard works on illness that informed Donne's contemporary world. It neither exclusively looks forward toward death and salvation, nor does it solely attend to the patient's daily medical treatments. Instead, Donne moves between earthly and heavenly concerns, alternating watchfulness over the health of the body with anxiety over the fate of the soul. Moreover, because the *Devotions* is composed as if it were a daily journal kept during the period of illness (and not, as was in fact the case, a recording done several weeks after the illness had passed), the experience of reading it comes as close as possible to the experience of having the illness ourselves. It is difficult to describe, in fact, the claustrophobic sense of immersion one feels within Donne's text, whose centripetal energy draws us further and further inside its orbit. The pressure of the writing reproduces, it would seem, the pressure of the disease, and we are never fully released from the intensity of its grip.

In his dedicatory epistle to Prince Charles, Donne describes the narrative recorded in the *Devotions* as a special form of rebirth. "Most Excellent Prince," he begins, "*I Have* had *three* Births; *One*, Naturall, *when I came into the* World; *One,* Supernatural, *when I entred into the* Ministery; *and now, a* preter-naturall Birth, *in returning to life, from this* Sicknes" (3). In the seventeenth century, the category of the "preternatural" referred to things or events that could not be explained by the ordinary course of nature, but did not belong to the realm of the supernatural.[13] The preternatural was not the work of God but of nature; and yet it was not what we regularly expect from the natural realm. The preternatural was, in short, the territory of the exceptional. The recovery that the *Devotions* records is positioned somewhere between a purely natural phenomenon and a supernatural one, and this position corresponds to Donne's treatment of his disease.

The overarching subject of the *Devotions* is crisis: Devotion 1 begins with Donne's discovery of his illness, and each subsequent entry charts the progression of the disease through his eventual recovery. The focus on crisis stems from Donne's interest in moments when the status of either body or soul undergoes some form of transition. These transitional moments attracted Donne because they provided an unusual occasion to negotiate both his bodily and spiritual health with God, who seemed at these times more accessible or present than during Donne's normal life. Donne's crisis in bodily and spiritual health also seemed to make possible a level of self-examination that otherwise eluded him. Some aspects of this attitude toward illness are already familiar to us from the contemporary devotional literature. Far less familiar, however, was Donne's implicit understanding of his illness as an opportunity to take divine judgment into his own hands, to rehearse for himself what his eschatological fate might be. The impression of circularity produced by the *Devotions*—the feeling that despite real changes in Donne's condition, we are never fully moving forward—can be traced to his efforts to contain his narrative, to create a closed if dynamic cycle of events that cannot easily be altered. In this respect, the act of writing the *Devotions* is an act of possession: Donne wants to claim for himself the rhetorical if not the actual power of determining his salvation.

It is altogether fitting that the *Devotions* begins with an act of self-diagnosis: Donne realizes, to his dismay, that both his body and soul are sick. The process through which he recognizes his condition is typical of the way that the *Devotions* works as a whole—he is initially confronted with his bodily sickness only then to discover a complementary sickness in his soul. The very first line in the text declares the sudden change in his physical state: "Variable, and therefore miserable condition of Man; this minute I was well, and am ill, this minute" (7). The immediacy of Donne's voice—"this minute I was well, and am ill, this minute"—speaks to his efforts to simulate the actual process of his experience. Far from recounting his illness with calm retrospection, he thrusts himself, and his readers, into its midst. The shift from past to present tense—"this minute I *was* well, and *am* ill, this minute"—within the tight constraint of *this* and not any other minute intensifies the quality of apprehending the present moment: we are made to feel as if we are witnessing the very instant that the disease manifested itself.

The first consequence of Donne's recognizing his illness is to reassess the benefits of inhabiting so complex an organism as the body. Meditation 1 reverses the conventional celebration of man's body as a microcosm, a commonplace in humanist thinking that had gripped Donne's imagination on and off throughout his writings.[14] The glory that this metaphor normally affords to man is entirely lost, Donne reasons, once the body becomes ill. "Is this the honour which Man hath by being a *litle world*," he asks with palpable derision,

> That he hath these *earthquakes* in him selfe, sodaine shakings; these *lightnings*, sodaine flashes; these *thunders*, sodaine noises: these *Ecylpses*, sodain offuscations, and darknings of his senses; these *blazing stars*, sodaine fiery exhalations; these *rivers of blood*, sodaine red waters? Is he a *world* to himselfe onely therefore, that he hath inough in himself, not only to destroy and execute himselfe, but to presage that execution upon himselfe[?] (7–8)

Far from elevating the nature of human experience, the microcosmic associations only intensify the anguish of the body; modest physical symptoms become ecological disasters in Donne's imaginative landscape. The body, moreover, is at once the victim and the perpetrator of the disease: the description is of disease not from without, but from within. Hence the language of suicide: man "destroy[s] and execute[s] himselfe."

This emphasis on—and magnification of—the physical symptoms of Donne's disease fades in the Expostulation that follows, where he shifts from lamenting the body's ability to "presage" its own demise to wishing the soul had similar capacities. We learn that the illness afflicting Donne is not only physical in nature: it is also spiritual. We learn as well that unlike the body, the soul has no mechanism to reveal its own sickness. *"My God, my God,"* Donne bemoans,

> why is not my *soule* as sensible as my *body?* Why hath not my *soule* these apprehensions, these presages, these changes, these antidates, these jealousies, these suspitions of a *sinne*, as well as my body of a *sicknes?*

why is there not alwayes a *pulse* in my *Soule*, to beat at the approch of
a tentation to sinne? (8)

Whereas the body intuits its own illness even before the illness has manifested itself in visible symptoms, the soul repeatedly fails to detect its own
sins. The resonant suggestion that the soul should have a pulse ("why is
there not always a *pulse* in my *Soule?*") conveys the extent of Donne's somatic imagination: the ideal soul is a corporeal soul, with its own heart
beating.

What began as a strictly physical disease has now evolved into a spiritual disease. Unlike the body's illness, moreover, which came on suddenly
and involuntarily, the soul's illness is both chronic and willful. "I go, I run,
I flie into the wayes of tentation, which I might shun," Donne confides,
"nay, I breake into houses, wher the plague is" (8–9). The horror of this last
metaphor cannot fully be grasped by modern readers, for whom the plague
is thankfully a historical fact and not a daily fear. But we can still feel the
overwhelming force of the scene he conjures up—the violent, voluntary, and
entirely inexplicable entry into a house that has been locked and quaran-
tined because it is contaminated by the most contagious disease—so much
so, perhaps, that we forget that he describes a metaphorical state of his soul
and not the actual condition of his body. This effect is not, I would argue,
accidental: as we see repeatedly in the *Devotions*, the language of bodily
disease is indispensable for describing the state of his soul. The problem of
diagnosing the soul is not only an ontological problem—that the soul is not
a bodily organ with a measurable pulse or temperature. It is also a metaphorical problem: the diseases of the soul cannot easily be imagined without the
language of pathology.

By the end of Devotion 1, Donne has established crucial continuities
between the respective illnesses of body and soul. Despite the devotional
tradition in which he lived and worked, he refuses to minimize or ignore the
physical symptoms of his disease, and he takes his bodily ailments seriously
on their own terms. One of the striking features of this text is that Donne
receives no spiritual ministers over the course of his illness, a feature that
no doubt derives largely from the contagiousness of his disease, but also
speaks to his implicit interest in the *Devotions* in self-ministering.[15] Donne
receives no shortage, however, of physical ministration: the first physician
arrives on the fifth day, and he is subsequently joined by others, including James I's personal doctor, whom the king sends to Donne on day eight.
This team of physicians performs all sorts of treatments upon their patient,
ranging from the use of cordials *"to keep the venim and Malignitie of the*

disease from the Heart" (56) to the application of dead pigeons, placed at his feet, in order *"to draw the vapors from the Head"* (62). The very structure of the *Devotions* is in fact driven by medical developments and procedures. The epigraphs preceding each station announce the arrival of the physicians (*"The Phisician comes,"* *"The Phisician desires to have others joyned with him"*); their reactions to the disease (*"The Phisician is afraid,"* *"They find the Disease to steale on insensibly"*); their diagnoses and treatments (*"They have so good signes of the concoction of the disease, as that they may safely proceed to purge"*); their success in healing (*"God prospers their practise, and he, by them, calls Lazarus out of his tombe, mee out of my bed"*). Donne watches his doctors carefully throughout his illness, gauging his health by their reactions, and at the end of Meditation 19 he expresses his gratitude for having such fine medical attention: "O how many farre more miserable, and farre more worthy to be lesse miserable than I, are besieged with this *sicknesse,* and lacke their *Sentinels,* their *Phisitians* to *watch,* and lacke their *munition,* their *cordials* to *defend,* and perish before the *enemies* weaknesse might invite them to *sally,* before the *disease* shew any *declination,* or admit any way of *working* upon it selfe?" (98–99).

At the same time that Donne shows passionate concern for his physical health, he also clearly regards the illness of the body as a medium for understanding the illness of the soul. On several occasions he imagines himself to have two separate illnesses—in Prayer 4, for example, he exclaims: "Behold mee under the vehemence of two diseases, and under the necessity of two *Phisicians"* (23). More often, however, he understands the treatment of one to affect the treatment of the other, just as the symptoms themselves overlap. Readers may be tempted to differentiate indications of bodily versus spiritual disease, to determine whether the "red rivers" described in Meditation 1, for example, are meant to signify the bloody color of the urine in typhus, or a world of sinners suffering from God's plagues.[16] But far more important than separating these symptoms from each other is to grasp how profoundly Donne believed them to belong together.

The continuity between bodily and spiritual disease pervades the *Devotions,* but it becomes Donne's exclusive concern in Devotion 13. After nearly two weeks in which both the patient and his physicians perceive the illness's development only "insensibly"—"The *pulse,* the *urine,* the *sweat,"* Donne laments in Devotion 10, "all have sworn to say nothing, to give no *Indication,* of any dangerous *sicknesse"* (52) —the material signs of the sickness finally manifest themselves, and Donne's body is covered with spots.[17] "In this *accident* that befalls mee now," he writes in Meditation 13, "that this sicknesse declares itself by *Spots,* to be a malignant, and pestilential disease, if there be a *comfort* in the declaration, that thereby the *Phisicians* see more cleerely what to doe, there may bee as much *discomfort* in this, That the malignity may bee so great, as that all that they can doe, shall doe *nothing*" (67). The relief Donne experiences from finally experiencing the visible proof of the otherwise invisible disease gives way by the end of the Meditation to unmitigated despair. "O poore stepp toward being well," he concludes, "when these *spots* do only tell us, that we are worse, then we were sure of before" (68).

Donne's intense focus on the literal spottedness of the body shifts in the Expostulation to the recognition of a metaphorical spottedness in the soul. *"My God, my God,"* he begins Expostulation 13, "thou hast made this sick bed thine *Altar*, and I have no other *Sacrifice* to offer, but my self; and wilt thou accept *no spotted sacrifice*?" (68). Here Donne at once anticipates and challenges God's rejection by comparing himself to the embodied Christ: "Doeth thy *Son* dwel bodily in this flesh, that thou shouldst looke for an unspottednes here? . . . or hath thy *Son* himself no *spots*, who hath al our stains, & deformities in him?" (68–69). The initial question of whether his flesh is inhabited by Christ and hence should be "unspotted" yields to the question of whether Christ himself remained without spots, having "al our stains, & deformities in him." It becomes clear by now (if it had not become clear already) that the spottedness in question is not physical but spiritual, and that we have moved from an external to an internal condition. "Thy mercy," Donne continues, "may goe a great way in my *Soule*, and yet not leave me without *spots*; Thy corrections may go far, & burn deepe, and yet not leave me spotles" (69).

Over the course of Devotion 13, Donne follows a standard pattern in this text: he proceeds from a troubled recognition of his bodily disease, to an equally if not more troubled discovery of his spiritual disease, to a resigned acceptance of his condition so long as he imagines that he will receive God's love. Having anticipated a demand from God for an unspotted "sacrifice," a demand that provoked his defensive account of both his own and Christ's condition, he reconceives his spots in Prayer 13 as signs of divine affection. "What a wretched, and disconsolate *Hermitage*," he begins, "is that *House*, which is not *visited* by thee, and what a *waif* and *Stray* is that *Man*, that hath not thy *Markes* upon him?" (70). The very spots that had seemed leprous and tainted become "markes" of God's grace, and he pities the clean-skinned man as he who is overlooked or disregarded.

The achievement of this single Devotion is the complete transforma-tion of the meaning of Donne's illness: he successfully reinscribes the signs of his disease as evidence of his election. This evidence is communicated, moreover, through bodily, not spiritual symptoms, as we learn at the end of the Prayer:

> These heates, *O Lord,* which thou hast brought upon this *body,* are but thy chafing of the *wax,* that thou mightest *seale* me to thee; These *spots* are but the *letters,* in which thou hast written thine owne *Name,* and conveyed thy selfe to mee; whether for a *present possession,* by taking me now, or for a future *reversion,* by glorifying thy selfe in my stay here. (70)

The principal metaphors in this passage derive from property law: Donne figures his disease as a deed of transfer that delivers him entirely to God. The heat of the body becomes the molten wax used by God to "seale me to thee"; the spots so recently lamented become the individual letters with which God signs his name across Donne's flesh. The Prayer concludes with a petition for God's presence, a presence that erases all distinction between earth and heaven: "Onely be thou ever present to me, *O my God,* and this *bed-chamber,* and thy bed-chamber shal be all one roome, and the closing of these bodily *Eyes* here, and the opening of the *Eyes* of my *Soule,* there, all one *Act*" (70).

Donne's longing for God to possess him fully in body and soul is certainly not limited to this period of illness—we need only recall "Batter my heart, three person'd God," for a similar instance of this desire, expressed with an unrivaled intensity. But illness seems to heighten Donne's sense of entitlement to a privileged communication with the divine. At the very end of his life, Donne reflects on his having suffered many illnesses as a devotional "advantage" for both himself and his friends. "By my frequent Fevers," he writes to a friend, "I am so much the oftener at the gates of heaven . . . [and] I am thereby the oftener at my prayers."[18] In the *Devotions,* however, he expresses anxiety over being abandoned by God at the moment of greatest need. "I am not able to passe this agony alone; not alone without *thee,*" he confides in Expostulation 5, and later cries out with palpable desperation and self-pity: "*O my God,* it is the *Leper,* that thou hast condemned to *live alone;* Have I such a *Leprosie* in my *Soule,* that I must die alone; alone without thee?" (27).

The notion that illness was an occasion to experience intimacy with God was by no means unique to Donne. As we have seen, Protestant authors repeatedly frame sickness as a coveted visitation, whereby physical symptoms become merely the medium for the divine to communicate with the spirit of his creatures. Donne's formulation in the second Prayer is in this sense largely conventional. "By stripping me of my selfe," he declares, "and by dulling my bodily senses to the meats and eases of this world; [Thou] hast whet, and sharpned my spirituall senses, to the apprehension of thee" (13–14). "Interpret thine owne worke," he pleads further with God, "and call this sicknes, correction, and not anger, & there is soundnes in my flesh" (14). The hope that his illness reflects God's "correction" and not his "anger" would seem to confirm, moreover, Donne's deep saturation in the Protestant tradition that figures disease as an opportunity for repentance and reform.

What is startling about Donne's account of his illness, however, is that he alternates between viewing it as an opportunity for intimacy with God, and viewing it as an opportunity for devotional autonomy. In the *Devotions*, as in some of the *Holy Sonnets*, Donne seems both to crave God's mediation and to resist it. Over the course of this text, Donne repeatedly arrogates to himself the power of judgment so that God's responses are not provoked so much as prevented. Immediately following his lament in Expostulation 5 over the possible "leprosie" in his soul that would hinder even God from visiting him, Donne ruminates on whether God's presence is necessarily desirable. Do I not recall, he chastises himself, that although God would not come to Jacob until he found him alone, "yet when he found him alone, *hee wrestled with him, and lamed him?*" (27). Applying the lesson of Jacob to his own condition, he continues:

> When in the dereliction and forsaking of friends and *Phisicians,* a man is left alone to *God, God* may so wrestle with this *Jacob,* with this *Conscience,* as to put it out of *joynt,* and so appeare to him, as that he dares not looke upon him face to face, when as by way of *reflection,* in the consolation of his temporall or spirituall servants, and ordinances hee durst, if they were there. (27–28)

The fear of God that Donne describes in this passage takes the form of his desire for indirection rather than direction, divine "reflection" rather than actual presence. On the one hand, this avoidance of intimacy represents one of the many obstacles Donne struggles to overcome as he reconciles himself to his illness. On the other hand, an indirect, mediated relation to the divine is perhaps what the *Devotions* implicitly strives to achieve. The intensity of Donne's focus on each day and the resolution he achieves within each Devotion ultimately serve to resist his subjection to a master narrative over which he has no control, and whose authorship he cannot himself possess.

The struggle between Donne's submission to God's judgment and his efforts to seize authority himself reaches its greatest intensity in Devotion

14. This Meditation begins with Donne's bemoaning the impossibility of ever fully inhabiting the present, which is no sooner articulated than it is past. Although time seems, he argues, to have "three *stations, past, present,* and *future,* yet the *first* and *last* of these *are* not (one is not, now, and the other is not yet) & that which you call *present,* is not *now* the same that it was when you began to call it so in this *Line,* (before you sound that word, *present,* or that *Monosyllable, now,* the present, and the *Now* is past)" (71). Donne struggles with the same issues that Augustine confronts in book 11 of the *Confessions,* in which he ponders the category of the present:

> Those two times therefore past and to come, in what sort are they, seeing the past is now no longer, and that to come is not yet? As for the present, should it always be present and never pass into times past, verily it should not by time but eternity. If then time present, to be time, only comes into existence because it passeth into times past; how can we say that also to be, whose cause of being is, that it shall not be?[19]

Donne's sickness, however, allows him imaginatively, if not literally, to slow down the passing of time. One of the peculiar features of illness as a bodily experience is its deceleration of the present so that each hour of the day can seem endless in its tedium or pain. Donne experiences this tedium as well, but he also seems to cherish the breadth of the day on the sickbed as a heightened opportunity both to dilate and shape his reckoning with God.

Having contemplated the fleeting nature of the present in Meditation 14, Donne turns in the Expostulation to demand that God give him a crisis that day. "Though thou have laid me upon my *hearse,*" Donne declares, "yet thou shalt not depart from mee, from this bed, till thou have given me a *Crisis,* a *Judgment* upon myselfe this *day* . . . and therefore, howsoever thou come, it is a *Crisis* to me, that thou wouldest not loose me, who seekst me by any means" (74–75). Donne draws upon Galen's theory that illnesses had "critical days," the result of which led either toward recovery or death. For Galen and his followers, the outcome of the crisis was based on whether it fell on a favorable or unfavorable astrological day; these calculations were based on a "medicinal month" of twenty-six days and twenty-two hours.[20] In Devotion 14, Donne does not experience a crisis given by God—he attempts to provoke one of his own making.

Donne's invocation of a crisis begins with his deliberation over whether the idea of critical days in a disease is permissible within a Christian worldview. The Galatians and Colossians were reprimanded, he reminds himself, for judging God in respect to particular days or moons, and yet he wants to

hold on to the idea of critical days as a means both to concentrate his devotion and test his hopes for salvation. "Though thou remove [critical days]
from being of the *Essence* of our *Salvation*," he contends,

> thou leavest them for *assistances*, and for the *Exaltation* of our *Devo-
> tion*, to fix ourselves, at certaine *periodicall* and *stationary times*, upon
> the consideration of those things, which thou hast done for us, and the
> *Crisis*, the *Trial*, the *Judgment*, how those things have wrought upon us,
> and disposed us to a spirituall recovery, and convalescence. (73)

Having just insisted that the crisis occur on that very day, Donne begs God
now to lengthen that day into seven days, to transform the present moment
into a full week that will simulate the entire process of death, resurrection,
and judgment. "Since *a day is as a thousand yeres with thee*," Donne begs,
"Let, O Lord, a *day*, be as a *weeke* to me; and in this one, let me consider
seven daies, seven *critical daies*, and *judge my selfe, that I be not judged
by thee*" (74–75).

There is an obvious tension between the idea of crisis—an intense, con-
centrated moment in the disease—and Donne's fantasy of extending a single day into seven. What lies behind this fantasy? It does not derive from
his impulse to create more opportunities for God to determine his fate, as
someone like Becon or Andrewes might suggest. Instead, it stems from what
we have already glimpsed in certain of the *Holy Sonnets:* Donne's desire to
"*judge my selfe, that I be not judged by thee*" (75). The shape that Donne's
self-judgment takes is dramatic: he strives to enact the entire cycle of eschatological experience, beginning with his illness and death, and followed
by resurrection, judgment, and final glory. This simulated "week" begins
on the first day with God's visitation, which Donne celebrates as a "*Crisis*
to me, that thou wouldest not loose me, who seekst me by any means" (75).
We need to remember that this visitation is not experienced so much as
willed or conjured—it is *as if* God had granted his request for a crisis, and
this hypothetical condition had then become the starting point for the exercise as a whole.

Once Donne assumes that his crisis has been delivered, he proceeds on
the imaginary second day to examine his conscience, and on the third, to
prepare himself to receive Christ's sacrament. He worries on this fictional
occasion about the dangers the day may bring, with its "many dark passages,
& slippry steps," but he reassures himself that the day is long: "there are
light houres inough, for any man, to goe his whole *journey* intended by thee"
(75). These first three days serve to strengthen Donne's resolve before con-

fronting the fourth, which is "the day of my *dissolution, & transmigration from hence*" (75). The text moves seamlessly from the horror of the body and soul's separation at death to their reunion on the fifth day. In this respect, the imaginary week answers to what we have identified as one of Donne's deepest desires: the desire to move quickly, even instantly, from death to rebirth—a blessing usually accorded only to those enviable creatures still alive on the eve of the apocalypse.

After imagining his body and soul effortlessly reunited on the day of resurrection, Donne proceeds to the day of judgment, which is "truely, and most literally, the *Critical,* the *Decretory day."* It is on this day, he asserts, "that *Judgement* shall declare to me, and possesse mee of my *Seventh day,* my *Everlasting Saboth* in *thy rest, thy glory, thy joy, thy sight, thy selfe"* (76). The confident, even triumphant tone of Donne's rhetoric helps disguise the fact that he has staged and resolved the entire cycle of his salvation without any reassurance from God. In the Prayer that follows, he expresses once again his wish to secure his election based on the spiritual drama he has himself authored. "May [this] bee a *Criticall day* to me," he implores, "a *day wherein,* and *whereby* I may give thy *Judgement* upon my selfe" (77). Donne repeats the petition that preceded the entire exercise—to "*judge my selfe, that I be not judged by thee."* What does this finally mean? It means to rehearse the drama of life, death, and rebirth. It means to conjure up and definitively settle the act of judgment reserved for the last day. It means to become the author of one's own eschatological script. It means, however temporarily, to take the place of God.

III

In Devotion 14, Donne attempts to anticipate his salvation by writing his own eschatological drama. What he successfully leaves behind is both the hardship of his current condition—he is an ill man on his sickbed—and his anxiety about the fate of his body after death. These concerns are not long dismissed, however, and once the triumph of this particular Devotion is behind him, his former worries come rushing back. As I have already suggested, one of the difficulties in reading the *Devotions* as a coherent narrative is its regressive or cyclical quality: just as we think Donne has achieved some resolution about his condition, new doubts or preoccupations arise. Hence Devotion 15 addresses one of the physical reminders of his sickness—the curse of insomnia—and Devotion 16 begins a several-day meditation upon death. This meditation is provoked by the tolling of church bells outside of his window, and culminates in the celebrated lines from Devotion 17:

No man is an *Iland*, intire of it selfe; every man is a peece of the *Continent*, a part of the *maine*; if a *Clod* bee washed away by the *Sea*, *Europe*
is the lesse, as well as if a *Promontorie* were, as well as if a *Mannor* of thy
friends or of *thine owne* were; any mans *death* diminishes *me*, because I
am involved in *Mankinde*; And therefore never send to know for whom
the *bell* tolls; It tolls for *thee*. (87)

That each death is not a singular event, but physically reduces the whole
of mankind; that one does not simply mourn the loss of a neighbor, but is
personally "diminished" by such a loss; that the bells tolling for the stranger
toll for Donne as well: each of these perceptions suggest an attachment to
earthly, mortal life that seems entirely outside the orbit of Christian metaphysics. Donne offers no consolation here about the dead man's soul, nor
does he address how fortunate the man was to be taken by God. Instead, he
dwells upon the material, physical significance of mankind.

We have seen Donne express his contempt for the idea of a collective
soul.[21] In this devotion, he seems intrigued by the idea of humankind as a
collective body, for which each loss would be felt as an unnatural severing
of a constitutive part. The gesture of the final "thee" is no doubt the rhetorical turn most responsible for this passage's enduring fame, and its power
lies in its reach from the confines of Donne's sickbed to the innumerable
"thee[s]" who will read his text. It is also a gesture of the egotistical sublime
of which Donne is often accused: everything in his world can be refracted,
absorbed into the universe of his own experience. Meditation 17 draws to
an end on this note of self-absorption: "this *bell*," he concludes, "that tells
me of his *affliction*, digs out, and applies that *gold* to *mee*: if by this consideration of anothers danger, I take mine owne into contemplation, and
so secure my selfe, by making my recourse to my *God*, who is our onely
securitie" (87).

Donne's consideration of the loss that one man's death inflicts both upon
humankind and himself leads in the next Devotion to the contemplation of
a parallel loss for the "continent" of the self: the separation of the soul from
the body. As we saw in the introduction, Meditation 18 is one of a handful of
occasions in Donne's collected works in which he directly addresses philosophical and theological theories about the origins and composition of the
soul. Here Donne considers the origin of the soul as but a context for mourning the body's posthumous fate. After briefly discussing what *"meere Philosophers"* would tell him about the soul's corporeal nature and what *"mixt
men, Philosophicall Divines"* would tell him about the soul's creation, he
dismisses all such inquiry with the abrupt declaration that we looked at

before: "It is the *going out*, more than the *comming in*, that concernes us" (91). The *"going out"* concerns him, of course, because it brings an instant end to the body. At this moment Donne seems sufficiently confident about his election—so confident in fact that he summarily affirms his belief that through his prayer and faith he does *"faithfully* beleeve, that that *soule* is gone to everlasting *rest*, and *joy*, and *glory"* (92).

But even this type of assurance does not compensate for the suffering Donne anticipates in his flesh from death. He now releases the imaginative power that he denied to his description of the soul, pouring out in words the horrific transformation of the body in the immediate aftermath of the spirit's departure:

> But for the *body*, How poore a wretched thing is *that?* wee cannot expresse it *so fast*, as it growes *worse* and *worse*. That *body* which scarce *three minutes* since was such a *house*, as that that *soule*, which made but one step from thence to *Heaven*, was scarse thorowly content, to leave that for *Heaven:* that *body* hath lost the *name* of a *dwelling house*, because none dwells in it, and is making haste to lose the name of a *body*, and dissolve to *putrefaction*. (92)

As I have argued in relation to *The Second Anniversarie*, the notion that the soul was "scarse . . . content" to leave the body for heaven was not a conventional Protestant position even if it may have reflected an existential truth—anyone who has been in the presence of someone dying, as Donne was many times, would have perceived the apparent resistance of the spirit, the holding on *in extremis* that often precedes the moment of death. Whatever the official theology or liturgy of the English church may hold, Donne does not rejoice unequivocally in the soul's liberation. Instead, he feels great pathos for the body. The passage from Devotion 18 continues: "Who would not bee affected, to see a cleere and sweet *River* in the *Morning*, grow a *kennell* of muddy land water by *noone*, and condemned to the saltnesse of the *Sea* by night? And how lame a *picture*, how faint a *representation* is that, of the precipitation of mans body to *dissolution?*" (92–93). The image of the body as a "cleere and sweet *River*" conveys Donne's loving attachment to the beauty of the flesh, a beauty that is horribly altered by the soul's hasty departure. *"Now* all the parts built up, and knit by a lovely *soule*," he concludes, *"now* but a *statue* of *clay*, and *now*, these limbs melted off, as if that *clay* were but *snow*; and *now*, the whole *house* is but a *handfull* of *sand*, so much *dust*, and but a peck of rubbish, so much *bone"* (93). "Now," "now," "now," "now"—Donne wants to produce the effect of a simultaneous narration, as if these events were passing directly before our eyes. This is very much in the spirit of the *Devotions'* very first sentence—"this minute I was well, and am ill this minute"—and speaks to Donne's preoccupation with capturing the exact instant of change. In Devotion 18 each phase of decomposition follows swiftly upon the last; the body moves from the relative durability of clay to the soft and fleeting medium of snow. We are left in the end with "a *handfull* of *sand*, so much *dust*," "a peck of rubbish, so much bone."

What solaces Donne is not the thought of the immortal soul travel- ing to heaven, but the recollection that the body—now consisting of only sand, dust, rubbish, bone—will also ultimately ascend. In Meditation 18 this hope seems far from Donne's mind, but in the Prayer that follows Donne recalls the theological solution that renders the body's miserable state only temporary. Although the soul "bee by *death* transplanted to thee, and so in possession of inexpressible happiness there, yet here upon earth thou hast given us such a portion of heaven, as that though men dispute, whether thy *Saints* in heaven doe *know* what we in earth in particular doe stand in need of, yet without all disputation, wee upon earth doe know what thy *Saints* in heaven lacke yet, for the *consummation* of their *happinesse*" (96). Even the saints in heaven, Donne argues, are not fully consumed with joy until they are reunited with their bodies. "That therefore this *soule*," he concludes, "now newly departed to thy *Kingdome*, may quickly returne to a joifull *reunion* to that *body* which it hath left, and that *wee* with *it*, may soone enjoy the full *consummation* of all, in *body* and *soule*, I humbly beg at thy hand" (96). Had we not encountered this sentiment on several earlier occa- sions in his writing, we might be surprised by the bold and uncompromised description of the reunion between body and soul as mutually joyful. The body, which rises from its state of decay and corruption, has obvious reasons to celebrate. But Donne insists here as elsewhere that the soul, which was already lodged in heaven, "quickly returne[s]" to the body and rejoices in the "consummation."[22]

This poignant anticipation of a "joifull reunion" in heaven immediately precedes Donne's first signs of recovery, a recovery that is itself figured as a form of resurrection. The epigram to Devotion 19 announces that the "*Physitians, after a long and stormie voyage, see land*" (97) and during the following days Donne's health begins to return. Once his recovery seems assured, he allows himself for the first time to consider the origins of his illness. "My *God*, my *God*," he asks in Expostulation 22, "what am I put to, when I am put to *consider*, and *put off*, the *root*, the *fuell*, the *occasion* of my *sicknesse*? What *Hypocrates*, what *Galen*, could shew mee that in my body?" (118). He resolves that the cause of disease lies neither all in the body, nor all in the soul. Instead, Donne concludes that disease results from the combination:

> It lies deeper than [the body], it lies in my *soule:* and deeper than so, for we may wel consider the *body,* before the *soule* came, before *inanima-tion,* to bee *without sinne;* and the *soule,* before it come to the *body,* before that *infection,* to be *without sinne; sinne* is the *root,* and the *fuell* of all *sicknesse,* and yet that which destroies *body* & *soule,* is in *neither,* but in *both together;* It is in the *union* of the *body* and *soule;* and, O my *God,* could I *prevent* that, or can I *dissolve* that? (118)

This is an extraordinary thing for Donne to say, not least because he seems to lament the very union that he longs so desperately throughout his life to sustain, and whose loss in death he so passionately fears. It is "the *union* of the *body* and *soule,*" he concludes, the very design of humankind, which causes our illness. The body was innocent before "inanimation," and the soul was sinless until its "infection" by the flesh. But the sheer act of putting body and soul together creates the disease from which only death can free us.

The inevitability of this disease creates the tone of futility in Donne's final question in this passage—"O, my God, could I prevent that, or can I dissolve that?" In the subtle shift from the conditional "could I" to the present "can I?" he moves from an event over which he had no control—the union of his body and soul—to an event that he could in fact initiate himself. To dissolve the union of body and soul would mean to take his own life. As we have seen, this was something Donne thought seriously about in *Biathana-tos,* in which he defends, under certain circumstances, the act of suicide as a legitimate Christian practice. In Expostulation 22, however, the initial lament for man's inherited predicament of sinfulness does not lead to an embrace of suicidal despair. Instead, it produces one of Donne's many positive assessments of human dualism. He concludes by explaining the importance of having a body in order to understand its less knowable partner: "I know that in the state of my *body,* which is more *discernible,* than that of my *soule,* thou dost *effigiate* my *Soule* to me" (119). To "effigiate" is to present a likeness of something by pictorial or sculptural representation. The state of the body therefore becomes an effigy of the soul, a necessary means to read what is otherwise invisible.

The problem of the soul's unknowability pervades the *Devotions.* We will recall that Donne began by lamenting that the soul, unlike the body, has no pulse. In Expostulation 21, he transforms the difficulty of knowing the state of his soul into a justification for having a body:

My *God*, my *God*, how large a *glasse* of the next *World* is *this?* As we
have an *Art*, to cast from one *glasse* to another, and so to carry the *Species* a great way off, so hast thou that way, much more; wee shall have a
Resurrection in *Heaven*; the knowledge of that thou castest by another
glasse upon us here; we *feele* that wee have a *Resurrection* from *sinne*;
and that by another *glasse* too; wee see wee have a *Resurrection* of the
body, from the *miseries* and *calamities* of this life. This *Resurrection* of
my *body*, shewes me the *Resurrection* of my *soule*; and both *here* severally, of both together hereafter. (112)

The force of the initial comparison between this world and the heavens turns
on the ability of humans to produce "species," by which Donne means outward, visible forms, or the reflection of a given object.[23] Just as humans can
reflect images in mirrors, all the more can God convey images of a world we
cannot otherwise glimpse. We see our future life in heaven, Donne suggests,
not through prophecy or inspiration, but through mediations, refractions,
experiences on earth. God has many "glasses," and each one shows us something new. But in one important context, Donne affirms, we learn directly
from ourselves. "This *Resurrection* of my *body*," he triumphantly declares,
"shewes me the *Resurrection* of my *soule*; and both *here* severally, of both
together hereafter" (112). The recovery of the body implies the recovery of
the soul; the experience of resurrection on earth forecasts the experience of
heavenly resurrection.

IV

In a letter to his friend Sir Robert Ker composed during his convalescence,
Donne explains his decision to publish the *Devotions*, which appeared in
print with unusual speed a few months after its composition:

Sir, Though I have left my bed, I have not left my bed-side, I sit there still,
and as a Prisoner discharged, sits at the Prison doore, to beg Fees, so sit I
here, to gather crummes. I have used this leisure, to put the meditations
had in my sicknesse, into some such order, as may minister some holy
delight. They arise to so many sheetes (perchance 20.) as that without
saying for that furniture of an Epistle, That my friends importun'd me to
Print them, I importune my Friends to receive them Printed.[24]

This is a wonderfully evocative image of the recovering but still infirm patient "discharged" from the strict confines of his bed but not yet free to

re-enter the world, using the "leisure" of this time in between sickness and health to gather the "crummes" of his thoughts. Donne explains his desire to publish the "meditations had in my sicknesse" so that they might "minister some holy delight," and we might assume that the "holy delight" they will give lies in the pleasure of witnessing his sweet return to health. But to claim this is to ignore the mood of the final Devotion, in which Donne moves from his triumphant recovery in Devotions 21 and 22 to his overwhelming fear of a relapse.

Devotion 23 begins with a warning from his physicians—*"They warne mee of the fearefull danger of relapsing"* (121)—and imagines the experience of re-experience: panting through the same heats, suffering through the same sweats, hoping against hope for the blessed recovery that he has already been given once before. The horror of relapse is not simply or even primarily one of physical discomfort. Instead, it results largely from spiritual failure, and sinks us back into a state of sin.[25] Hence he who relapses reprimands himself: *"Alas, how unprovident, and in that, how unthankfull to God and his instruments am I, in making so ill use of so great benefits, in destroying so soone, so long a worke, in relapsing, by my disorder, to that from which they had delivered mee"* (122). The idea that God could forgive Donne his sins, and yet despite this forgiveness he could choose to sin once again, places him below even the fallen angels, who would certainly have *"fixed* themselves upon thee, if thou hadst once *re-admitted* them to thy *sight"* (125).

At the same time, however, that Donne seems gripped by a fear of relapse that may exceed earlier fears of never recovering, there is an unspoken sense in which relapse corresponds to a secret wish. This is not to say that Donne would actually welcome the opportunity to suffer again the physical pain of this disease, nor is it to imply that he is indifferent to provoking God's wrath by disregarding the blessing of health. It is to suggest that the purpose of the text is to create a narrative of sickness and recovery that can, in every reading, be renewed. And this potential for renewal is perhaps the source of the *Devotions'* intended "holy delight." For the delight that the *Devotions* provides is not the delight that comes from witnessing a straightforward recovery, nor is it the delight that comes from watching the ill man make peace with his fate in the manner of the Protestant *ars moriendi*. Instead, it is the delight of being thrust in the middle of a crisis, of witnessing the vicissitudes of falling and rising, of understanding the struggle of sickness as something imaginatively and devotionally productive. It is the delight of being invited into the mind of someone who thrives on the sensitivity that illness effects in body and soul, someone who welcomes, rather than shuns, the opportunity to rehearse for his death.

CHAPTER SIX

Deaths Duell

When Donne became a minister in the Church of England, he pursued his lifelong preoccupation with the resurrection of the flesh in a manner unprecedented in his earlier works. To read the ten volumes of Donne's surviving sermons is to experience an intensity of focus on the posthumous body that has no parallels in early modern Protestant literature. Whether the occasion was Good Friday or a funeral, Easter Day or a wedding ceremony, Donne made his central theme again and again the subject of resurrection. We have seen examples of such sermons in many of the preceding chapters, and we have noted his concern with retrieving his own flesh and blood as well as his own soul on the last day. The final proof of how profound an obsession the resurrection was for Donne comes in the last sermon he ever wrote. In this sermon, Donne not only rehearses his fears about bodily corruption and his hopes for divine reconstitution, as he had on earlier occasions. He also attempts to stage his own death in the pulpit, to perform his valediction to the world.

On the first Friday of Lent in February 1631, Donne preached before King Charles I and hundreds of listeners at Whitehall Palace a sermon that was published one year later with the posthumous title *Deaths Duell, or A Consolation to the Soule against the Dying Life and Living Death of the Body*.[1] This Friday was Donne's regular assignment in the Lenten sermons, and Walton refers to it as Donne's "old constant day." Indeed, Donne seems to have felt an unusually strong commitment to preaching on this occasion, as if it held a particularly strong place in his sense of vocation. Hence he writes to a friend in the weeks between Christmas and Lent that although his illness had forced him to arrange a substitute for his annual Christmas Day sermon at St. Paul's, he was determined to keep his "Lent Sermon, except my

Lord Chamberlaine believe me to be dead, and leave me out; for as long as I live, and am not speechlesse, I would not decline that service" (243–44).[2]

As Walton relates it, when the sickly dean entered the pulpit that day at Whitehall, the audience responded as if encountering a ghost:

> Many of them thought he presented himself not to preach mortification by a living voice, but mortality by a decayed body, and a dying face. And doubtless many did secretly ask that question in Ezekiel: 'Do these bones live?' . . . many that then saw his tears, and heard his faint and hollow voice, professing they thought the text prophetically chosen, and that Dr. Donne had preached his own Funeral Sermon.[3]

The notion that Donne might have "preached his own Funeral Sermon" is obviously fantastic, but the fantasy did not belong to the congregation alone. In the letter in which he expresses his commitment to preaching his Lent Sermon, Donne responds to a rumor that he had already passed away. "Yet, I perceive it [the rumor] went not through all," he writes, "for, one writ unto me, that some (and he said of my friends) conceived, that I was not so ill, as I pretended, but withdrew my self, to save charges, and to live at ease, discharged of preaching" (242). "This," he exclaims, is an "unfriendly, and God knows, an ill-grounded interpretation," not least because "it hath been my desire, (and God may be pleased to grant it me) that I might die in the Pulpit" (242–43). If such a death cannot be granted, he prays that he might at least meet his death through his exertions in the pulpit: "that is," he explains, "die the sooner by occasion of my former labours" (243).

Donne had long expressed his desire to have an active death. In an early letter to Goodyer, he explains,

> I would not that death should take me asleep. I would not have him meerly seise me, and onely declare me to be dead, but win me, and overcome me. When I must shipwrack, I would do it in a Sea, where mine impotencie might have some excuse; not in a sullen weedy lake, where I could not have so much as exercise for my swimming. (50)

At the time of this letter, Donne was immensely frustrated with his lack of career advancement. The shipwreck analogy corresponds to the letter's overarching spirit of melancholy, a melancholy that has its roots in his desire to find his vocation. "Therefore I would fain do something," he continues, "but that I cannot tell what, is no wonder. For to chuse, is to do: but to be no part of any body, is to be nothing" (50–51). By contrast, in the letters Donne wrote in response to the rumor that he had died, he expresses his hope to meet his end while he is actively practicing his profession. Writing on January 15, 1631, to his friend Mrs. Cokayne—the widow of Sir William Cokayne, for whom Donne preached the 1626 funeral sermon we have returned to several times—Donne explains that he shall come to London "not onely to be nearer [my] grave, but to be nearer to the service of the Church, as long as I shall be able to do any . . . I know nothing to the contrary, but that I may be called to Court, for Lent service" (317).

Although Donne is not responsible for the title of his final sermon, there is nothing in his collected works that better warrants its name. This is not to diminish the challenge posed to death in poems like "Death be not proud" or in the final Meditations of the *Devotions*. But nowhere does Donne offer so sustained a contemplation of death as he does in *Deaths Duell*, and nowhere does he describe in such vivid terms death's eventual defeat through resurrection. In this climactic sermon, a sermon that Donne wrote with the understanding that it would be his last, he poses the questions that plagued him throughout his life. How do we survive the separation of our body and soul? How do we assure that death will not be the end of us, but merely a period between life and rebirth? How do we arrive in heaven as the identical people we were in this life, albeit in perfected form? Donne answers these questions by condensing into a single text the meditations that have pervaded both his secular and religious writings. He does so, moreover, by translating these meditations into a dramatic form in which he and his listeners are all participants.

The sermon is a dramatic form—the presence of an audience demands this—but nowhere is Donne more dramatic than in *Deaths Duell*. More than any of his other sermons, *Deaths Duell* reminds us again and again that the text we have received is merely a script of what was originally a live performance. In his elegy appended to the 1633 edition of Donne's *Poems*, the poet and clergyman Jasper Mayne describes Donne the preacher as above all a consummate performer:

Who with thy words could charme thy audience,
That at thy sermons, eare was all our sense;
Yet have I seene thee in the pulpit stand,
Where wee might take notes, from thy looke, and hand;
And from thy speaking action beare away
More Sermon, then some teachers use to say.
Such was thy carriage, and thy gesture such

As could divide the heart, and conscience touch.
Thy motion did confute, and wee might see
An errour vanquish'd by delivery. (55–64)

When Donne was in the pulpit, the power of his "looke," "hand," "carriage," and "gesture" had the argumentative force to defeat error. We do not
know whether Mayne was present to hear *Deaths Duell*, but it seems altogether clear that this sermon provides the consummate example of what he
describes as Donne's "speaking action." It is our most enduring and most
evocative trace of Donne in motion.

I

Donne was first ordained as a priest in the Church of England in 1615, and
began preaching almost immediately thereafter. His first sermon before a
congregation was during the summer of that same year, when he preached
at the Inns of Court, and there is evidence that he began preaching before
James I in 1616 if not sooner.[4] His lifelong appointment as a Royal Chaplain
meant that he had regular preaching duties before the king: there were forty-
eight Chaplains in Ordinary assigned to the king's court, each of whom was
in attendance for either one or two months a year, during which period he
would preach on multiple occasions.[5] In 1616 Donne was chosen Divinity
Reader at Lincoln's Inn, a position he held until several months after his
installation as Dean of St. Paul's in late 1621, and one that involved preaching approximately fifty sermons per year.[6] In addition to his official duties,
Donne found time to freelance, so to speak, throughout his career at chris-
tenings, weddings, and funerals of friends; during trips abroad by members
of court; at the private house of the queen or prince; as a temporary preacher
for parishes with a vacant pulpit; and even possibly on hunting trips with
his king.[7] After years of social isolation, this intensely social man must have
seized with fervor every opportunity for preaching. Donne's embrace of the
pulpit was motivated even more profoundly by his conviction that his words
could transform the lives of his listeners.

However deeply Donne valued the sacraments of baptism and commu-
nion, he regarded the sermon as the high road to grace. Paraphrasing St.
Paul in Romans 10:17—"faith cometh by hearing, and hearing by the word
of God"—Donne declares in January 1627 in the fourth of his Prebend Sermons, on Psalm 65:5, "there is no salvation but by faith, nor faith but by
hearing, nor hearing but by preaching; and they that thinke meanliest of the
Keyes of the Church, and speake faintliest of the Absolution of the Church,

will yet allow, That those Keyes lock, and unlock in Preaching" (7:320). Although the sacraments are by no means *adiaphora*—things indifferent to salvation—Donne regards them as secondary in importance to the preaching of God's word. As he explains in an undated sermon preached on Candlemas Day, Christ instituted the sacraments as "subsidiary things" to accompany the power of the Word: the sacraments serve "our infirmity, who stand in need of such visible and sensible assistances" (10:69).

This privileging of preaching (versus a liturgical or sacramental emphasis) had been central to church piety under Elizabeth and James, but came under attack when Charles ascended the throne. As Peter McCullough has shown, when Donne gave the Prebend sermon in 1627 advocating the power of preaching above all else, he was directly flouting the new emphasis in the Carolinian church under the leadership of William Laud, who would two years later institute a nationwide "suppression" of preaching.[8] In her study of Jacobean sermons, Jeanne Shami convincingly argues that Donne resisted using the pulpit as a platform to engage in polemic, and that he tended on the whole to tow a middle line of conformity.[9] Hence it is all the more striking that he took the unusual risk of offending both Charles and Laud by so unequivocal an endorsement of preaching.

Why would Donne take such a risk? The most compelling answer is that he genuinely believed his vocation was defined by the act of preaching God's Word. He explains this in a sermon delivered "to the Houshold at Whitehall" in 1626, in which he declares that "our ordinary commission is *Ite, praedicate, Go and preach the Gospel*, and bring men in so" (7:156).[10] By "ordinary," Donne does not mean "regular" or "unexceptional"; he means that this is his official, ordained, and indeed commanded duty. Christ comes to us by calling, he continues, and this calling is not conveyed only through the words of scripture, but requires a voice as well as a word. "It is by the Word," he allows, "but not by the Word read at home, though that be a pious exercise; nor by the word submitted to private interpretation; but *by the Word preached*, according to his Ordinance, and under the Great Seal, of his blessing upon his Ordinance. So that *preaching* is this *calling*" (7:157). Reading the scriptures at home, however edifying, pales in comparison to the power of hearing God's Word preached in the church. "If Christ do appear to any man, in the power of a miracle, or in a private inspiration," he explains, "yet he appears but in weakness, as in an infancy, till he speak, till he bring a man to the hearing of his voice, in a settled Church, and in the Ordinance of preaching" (7:157).

For Donne, preaching was not simply a monologue: it was a shared activity between preacher and listener. In a 1624 sermon on Psalm 34:11,

"Hearken unto me, I will teach you the fear of the Lord," he declares: "To every Minister and Dispenser of the Word of God, and to every Congregation belong these words; And therefore we will divide the text between us: To you one, to us appertains the other part. You must *come*, and you must *hearken*; we must *teach*, and teach to *edification*; There is the *Meum & Tuum*, your part, and our part" (6:95). Later in the sermon, he explains that both body and soul must be engaged in the act of "hearkening"—which in the seventeenth century meant not simply to listen but "to hear with attention," or "to apply the mind to what is said."[11] Donne lambastes those who pursue "perverse extasie[s]," during which the soul departs from the body while they are attending church services: "It were a strange and a perverse extasie, that the body being here, at a religious exercise, and in a religious posture, the soul should be gone out to the contemplation, and pursuit of the pleasures or profits of this world."

Needless to say, Donne is not imagining the kind of ecstasy described by Plotinus—the soul that he criticizes is not pursuing divine enlightenment so much as searching for earthly delights, perhaps not so far off, while the body sits confined in the pews. But the indictment is directed primarily at the negative consequences of separating soul from body while attending a sermon, whatever the object of the soul's attentions may be. "You come hither but to your own funerals," Donne warns, "if you bring nothing hither but your bodies; you come but to be *enterred*, to be *laid in the earth*" (6:101). In an Easter Day sermon preached the same year, Donne attacks those listeners who are not receptive to the message of a sermon as spiritually dead. "It is not evidence enough," he declares, "to prove that thou art alive, to say, I saw thee at a Sermon; that spirit, that knows thy spirit, he that knows whether thou wert moved by a Sermon, melted by a Sermon, mended by a Sermon, he knows whether thou be alive or no" (6:71). Adopting an argument long embraced by the Church of England in relation to participating in public prayer, Donne contends that mere attendance at sermons is inconsequential if one's spirit is not "moved," "melted," or "mended." "To be alive"—which means here to be resurrected in this life from spiritual death—is to be penetrated by the Word preached.

This does not mean, however, that all sermons have the power to penetrate all listeners, nor does Donne imagine that his listeners will attend to every word that he speaks. Here I disagree with Debora Shuger's conclusion that "Donne sets the standard of obedience so high that no one can perform his part of the bargain."[12] For it seems clear that one of Donne's more endearing qualities as a minister was his tolerance for human imperfections. Hence he tells Charles and his courtly audience on April 1, 1627, that one need not understand or remember an entire sermon, so long as one "layeth hold upon such Notes therein as may be applicable to his own case, and his own conscience, and conduce to his own edification" (7:393). "That poore soule that gathers a stick or two, for the baking of her own cake," he continues, "that layeth hold upon any Note for the rectifying of her own perverseness hath performed the commandment of this Text, *Take heed what ye heare*" (7:393). It is a bitter irony that this sermon in which Donne advocates the listener's ability to single out passages for his personal edification was for other reasons deemed a deliberate attack on Laudian high church ecclesiology, and after being commanded to provide the king with a copy of the sermon, Donne was forced to apologize.[13] In Laud's diary entry for April 4, three days following the sermon, he notes: "When his Majesty King *Charles* forgave to Doctor *Donne* certain slips in a Sermon Preached on *Sunday, April 1*."[14]

Notwithstanding the offense given to Charles, Donne's injunction to learn what one can without worrying about comprehending the whole speaks to his overarching desire to reach as many listeners as possible. How does he do this? In her influential study of Donne's prose style, *Contrary Music*, Joan Webber describes a wide range of classical rhetorical techniques that Donne employed in crafting his sermons, including *antimetabole* (reversing the order of a phrase just spoken), *paranomasia* (playing on words that sound almost identical), *apostrophe* and *hypotyposis* (conjuring up of scenes before his listeners' eyes), and the alternation of the Senecan and the Ciceronian sentence.[15] Each of these is rightly adduced as contributing to Donne's success in the pulpit, although we can certainly imagine a preacher who employs all of these techniques but possesses none of Donne's ability to seize the attention of his listeners.

In addition to these classical devices, Donne also regularly uses a technique advocated in many contemporary preaching manuals: to include himself among the members of the congregation when he describes sins or imperfections that afflict them. Hence the Puritan divine Richard Bernard recommends in his 1607 work, *The Faithfull Shepheard*, that in order for a minister to preach profitably, "he must preach to [his hearers] from knowledge out of himselfe, feeling the corruption of nature."[16] Likewise in his *Practis of Preaching*, the Flemish reformer Andreas Hyperius recommends that the preacher, before speaking, must "conceive such lyke affections in his mynde, and rayse them upp in himselfe," so that they may be "translated into the myndes of his auditors." "He that burneth wholly in himself," Hyperius concludes, "by his oration and (as it were) by his owne example may incense others to enterprise the lyke."[17]

There are many concerns or fears that Donne confesses to experiencing himself when he preaches about them to his listeners, but no single subject surfaces so regularly as the fear of what awaits us after death. As we saw in the introduction, one reason that Donne preaches so fervently on the doctrine of bodily resurrection is that he knows how difficult a doctrine it is to believe—he declares, we will recall, that it is the "hardest Article" of the entire Creed to teach, and that it was for this reason that Christ performed his miracle of raising Lazarus from the dead. If we consider the 160 extant sermons as a whole, we see how persistently Donne attempts to convince his listeners that however decayed and scattered the posthumous body may be, it will return intact on the last day.

Donne's habit of rehearsing the anxieties that surround the prospect of mortality in order to offer a vision of eventual reconstitution, of sharing with his audience the horrors of bodily corruption and disintegration in the grave in order to take pleasure in the miracle of that body's perfection in heaven, lies at the very heart of his preaching style. T. S. Eliot complained in an essay on Lancelot Andrewes that Donne's sermons are "certainly known to hundreds who have hardly heard of Andrewes; and they are known precisely for the reasons because of which they are inferior to those of Andrewes. He is a little of the religious spellbinder," Eliot declares, "the Reverend Billy Sunday of his time, the flesh-creeper, the sorcerer of emotional orgy."[18] The contemptuousness of Eliot's language bespeaks something powerful about Donne's: even for his modern readers, let alone for his contemporary listeners, there is at times an alarming intensity in his sermons that may indeed make the flesh creep, or provoke a momentary loss of emotional control. If Donne denies us the detachment that Andrewes reliably supplies, the effect of this is to draw us into the drama he unfolds, to force us to participate in a confrontation for which we have had no warning, and in which we may not have been prepared to engage. We are brought to unfathomable lows and soaring highs in Donne's journeys through the cycle of life, death, and rebirth, and the sweeping power of his voice seems somehow to reverberate even on the printed pages of his volumes today. This can be said of so many of the sermons, but nowhere is more extravagantly true than in the case of *Deaths Duell.*

II

When Donne entered the pulpit to preach *Deaths Duell*, his deathlike appearance made his text—"And Unto God the Lord Belong the Issues of Death" (Psalm 68:20)—conspicuously self-referential. Except for his Prebend

Sermons on the five Psalms that were assigned to him as dean of St. Paul's (Psalms 62–66), the choice of scriptural text was Donne's own. According to Walton, Donne "never gave his eyes rest [after preaching] till he had chosen out a new Text, and that night cast his Sermon into a form, and his Text into divisions; and the next day betook himself to consult the Fathers, and so commit his meditations to his memory, which was excellent."[19] Although Walton's hagiographic account of Donne's life cannot necessarily be trusted, the memorization of sermons was standard practice for the accomplished preachers of Donne's age, and it is generally assumed that Donne preached *Deaths Duell* without any notes at hand. In the established church, there was a widespread prejudice both against reading sermons, and against *ex tempore* preaching. Auditors expected neither spontaneity nor script: they expected the preacher to know his sermon by heart.

Donne's decision to preach during what would turn out to be his final illness meant not only having the physical stamina to deliver the sermon from the pulpit, but also having the mental stamina to commit the sermon to memory. He provides us with an interesting glimpse of the labor involved in composing and learning his sermons in a letter to Sir Robert Ker written on April 2 or 3, 1627, in the immediate aftermath of the sermon that gave offense to Charles, preached on Mark 4:24, "Take heed what you heare." Donne expresses his anxiety to Ker about the king's disapproval, but claims he can find no grounds for the complaint. "I am still upon my jealousie," he writes,

> that the King brought thither some disaffection towards me, grounded upon some other demerit of mine, and took it not from the Sermon. . . . I have cribrated, and recribrated, and post-cribrated the Sermon, and must necessarily say, the King who hath let fall his eye upon some of my Poems, never saw, of mine, a hand, or an eye, or an affection, set down with so much study, and diligence, and labour of syllables, as in this Sermon.[20]

To "cribrate" is another of Donne's neologisms, from the Latin *cribrare*, "to pass through a sieve." What is revealing is the comparison between the "study, and diligence, and labour" involved in composing a poem and writing a sermon. (As this letter suggests, Charles seems to have taken an interest in Donne's poetry, and his personal copy of the 1635 edition of the *Poems* is in London today.)[21] Both poems and sermons demand the weighing of syllables, Donne explains to Ker, and both require a good deal of premeditation and care. "I remember I heard the old King [James] say of a good Sermon," he continues, "that he thought the Preacher never had thought of his Sermon, till he spoke it; it seemed to him negligently and extemporally spoken. And I knew that he had weighed every syllable, for half a year before, which made me conclude, that the King had before, some prejudice upon him" (309).

Whatever Charles may have thought when he heard Donne preach *Deaths Duell* in February 1631, it is unlikely that he regarded the sermon as either "negligently [or] extemporally spoken." Among its other qualities, *Deaths Duell* is a masterpiece of premeditation. Donne organized the sermon around three alternative interpretations for the scriptural phrase, "the issues of death" (*exitus mortis*)—deliverance from death, deliverance in death (i.e., through the manner of our death), and deliverance by or through death—and he adheres rigorously to this tripartite structure. The sermon begins by bombarding its listeners with arguments for death's pervasiveness. On other occasions Donne speaks of death as a clearly demarcated transition between one state and the next. We might recall, for example, the stirring passage in the *Devotions* in which he laments how quickly the body, a "clear and sweet *River*" in the morning, becomes a "*kennel* of muddy land water by *noone.*" In *Deaths Duell*, however, he insists that what we regard as life is indistinguishable from death, and he rewrites the entire life cycle as a continuous act of dying.

The idea of life as indistinguishable from death was not an invention of Donne's. In *The City of God*, St. Augustine argues that "no sooner do we begin to live in this dying body, than we begin to move ceaselessly towards death." "Man," he declares, "is never in life from the moment he dwells in this dying rather than living body."[22] Augustine himself would have encountered the idea in Seneca, whose Epistle 24 recounts what Seneca already regarded as a commonplace. "Every day," writes Seneca, "a little of our life is taken from us; even when we are growing, our life is on the wane."[23] Donne's contribution to the tradition is to slow down and particularize the phenomenon of continuous dying; to vivify the experience for his listeners by describing its daily horror.

In *Deaths Duell*, Donne describes even our time in the womb as overshadowed by the prospect of death. "In our mothers wombe," he begins, "we are dead so, as that wee doe not know wee live. . . . In the wombe wee have eyes and see not, eares and heare not; There is the wombe wee are fitted for workes of darkenes, all the while deprived of light" (10:233). If the womb is a place of death, we might imagine that our birth into the world would be an entrance into life. But this too is regarded as another phase of dying. "This *exitus a morte*," he continues, "is but *introitus in mortem*, this *issue*, this deliverance *from* that *death*, the death of the *wombe*, is an *entrance*, a delivering over to *another death,* the manifold deathes of this *world.*" The occasion of birth becomes indistinguishable from the occasion of death, as Donne connects the birth caul covering the head of the newborn infant with the winding sheet covering the corpse: "Wee have a winding sheete in our Mothers wombe, which growes with us from our conception, and wee come into the world, wound up in that *winding sheet,* for wee come to *seeke a grave*" (10:233).

Donne is not always so dismissive in his sermons of the pleasures of being alive. At times his invocations of earthly loveliness are almost unbearably poignant, because they are seen under the mantle of loss. Consider, for example, these lines from a sermon preached to the Prince and Princess Palatine during his trip to Germany with Lord Doncaster in 1619: "The sun is setting to thee, and that for ever; thy houses and furnitures, thy gardens and orchards, thy titles and offices, thy wife and children are departing from thee, and that for ever" (2:267). It is not the dying man who departs from his gardens and orchards and wife and children—the gardens and orchards and wife and children depart from him. This passage comes from a sermon preached on Romans 13:11, "For now is our salvation nearer then when we believed," and Donne frames his description of the man's losses within the context of welcoming his salvation. Hence the passage is prefaced with the reassurance "Behold thy Salvation commeth," and followed with the reassurance "*Ecce Salvator tuus venit,* behold then a new light, thy Saviours hand shall open thine eyes." Between these two promises of heavenly peace, however, is a moving lamentation for the pleasures of the mortal world.

In *Deaths Duell,* by contrast, Donne delivers a crushing negation of earthly joys. In his desire to represent all of life as a series of deaths, there is no room whatever for acknowledging the *praemia vitae.* "The whole world is but an universall church-yard, but our common grave," he declares, "and the life and motion that the greatest persons have in it, is but as the shaking of buried bodies in their graves by an earth-quake" (10:234). This startlingly bleak image in which the bustle and activity of life on earth are reduced to the rattling of bones underground empties all meaning from human vitality and achievement. Gone is the wistful voice from the *Devotions* of the man who regretted the loss of his neighbor: "any mans *death* diminishes *me,* because I am involved in *Mankinde*" (87). In a world already peopled by the dead, there is no room for the sentiment of loss.

By emphasizing the lack of distinction between living and dying, Donne seeks to minimize the significance of what is normally regarded as the single moment of death—the moment when the soul separates from the body. Elsewhere in his writings—in *The Second Anniversarie,* the *Holy Sonnets,* and the *Devotions,* to name a few prominent examples—Donne focuses intensely on the moment of death as one of profound and immediate transformation. In *Deaths Duell,* by contrast, he treats it as simply another phase in the cycle of deaths to which we are subjected. In response to the possibility that we might be liberated "from the manifold deaths of this world . . . by that *one death,* the *final dissolution* of body and soule," he exclaims: "Though this be *exitus a morte,* it is *introitus in mortem:* though it bee an *issue from* the manifold *deaths* of this *world,* yet it is an *entrance* into the *death of corruption* and *putrefaction* and *vermiculation* and *incineration,* and dispersion in and from the *grave,* in which every dead man dyes over againe" (10:235–36).

This wormy "vermiculation"—another of Donne's neologisms—is appalling, but worse still is the prospect of our vermiculated remains being contaminated by the remains of others.[24] As if temporarily suspending his belief in the promise of personal resurrection, Donne treats the integrity of the corpse as the defining feature of our eschatological fate. Hence, to return to a passage we looked at in chapter 2, Donne conjures up with real horror the mingling of family remains as a violation to our posthumous identity:

> When those bodies that have beene the *children* of *royall parents,* and the *parents* of *royall children,* must say with *Iob, to corruption thou art my father,* and to *the Worme thou art my mother and my sister. Miserable riddle,* when the *same worme* must bee *my mother,* and *my sister,* and *my selfe. Miserable incest,* when I must bee *married* to my *mother* and my *sister,* and bee both *father* and *mother* to my *owne mother* and sister. (10:238)

Although James I's death was five years in the past, it is possible that this description of royal parents and children was meant to remind Charles, sitting prominently in Donne's audience, of his own father's plight underground. Donne then moves from the fate of kings and queens to a more personal, family scene of necrological incest. The commingling he envisions entails a total negation of discrete, individuated roles within the familial structure: the worm is the eater and the eaten—at once Donne's mother, sister, and himself—and Donne is at once vermicular husband and parent to both mother and sister.

The contamination wrought by death is not limited to family members—death knows no limits in its disruption of bodily integrity. Once again beginning with an implicit address to Charles, Donne imagines the grotesque dispersal of the king:

> That that *Monarch,* who spred over many nations alive, must in his dust
> lye in a corner of that *sheete of lead,* and there, but so long as that lead
> will laste, and that private and *retir'd man,* that thought himselfe his
> owne for ever, and never came forth, must in his dust of the grave bee
> published, and (such are the *revolutions* of the *graves*) bee mingled in his
> dust, with the dust of every high way, and of every dunghill, and swal-
> lowed in every puddle and pond. (10:239)

Donne's real sympathies seem to lie not with the imagined monarch, however, but with the "private and *retir'd man,* that thought himselfe his owne
for ever." Death does nothing less, he argues, than "publish" us to the world,
and hence strip us of self-possession. "This is the most inglorious and contemptible *vilification,*" he concludes, "the most deadly and peremptory *nullification* of man, that we can consider . . . in this death of *incineration,* and
dispersion of dust, we see *nothing* that we can call *that mans*" (10:239).
Perhaps it was as a result of this type of anxiety that Donne specifies in his
Last Will and Testament that he be buried "in the moste private manner that
maye be" in St. Paul's.[25] For Donne, nothing can approximate the horror of
losing himself in the heaving mass of the dead.

Deaths Duell is by no means the first time that Donne considers the
posthumous state of the body. In the 1620 sermon on Job 19:26 that culminates with the description of his own distraction while preaching,[26] he
refers to the foulness of the decomposed flesh as something no visual artist
could ever convey:

> Painters have presented to us with some horrour, the *sceleton,* the frame
> of the bones of a mans body; but the state of a body, in the dissolution of
> the grave, no pencil can present to us. Between that excrementall jelly
> that thy body is made of at first, and that jelly which the body dissolves
> to at last; there is not so noysome, so putrid a thing in nature. (3:105)

We know from Donne's will that he himself owned a "Picture call'de the
Sceleton" that he bequeathed to the dean of Gloucester, Thomas Winniff, and
we know from Walton that he kept the picture of himself dressed in his shroud
next to his bed in his final weeks of life.[27] These two states of being—the skel-
etal and the fully embodied—pose no problem to the painter. What cannot
be captured pictorially is the state of "dissolution of the grave." This is what
Donne wants to conjure up not in images but in words. Once again, he does
so by braiding together the process of procreation and putrefaction. Earlier he

linked the birth caul and the winding sheet, and now he connects semen, described as "excrementall jelly," with the putrified substance of our corpse.

Why is Donne so preoccupied with the posthumous state of the body? The most obvious answer is that however much he claims to trust in the promise of resurrection, he is still fraught with anxiety about the logistics of his material reassemblage. In the sermon on Job 19:26, this anxiety takes the form of concern for the inevitable scattering over time of his flesh and blood and limbs. After describing the "noysome" and "putrid" qualities of the corpse, he reassures both his listeners and himself of the resurrected body's continuity with its mortal self. In a passage we looked at in chapter 4, Donne asks, "Shall I imagine a difficulty in my body, because I have lost an Arme in the East, and a leg in the West? because I have left some bloud in the North, and some bones in the South?" "Doe but remember," he commands his Lincoln's Inn congregation,

> with what ease you have sate in the chaire, casting an account, and made a shilling on one hand, a pound on the other, or five shillings below, ten above, because all these lay easily within your reach. Consider how much lesse, all this earth is to him, that sits in heaven, and spans all this world, and reunites in an instant armes, and legs, bloud, and bones, in what corners so ever they be scattered. (3:109)

Donne regularly presents his listeners with images from their daily lives, as here where he compares God's reconstitution of the self to a merchant sitting in a chair, gathering the appropriate change to make a payment of one sort or another. Although on the surface of things this technique might render God's actions more familiar and hence less unfathomable, the effect in this case may well have been the opposite. The wild, potentially terrifying vision of arms, legs, blood, and bones rising from the corners of the earth bears so little resemblance to the merchant's counting of his coins that the strangeness of God's power is intensified. (This is precisely the kind of *"discordia concors"* that Dr. Johnson finds disturbing in Donne's poems—the yoking together of images that, outside of Donne's writings, are not likely to be found in the service of a single description.)

A similar set of concerns about bodily scattering arises in the 1627 sermon preached at the wedding of the Earl of Bridgewater's daughter on Matthew 22:30: "For, in the resurrection, they neither mary nor are given in marriage, but are as the angels of God in heaven."[28] The fact that Donne chose to preach a wedding sermon on a text almost comically inappropriate speaks to the depths of his obsession with the subject of our posthumous fate. Donne begins this joyful occasion not by celebrating the earthly union consecrated by the marriage, but by affirming the certainty of our eventual resurrection when, according to Matthew, there shall be no further bonds of matrimony. Having established this early on in the sermon, he shifts to his personal preoccupation with the posthumous scattering of the body across the globe:

> Where be all the splinters of that bone, which a shot hath shivered and scattered in the Ayre? Where be all the Atoms of that flesh, which a *Corrasive* hath eat away, or a *Consumption* hath breath'd, and exhal'd away from our arms, and other limbes? In what wrinkle, in what furrow, in what bowel of the earth, ly all the graines of the ashes of a body burnt a thousand years since? In what corner, in what ventricle of the sea, lies all the jelly of a Body drowned in the *generall flood?* What cohaerence, what sympathy, what dependence maintaines any relation, any correspondence, between that arm that was lost in Europe, and that legge that was lost in Afrique or Asia, scores of years between? (8:98)

The macabre character of this meditation—the concern for the bits of bone lost in a gunshot or the atoms exhaled from our limbs by a consumption—is further intensified by the description of the earth itself as a wrinkled, furrowed body, whose bowels contain the remains of human flesh. Although these concerns about retrieval are familiar, Donne's central concern here is unique in his wide-ranging musings on the difficulties of resurrection: that there will be no principle of "cohaerence," "sympathy" or "dependence" that will motivate the various pieces of the self to find one another again.

Before turning to the only hope that can resolve this otherwise dismal picture of natural disintegration, Donne delves even deeper into the processes of decay:

> One humour of our dead body produces worms, and those worms suck and exhaust all other humour, and then all dies, and all dries, and molders into dust, and that dust is blowen into the River, and that puddle water tumbled into the sea, and that ebbs and flows in infinite revolutions, and still, still God knows in what *Cabinet* every *seed-Pearle* lies, in what part of the world every graine of every mans dust lies; and *sibilat populum suum,* (as his Prophet speaks in another case) he whispers, he hisses, he beckens for the bodies of his Saints, and in the twinckling of an eye, that

body that was scattered over all the elements, is sate down at the right hand of God, in a glorious resurrection. (8:98)

We might well ask whether the comfort finally delivered sufficiently compensates for the imaginative dread that has been stirred up: here and elsewhere in Donne's sermons, the assuaging conclusion seems vastly outweighed by the physical horror that precedes it. This may reflect Donne's belief in the salutary effects of anxiety, but more likely reflects his preference for imagining horror over other forms of imagining. The eschatological message we derive, however, from both this sermon and the sermon on Job 19:26 is perfectly clear: notwithstanding the body's "scatter[ing] over all the elements," Donne wants to assure his listeners that they will be resurrected with all of their parts intact.

Donne's preoccupation with the material continuity of the self is unusual for a seventeenth-century Protestant minister, whose church did not emphasize in either doctrine or liturgy the significance of bodily resurrection. The only resurrection mentioned in the *Thirty-Nine Articles*, the definitive doctrinal statement of the Church of England, is the resurrection of Christ.[29] The 1553 draft of the Articles, which numbered forty-two in all, includes the following as Article 39: "The Resurrection of the dead is not as yet brought to passe, as though it only belonged to the soul, but it is to be looked for at the last daie: for then (as Scripture doeth moste manifestlie testifie) to all that be dead their owne bodies, flesh, and bone shalbe restored." This article was omitted, however, from the authoritative version of the text published under Elizabeth, first in Latin in 1563, and in English in 1571. The explanation historians give for this omission is that the original article, along with several others, was designed to combat Anabaptist heresies on several doctrinal matters, and that by the later date the Anabaptist threat had died down.[30] But this explanation seems to overlook the general discomfort that Protestants evince around the subject of the resurrected body. If we look at the Church of England's official liturgy, this discomfort is sharpened into an outright dismissal of the idea that we might retain our own body parts. Hence the Book of Common Prayer's "Order for the Burial of the Dead" includes the promise of a "sure and certain hope of resurrection to eternall lyfe, through our Lord Jesus Christ," but denies the material continuity of this resurrected body: Christ "shall change our vile body," the liturgy reads, "that it may be like to his glorious body."[31]

Donne owes his commitment to the idea that his resurrected flesh will be materially continuous with his earthly body not to English Protestant-

ism, but to a much older tradition in Western Christianity that lasted from
the early third century well into the Middle Ages. As Carolyn Bynum has
richly documented, as early as 200 AD the Latin fathers began to reject the
idea that the resurrection of the flesh involved a full transformation of the
body in the manner described by Paul in 1 Corinthians 15:

> 42. So also is the resurrection of the dead, it is sowen in corruption, it is
>   raised in incorruption.
> 43. It is sowen in dishonour, it is raysed in glorie: it is sowen in weake-
>   nesse, it is raysed in power.
> 44. It is sowen a naturall body, it is raised a spirituall bodie. There is a
>   naturall bodie, and there is a spirituall bodie. . . .
> 51. Behold, I shew you a mysterie: we shall not all sleepe, but wee shall
>   all be changed.
> 52. In a moment, in the twinckling of an eye, at the last trumpe, (for the
>   trumpet shall sound, and the dead shall be raised incorruptible, and
>   we shall be changed).[32]

Paul's emphasis on the metaphor of the seed, and his deprecation of the
natural body in favor of the spiritual body, made explicit in verse 44, suggest that the resurrected self would have little if any material resemblance
to its earthly predecessor. The resurrected body may be continuous with the
earthly body, that is, but it will be as different as the full-grown plant from
its seed. According to Dale B. Martin's *The Corinthian Body*, Paul unambiguously rejects the idea that our human flesh (*sarx*) will be resurrected, proposing instead that we will assume the form of heavenly bodies (*soma*). This
distinction between *sarx* and *soma* was not maintained, however, by many
of the church fathers, who insist that our resurrected body will be constituted by our own flesh and bones. Outside of perfecting our flaws, there will
be no material distinction between the "naturall" and "spirituall" self.[33]

Writing around 200 AD, Tertullian denounces the idea that we might be
reborn in a body other than our earthly one. "How absurd," he declares in
De Carnis Resurrectione, "to suppose that the same soul as has gone through
the whole course of life in this flesh, as has learned of God in this flesh and
has 'put on Christ' and has sown the hope of salvation, should reap the fruit
in some other flesh!"[34] In a wonderfully skeptical passage that resembles the
kind of questions we might expect from Montaigne, Tertullian paraphrases
the objections raised by nonbelievers. For what purpose, they ask, will we
retain our organs,

when there will be no opportunity for eating and drinking? To what purpose do such organs admit, masticate, pass down, break up, digest, discharge? What will be the use of the hands themselves and the feet and all the working parts of the body, when even trouble about food will cease? What will be the use of the kidneys with their knowledge of the seeds they contain, and of the other genital organs of both sexes and the dwelling places of foetus and the streams from the nurse's breasts, when sexual intercourse and conception and upbringing alike will cease to be? Finally, what use will the whole body be, which will of course have absolutely nothing to do? (153–54)

Tertullian's response is rather unsatisfying—he explains that these parts of the body will "be freed from their functions, but they will not therefore cease to be necessary." It is not "of their functions, but of their substance that a man is composed," he concludes, and he reminds his readers that "'God's tribunal' demands that a man shall be whole, but without the various parts of the body one cannot be whole" (154).

Nearly two hundred years later, Augustine defends the idea of bodily resurrection against continued attacks from nonbelievers. In *The City of God*, he addresses the logistical problems raised by aborted fetuses and infants, and responds that they will not be resurrected in the size they were at their deaths, "but shall receive by the marvelous and rapid operation of God that body which time by a slower process would have given them."[35] Turning to the derision heaped upon Luke 21:19—"Verily I say unto you, not a hair of your head shall perish"—he declares that "there will not be a simple restoration of what formerly existed, but, on the one hand, an addition of what had no existence, and, on the other, a loss of what did before exist" (836). Hairs and nails that were cut off in this life and would render the body unseemly will not be restored, nor will any feature of the body that might cause a deformity. As for those body parts that have been eaten by animals or have deteriorated through the natural processes of decay, Augustine exclaims, "Far be it from us to fear that the omnipotence of the Creator cannot, for the resuscitation and reanimation of our bodies, recall all the portions which have been consumed by beasts or fire, or have been dissolved into dust or ashes, or have decomposed into water, or evaporated into the air" (843–44).

Many more examples could be adduced of both patristic and scholastic theologians who defend the material continuity of the resurrected self. In particular, the twelfth-century *Sentences* of Peter Lombard provides a virtual manual for details about the resurrected body's probable age, its size, and its

number of hairs: Peter even assures his clerical readers, who were presumably worried about losing their elevated status in the heavenly hierarchy,
that no hair will return "that so far as detracts by crowding the tonsure."[36]
In the first Constitution of the Fourth Lateran Council in 1215, the church
unambiguously affirms the identity of the resurrected body with the earthly:
"All of them will rise with their own bodies, which they now wear."[37] By the
early fourteenth century, however, this emphasis began to give way to a new
conception of the soul as the determining feature of the resurrected self, and
the commitment to bodily integrity lost some of its force.

The reasons for this shift toward the soul extend well beyond the subject
of this book.[38] But it is reasonably clear that belief in the continuity of the
flesh was by no means eradicated in the fourteenth century. It is also clear
that three hundred or so years later in a very different religious climate,
someone like Donne remained deeply drawn to the materialist arguments
formulated by Tertullian and Augustine and codified by Peter Lombard.
Hence at the end of the 1627 wedding sermon for the Earl of Bridgewater's
daughter, he splendidly declares: "I shall have mine old eies, and eares, and
tongue, and knees, and receive such glory in my body my selfe" (8:97–98).
Even if the heavenly equivalent of seeing and hearing and tasting and moving
will no longer require bodily mechanisms, Donne wants to keep his "old eies,
and eares, and tongue, and knees" all the same. It is tempting to conclude
that he resembles neither an early modern Protestant nor an early modern
Catholic so much as a medieval church father, and arguments to this effect
have over the years been made.[39] It seems closer to the truth, however, to say
that Donne found in the Latin fathers a source of comfort for his anxieties
about his posthumous identity, and that he excavated from these materials
a vocabulary for formulating his own beliefs.

In *Deaths Duell*, Donne transforms his personal obsession with the nature of the resurrected body into a collective event. Perhaps more than any
other single feature, the intensity of his engagement with his listeners differentiates *Deaths Duell* from the writings of his medieval counterparts—the
sermon is less an exposition of doctrine than it is the vicarious experience of
that doctrine in one's flesh. After guiding his audience through the horrific
processes of bodily scattering and decay, Donne directs their attention to the
miraculous nature of rebirth. "This death of *incineration* and dispersion is,
to naturall *reason*, the most *irrecoverable death* of all," he declares.

> And yet, *Domini Domini sunt exitus mortis, unto God the Lord be-
> longs the issues of death,* and by *recompacting* this *dust* into the *same
> body,* and *reanimating* the *same body* with the *same soule,* hee shall in a

blessed and glorious *resurrection* give mee such an *issue from* this *death*, as shal never passe into any other death, but establish me into a life that shall last as long as the Lord of life himself. (10:239–40)

However debilitating the effects of death may seem to be, God will effortlessly overcome them—"*recompacting* this *dust* into the *same body*, and *reanimating* the *same body* with the *same soule*." The threefold repetition of the adjective "same" is not accidental: Donne insists that he will not simply be resurrected, but that he will be resurrected with the body and soul that he currently has. It is striking, moreover, that he specifies his own and not his listeners' resurrection by using the first-person singular "me": "give mee such an *issue*"; "establish me into a life." After a lifetime of pondering the hypothetical moment of passing from one world to the next, Donne now declares before hundreds of listeners that his moment to triumph over death has come. The prospect of dying and rising is no longer abstract. It is both personal and imminent.[40]

Donne's affirmation of his impending death and subsequent resurrection concludes the first of *Deaths Duell*'s three explications of his scriptural verse, "And unto God the Lord Belongs the Issues of Death": namely, that God will deliver us from death not by sparing us its immediate posthumous consequences, but by promising our eventual rebirth. This is followed by a surprisingly abbreviated discussion of the second possible meaning for this verse—that "it *belongs* to *God*, and *not* to *man* to *passe a judgement* upon us at our death." Donne argues here, in effect, against the importance of a "good death"—our hopes for salvation are not to be determined, he contends, by whether we die peacefully or violently, suddenly or slowly; whether we seem reluctant to die or embrace it willingly. "Make no *ill conclusions*," he warns his audience, "upon any mans *loathnes* to dye." Christ himself, he continues, forbids us to judge a man by the manner of his death, for his own death was marked by false impressions. Speaking once again in a first-person singular that must have had a particular resonance coming from the mouth of a visibly dying man, he declares: "Whether the *gate* of *my prison* be opened with an *oyld key* (by a gentle and *preparing sicknes*) or the gate bee *hewen downe* by a *violent death*, or the gate bee *burnt downe* by a *raging* and *frantique feaver, a gate into heaven I shall have*" (10:241–42).

Elsewhere in his writings Donne gave more thought to the manner in which one died. Recall, for example, the opening stanza of "A Valediction: forbidding mourning," in which the soul of the virtuous man departs from his body without any noise or sign of resistance, and this quiet melting away is assumed to be a sign of grace. Early modern English culture took the art of dying very seriously as did its medieval predecessor—there was no short-age of *ars moriendi* literature in English Protestantism, as we saw in chapter 5, and Donne was certainly familiar with the conventions for preparing for death. But if Jeremy Taylor declares in *Holy Dying* that "no story tells of any godly man, who living in the fear of God fell into a violent and unpardoned impatience in his naturall sicknesse" (42), Donne in *Deaths Duell* rejects the idea that the manner of our death might have any bearing on our hope for salvation. "Our *criticall* day is *not* the *very day* of our *death,*" he declares, "but the whole course of our life. I thanke him that *prayes* for me when my bell tolles, but I thank him much more that *Catechises* mee, or *preaches* to mee, or *instructs me how to live.*" The tolling bells so hauntingly described in the *Devotions* as a reminder of our own mortality are invoked only to be dismissed, and he moves to his third, and preferred interpretation for his scriptural verse: "that this *issue of death* is *liberatio per mortem,* a *deliverance by the death* of another, by the *death* of *Christ*" (10:241–42).

III

It is hard to imagine how Donne's audience would have responded to the final part of *Deaths Duell.* In both its description of bodily dispersion and corruption and its forceful affirmation of resurrection, the sermon had already no doubt achieved an unusually high level of dramatic power. But Donne had not yet made explicit demands of his listeners. In the third and last section of the sermon, Donne adopts an unabashedly confrontational style: he conflates sacred and historical time to compare the last day of Christ's life, hour by hour, with the activities of his audience. "It is good to dwell here," he declares, "in this consideration of his death, and therefore transferre wee our tabernacle (our devotions) through some of those steps which God the Lord made to his issue of death that day" (10:245). In what follows, Donne transforms a traditional *imitatio Christi* instruction into an intense scrutiny of his listener's individual conscience. His role as someone standing apart from his audience, moreover, becomes unusually pronounced. No longer identifying his own condition with that of his listeners, Donne uses this climactic meditation on the Passion to bid his own farewell.

"Take in the *whole day,*" Donne begins, "Make *this* present *day* that *day* in thy *devotion,* and consider what *hee did,* and remember what *you have done*" (10:245). Each step of Christ's becomes a model against which Donne's listeners judge themselves, and the result that he anticipates is the recognition of their sinfulness and inadequacy. "*At night* hee *went into the garden* to *pray,*" he remarks,

and he prayed *prolixius;* he spent *much time* in prayer. I dare scarce aske
thee *whither* thou *wentest,* or *how* thou *disposedst* of *thy self,* when it
grew darke and after *last night.* If that time were spent in a holy recom-
mendation of thy selfe to God, and a submission of thy will to his, it was
spent in a conformity to him. (10:246)

At moments like this, Donne stresses the enormous chasm that falls between his audience's behavior and Christ's. At other times, with palpable
irony, he identifies similarities. "About midnight," he recounts, "he was
taken and bound with a kisse." Turning upon his listeners, he hints at their
sexual improprieties: "art thou not too conformable to him in that? Is not
that too literally, too exactly thy case? At midnight to have bene taken and
bound with a kisse?" (10:246). The suggestion of sexual wrongdoing then
becomes more explicit. "How thou passedst all that time last night," he exclaims, "thou knowest." Referring to Christ's prediction in the Gospels that
Peter would deny him three times before the cock crows, Donne warns, "If
thou didst any thing then that needed *Peters teares,* and has *not shed them,*
let me be thy *Cock.*" "Doe it now," he commands, assuming the role of both
the cock and Christ: "Now thy *Master* (in the unworthiest of his servants)
lookes back upon thee, doe it now" (10:246–47). Donne orders his listeners
to break down in tears in exactly the manner that unsettled Eliot—there is
no room for emotional detachment or withdrawal.

As Donne approaches the hour of the crucifixion, he intensifies the sense
of drama by shifting from the past tense to the present. In so doing, he closes
any remaining gap between biblical and personal time, rendering the slope of
Mount Calvary inseparable from his own surroundings at Whitehall. After
reporting that "Towards *noone Pilat* gave *judgement,* and they made such
hast to execution, as that *by noone* hee was *upon the Crosse,*" Donne conjures the scene for his listeners as if it were transpiring before their eyes:

> There now hangs that sacred Body upon the Crosse rebaptized in his
> owne teares and sweat, and embalmed in his owne blood alive. There are
> those *bowells of compassion,* which are so conspicuous, so manifested,
> as that you may *see them through his wounds.* There those *glorious eyes*
> grew faint in their light: so as the *Sun ashamed* to survive them, *departed
> with his light too.* (10:247–48)

Like the most gruesome baroque altarpiece, this Christ is covered in bodily
fluids of tears, sweat, and blood. He is not only visibly wounded, but his
wounds are so open and transparent as to allow us to gaze through to his

bowels. The scene may remind us of Donne's great poem "Good Friday, 1613. Riding Westward," in which he also conjures up a vision of a bloody Christ upon the cross, but in the poem he cannot bear to look: "Yet dare I'almost be glad, I do not see / That spectacle of too much weight for mee" (15–16). In *Deaths Duell*, there is no alternative to facing Christ directly— Donne's listeners are confronted with the weighty spectacle whatever their spiritual readiness.

But, we may well ask, when Donne instructed his listeners to look "there," where was he pointing? Was there in fact a crucifix or altarpiece hanging before them? The answer to this question depends on where exactly at Whitehall Palace *Deaths Duell* was preached. There are two possibilities: indoors in the Chapel Royal, or outdoors in the so-called Preaching Place. If Donne preached this sermon indoors, it is conceivable that when he instructs his listeners to gaze upon Christ's sacred body hanging on a cross, he may have been pointing at a crucifix in the Chapel Royal, although this crucifix would have had none of the fleshy details that he describes. His contemporary Sir Thomas Knyvett recounted in a letter from 1621 that the renovations to the king's chapel at that time included the planned addition of both new images and a silver crucifix, all done "against the spannish Ladys coming."[41] The so-called Spanish Match—the proposed marriage between Charles, Prince of Wales, and the Spanish Infanta—was not in the end successful. But the ecclesiastical ornamentation it helped to spawn was certainly consistent with the High Church direction of the church under Andrewes and Laud, the successive deans of the Royal Chapel. Arguing against the presence of an actual cross is this testimony from W. Hawkins to the Earl of Leicester in April 1637, six years after *Deaths Duell* was preached: "Upon Sunday last," he writes, "was hanged up a peece of hangings over the alter in the Kings Chappell, the likest a Crucifix that hath been seen there these fortie yeares."[42]

Given, however, both the popularity of Donne as a preacher and the occasion, it is very likely that the sermon was planned for the outdoor pulpit.[43] The outdoor Preaching Place was used regularly during Lent, when the court sponsored a particularly important series of sermons, which were delivered every Sunday, Tuesday, and Friday by the most prominent preachers. According to McCullough, by 1642, the Preaching Place was so deeply associated with the Lenten sermons that it was referred to in one contemporary account author as "the Lenten pulpit." The afternoon sermons during Lent were unique in drawing a large, public audience to Whitehall, rendering the courtly space more like the sprawling space of Paul's Cross than we might normally imagine for a courtly site. According to a contemporary account, the space could accommodate "four times so many people as could have stoode in the Kings Chappell." If the chapel could hold somewhere between 300 and 500 people depending on how packed the aisles might have been, the Preaching Place may well have held 2,000, although the Venetian ambassador claims that the space held upwards of 5,000 when he attended a sermon there in 1559.⁴⁴ This was no doubt an exaggeration, but the impression that the place made on him as vast and crowded is important to keep in mind when we conjure the possible scene of *Deaths Duell*.

The Preaching Place was built by Henry VII in a courtyard that had originally been designed as a garden. The pulpit was roofed, and the courtyard was surrounded by buildings on all four sides that were several stories high. The decorations that we know of are secular in nature—heraldic beasts, for example, were carved into the posts that adorned the outdoor space. If, then, Donne preached *Deaths Duell* in the Preaching Place, there would almost certainly have been no crucifix or image of Christ visible to him. When he instructed his listeners to look "there" at Christ's body, he was likely not to be pointing anywhere at all. The Christ he conjures up, in short, would be constituted entirely by words.

We have no contemporary account of the physical conditions of *Deaths Duell*'s performance, but one way to glimpse its symbolic arrangement of preacher, crucifix, and congregation is to compare it with a Lutheran altarpiece painted by Cranach the Elder and erected in Wittenberg some eighty years earlier. In the predella of this altarpiece, Luther stands in the pulpit in the far right of the canvas, while the congregation stands in a huddle on the far left. In the center of the painting is Christ hanging on the cross (figure 3). In his magisterial study *The Reformation of the Image*, Joseph Koerner has described the ways in which Cranach's crucifix, despite its central position, insists upon its own absence from the ecclesiastical space. It is not, in other words, meant to be understood as part of the church scene that Cranach represents. Instead, it is meant as a "visual quotation, an image of an image rather than the thing itself."⁴⁵ Cranach did not want us to think, Koerner argues, that Christ himself was visible to the congregation, nor does he want the crucifix to resemble an artifact positioned in the church. The way in which the cross stands without a firm foundation in the ground and the manner in which Christ's flow of blood comes to a sudden stop just above the base convey the artist's decision to represent a crucifix that was neither a wooden monument standing in the room nor a miraculous vision of Christ in his Passion.

What Cranach's predella strives to represent is the power of preaching to produce the image of Christ. "Whether I want to or not," Luther confesses,

Figure 3. Lucas Cranach the Elder, Luther preaching to the Wittenberg congregation,
predella of the *Wittenberg Altarpiece*, 1547.

"when I hear the word Christ, there delineates itself in my heart the picture of a man who hangs on the cross."[46] The painting is in effect a visual
translation of this sentiment. Or, more precisely, it is a visual translation of
the ways in which what happens in Luther's heart is shared with the congregation. Through preaching, Luther's personal experience becomes a common experience. Cranach's predella is ultimately, then, the representation
of what preaching can do. "Behold," said John the Baptist, "behold," echoes
Cranach's Luther, as he points his finger at a Christ that is not really there:
"Behold the lamb of God."

    "There now hangs that sacred Body upon the Crosse." When Donne
preached *Deaths Duell*, he too points his finger at a crucifix that is not physically present. Like Cranach's Luther, he too gives his listeners the imaginative tools to meditate upon a Passion scene that they can collectively
internalize. In Donne's case, of course, this crucifix is verbally, not visually
constructed. But the parallels between what Cranach wants to represent
in his predella and what Donne wants to achieve in his sermon are significant. Both are Protestant artists who convey the power of sermons to bring
Christ's Passion to life. Both transform the Catholic altarpiece of the cruci-
fied Christ from an actual image beheld by the congregation into the imaginative product of preaching.

    In another sense, however, the scene that Cranach depicts in Wittenberg
and the scene when *Deaths Duell* was preached at Whitehall are importantly
different. This difference turns on the figure of Donne himself. In the Cranach painting, the center of the space is filled by the crucifix, which—whatever the status of its actual presence for the Wittenberg congregation or for
Luther—dominates the eerily emptied out space at the heart of the canvas.

At Whitehall, it was Donne who stood at the center of the crowd. If he were indoors, he preached from a pulpit placed in the very front of the chapel at the top of the three steps leading to the altar, with rows of stalls before him, and behind the stalls the elevated royal closets—private galleries placed over antechambers—in the rear west end of the gallery symmetrically opposite the pulpit. If he were outdoors, as he is likely to have been, he preached in a square pulpit located at the center of the courtyard, surrounded by hundreds and possibly even thousands of listeners. The elevation of the pulpit, the presence of a roof, and the paved or graveled floor of the courtyard would all have helped with the acoustic challenge that the occasion may have provided, but Walton's comment about Donne's "faint and hollow voice" takes on new meaning in the context of this vast space. (The king and his guests, however, would have had little problem hearing the sermon: they sat some twenty feet away from the pulpit in the council chamber reached by an elevated terrace.[47]) Whatever the acoustical challenges, it is clear that all eyes would have been directed toward Donne. He is not in the position of Cranach's Luther. He is in the position of Cranach's Christ.

When Donne came to the end of *Deaths Duell*, he points his finger not only at an invisible Christ on the cross. He also points his finger at himself. "There," he begins the last sentence he will ever preach,

> wee leave you in that *blessed dependancy*, to *hang* upon *him* that *hangs* upon the *Crosse*, there *bath* in his *teares*, there *suck* at his *woundes*, and *lye downe in peace* in his *grave*, till he vouchsafe you a *resurrection*, and an *ascension* into that *Kingdome*, which hee *hath purchas'd for you*, with the *inestimable price* of his *incorruptible blood*. AMEN. (10:248)

Although the Lenten series of sermons as a whole was geared toward the event of Christ's Passion, the overwhelmingly physical interaction that Donne describes would have been anathema to mainstream English Protestants, for whom the prospect of hanging on the cross and sucking Christ's wounds was a grotesquely literal participation in the Passion.

Listeners familiar with medieval *ars moriendi*, manuals like the immensely popular *Book of the Craft of Dying* may have been struck, in fact, by the similarities between Donne's injunction and the words of the fifteenth-century text. "In truth," wrote Caxton, who translated the text from the French in 1490, "the disposition of the body of our Lord Jesu Christ hanging on the cross ought much to induce a sick person, paining to the death, to have very hope and confidence in God. For He hath the head inclined and bowed to kiss us; the arms stretched abroad for to embrace us; the hands pierced and opened for to give us; the side open for to love us; and all His body stretched for to give Himself all to us."[48] Caxton's Christ, however, is much more loving than Donne's, who is remarkably passive. For Donne does not comfort his listeners with an account of Christ's mercy. He instructs them, by contrast, to become actively engaged themselves. What he advocates, moreover, is not simply an immersion in Christ's wounds—this is not a literal description of Eucharistic piety, a partaking in Christ's body and blood. Instead, he recommends a type of substitution for Christ's own corpse: "lye downe in peace in his grave, till he vouchsafe you a resurrection."

These are his final words to his listeners, but where do they leave Donne? "Wee," he began, "leave you in that blessed dependancy," but who is this "wee"? And, given his own proximity to death, why does he not include himself among the "blessed" dependents? English preachers often speak in the collective, clerical "we"—this is the voice of the church's authority comparable to the "royal we" of the monarch—and we could easily assimilate Donne's voice to this conventional model. The particular circumstances of *Deaths Duell*, however, suggest otherwise. Remember that earlier in the sermon Donne had singled himself out as he who would be resurrected, using the singular "mee." Remember also that he desired nothing more than to anticipate death, to leap from one world to the next without falling prey to death's ravaging hands. Remember, finally, that he stands in the position of Christ, weakened and feeble, but full of God's grace as he prepares for his own death. "Wee leave you." In his ultimate theatrical coup, Donne stages his departure by assuming a voice that he has long denied himself: the "wee" of himself and his God. This voice is only conceivable, of course, for those who have completed their *exitus a morte*, those who have arrived triumphant on the other side of the grave.

IV

In the weeks following *Deaths Duell*, Donne rehearsed for his death in the privacy of his home. According to Walton, he not only followed a serious regimen of spiritual exercises to prepare his soul for the afterlife, but also made plans for the posthumous fate of his flesh. To this end, Walton relates in an oft-quoted passage from his *Life*, Donne designed and posed for his own funerary monument:

A Monument being resolved upon, Dr. Donne sent for a carver to make for him in wood the figure of an urn, giving him directions for the compass and height of it; and to bring with it a board of the just height of his body. These being got, then without delay a choice painter was got to be in readiness to draw his picture, which was taken as followeth.——— Several charcoal fires being first made in his large study, he brought with him into that place his winding-sheet in his hand, and, having put off all his clothes, had this sheet put on him, and so tied with knots at his head and feet, and his hands placed as dead bodies are usually fitted, to be shrowded and put into their coffin, or grave. Upon this urn he thus stood, with his eyes shut, and with so much of the sheet turned aside as might shew his lean, pale, and death-like face, which was purposely turned toward the East, from whence he expected the second coming of his and our Saviour Jesus. (234)

Why would Donne, gravely ill and extremely feeble, strip naked and pose in a shroud with knots tied at his head and feet (figure 4)? The only plausible explanation, and one that corresponds to impulses we have seen throughout his writing, is that he wanted to experience being clothed as a corpse—to have the strange thrill of being simultaneously dead and alive. Given the further detail that he "caused [the picture] to be set by his bed-side, where it continued and became his hourly object till his death"—he must also have wanted to serve as his own *memento mori*. Yet, this engraving of Donne clothed in a shroud is hardly a standard image for deathbed contemplation. Conventional *memento mori* images picture a full-length skeleton or skull, but not a man with his body intact. Moreover, as Donne reminds us in *The First Anniversarie* and elsewhere, the corpse could retain its flesh intact for a handful of days before beginning to rot, so what he kept by his bedside could not have been a projected image of his corpse during the long period he expected between death and rebirth. What, then, did he imagine this picture to depict?

Our best clue may lie in the funerary urn that served as the monument's pedestal. The balance that would be required to stand atop a wooden urn casts doubt on whether Donne actually posed in the manner Walton describes. But there is evidence corroborating Walton's claim that Donne designed the monument himself,[49] and hence we can reasonably ask why he chose to be figured in this posture. As we have seen, Donne was preoccupied with the posthumous scattering and reassembling of his decomposed body, and he reassured himself repeatedly that God would on the last day reconstitute him. In light of this preoccupation, it makes sense that the standing, shrouded figure rising from a funerary urn cannot represent Donne's corpse. Instead, it must represent his resurrected body.[50] Resurrection monuments

Figure 4. Portrait of Donne, frontispiece to *Deaths Duell*, engraved
by Martin Droeshout, London, 1631. Courtesy of Houghton Library,
Harvard College Library (STC 7031 Lobby XII.1.20.A2v).

were not uncommon in the mid-seventeenth century; as Gardner has documented, a number of shrouded figures standing on top of shallow bowls
were erected at roughly the same time as Donne's.[51] In each of these other
examples, however, the figure's eyes are open, indicating that he or she has
heard the sounding of the trumpet, and has awoken in perfected flesh. But
Donne's eyes are closed.

How can we explain the strange combination in Donne's monument of
dormant corpse and resurrected body? Gardner dismisses the question by arguing that the monument is incoherent, and she proposes that it must have
been initially designed as a recumbent, sleeping figure, but due to logistical issues of space in St. Paul's, was later converted to be standing. There
are problems, however, with this argument, having to do with the curved
shape of the back of the figure's head. Even with a marble pillow beneath it,
Gardner concedes, Donne's head could never have been laid prostrate, and
she ultimately retreats from her own hypothesis. If, however, we accept the
monument as we find it in St. Paul's today, where it was re-erected around
1818 after having been stored in a niche for over a hundred and fifty years
following the Great Fire of 1666, its posture and expression resonate deeply
with aspects of Donne's imaginative life. For the posture and expression
of the monument suggest one of the moments that Donne most loved to
imagine: the moment between the reassembly of his scattered body and its
reunion with his soul.

What Donne has asked the artist to capture is not the moment that he
will open his eyes and be reanimated, but the moment preceding this, when
his very body is filled with joy and anticipation. It is the sacred equivalent
of where Elegy 19, "To his Mistris going to Bed," leaves off—in the delighted
expectation of what awaits him. As he explains in his sermon commemorating Magdalen Herbert, "creatures of an inferiour nature are possesst with
the *present*; Man is a *future Creature*" (8:75). Our final image of Donne pre-
serves for posterity his tremendous pleasure in looking toward, but not yet
arriving at, the heavenly resurrection of his body and soul. It is the material
realization of the dream he shares with his listeners in a 1626 sermon at St.
Paul's (7:71): "in the agonies of Death, in the anguish of that dissolution, in
the sorrowes of that *valediction*, in the irreversibleness of that transmigration, I shall have a joy."

꽃

NOTES

INTRODUCTION

1. *The Sermons of John Donne*, ed. George R. Potter and Evelyn M. Simpson, 10 vols. (Berkeley: University of California Press, 1953–62), 2:261–62.

2. See, for example, Gilbert Ryle's classic midcentury treatment of the subject, *The Concept of Mind* (Chicago: University of Chicago Press, 1949).

3. T. S. Eliot, *Selected Essays* (London: Harcourt, Brace and Co., 1932), 247.

4. Dryden criticized Donne for "affect[ing] the Metaphysicks, not only in his Satires, but in his Amorous Verses, where Nature only shou'd reign; and perplexes the Minds of the Fair Sex with nice Speculations of Philosophy, when he shou'd ingage their hearts, and entertain them with the softnesses of Love." A. J. Smith, *John Donne: The Critical Heritage* (London: Routledge & Kegan Paul, 1975), 151.

5. Samuel Johnson, *Lives of the Poets*, ed. George Birbeck Hill (Oxford: Clarendon Press, 1905), 20.

6. The notable exception was Samuel Taylor Coleridge, who annotated a copy of Donne's poems as well as his sermons.

7. Cited in Smith, *John Donne: The Critical Heritage*, 351.

8. *Metaphysical Lyrics and Poems of the Seventeenth Century, Donne to Butler*, ed. Herbert J. C. Grierson (Oxford: Clarendon Press, 1921), xiv.

9. See Dayton Haskin's essay "Donne's Afterlife" for a fascinating account of the American role in re-stimulating Donne studies in the United Kingdom (*The Cambridge Companion to John Donne*, ed. Achsah Guibbory [Cambridge: Cambridge University Press, 2006], 233–46; see especially 239–41).

10. T. S. Eliot, *The Varieties of Metaphysical Poetry*, ed. Ronald Schuchard (New York: Harcourt Brace & Co: 1993), 47; "Shakespeare and the Stoicism of Seneca," in *Selected Essays* (London: Faber & Faber, 1951), 139.

11. On Donne and the new science, see C. M. Coffin, *John Donne and the New Philosophy* (New York: Columbia University Press, 1937), William Empson, "Donne the Spaceman," *Kenyon Review* 19 (1957): 337–99, and George Williamson, "Mutability, Decay, and Seventeenth-Century Melancholy," *ELH* 2, no. 2 (Sept. 1935): 121–50, to name

a few. On Donne's Petarchism, see Donald Guss's classic study, *John Donne, Petrarchist* (Detroit: Wayne State University Press, 1966), and also chapter 6 of Heather Dubrow's revisionist account, *Echoes of Desire* (Ithaca: Cornell University Press, 1995). On Donne's relationship to Catholic devotional practices, see Louis Martz, *The Poetry of Meditation* (New Haven: Yale University Press, 1954). On Donne and Protestantism, see Barbara Lewalski, *Protestant Poetics* (Princeton: Princeton University Press, 1979); Debora Shuger, *Habits of Thought in the English Renaissance* (Berkeley: University of California Press, 1990); Jeffrey Johnson, *The Theology of John Donne* (Rochester: D. S. Brewer, 1999); Mary Arshagouni Papazian, ed., *John Donne and the Protestant Reformation: New Perspectives* (Detroit: Wayne State University Press, 2003); and Theresa DiPasquale, *Literature and Sacrament: The Sacred and the Secular in John Donne* (Pittsburgh: Duquesne University Press, 1999).

12. All references to Donne's poetry, with the exception of the verse epistles, are from *The Poems of John Donne*, ed. Herbert J. C. Grierson, 2 vols. (Oxford: Clarendon Press, 1912), and are cited in text.

13. T. S. Eliot, "The Metaphysical Poets," in *Selected Essays* (London: Faber and Faber, 1951), 283.

14. Cited in R. C. Bald, *John Donne, A Life* (Oxford: Clarendon Press, 1970), 563, 560.

15. *Letters to Severall Persons of Honour*, A Facsimile Reproduction with an introduction by M. Thomas Hester (Delmar: Scholars' Facsimiles & Reprints, 1977), 51. All references to Donne's prose letters are from this volume and cited in text unless otherwise noted.

16. Izaak Walton, *Life of Donne*, in *The Complete Angler and The Lives of Donne, Wotton, Hooker, Herbert, & Sanderson* (London: Macmillan and Co., 1925), 226. Jessica Martin questions the extent of Walton's familiarity with Donne in her *Walton's Lives: Conformist Commemorations and the Rise of Biography* (Oxford: Oxford University Press, 2001), 169.

17. Geoffrey Keynes lists 219 titles in his appendix on Donne's library (*A Bibliography of Dr. John Donne, Dean of St. Paul's*, 4th rev. ed. [Oxford: Clarendon Press, 1973]). Among the volumes known to have belonged to Donne is a single group of sixty-nine titles that was either purchased by or given to Robert Ashley, a lawyer at the Middle Temple in London, who died in 1641, and left his library to the Middle Temple, where he lived as a bachelor for many years. With the exception of a decision in 1958 to replace the original limp vellum—Donne's favorite binding—with a more durable brown leather, these volumes have been preserved at the Middle Temple Library without significant changes in condition for more than 350 years. I am grateful to Mr. Stuart Adams, the senior librarian at the Middle Temple Library, for assisting me with the Donne collection.

18. The very first of the fictional titles meant to fill the fatuous courtier's shelves is none other than "Nicholas Hill, the Englishman, *How to differentiate sex and hermaphroditism in Atoms. The same, On their anatomy and midwifery in buried embryons . . .*" *The Courtier's Library*, ed. Evelyn Mary Simpson (London: Nonesuch Press, 1930), 43.

19. Charles Hardwick, *A History of the Articles of Religion* (Cambridge: Deighton, Bell, and Co., 1859), Appendix III: "Articles of Religion in the Reigns of King Edward VI and Queen Elizabeth," Article 40, 328.

20. Calvin, *Institutes of the Christian Religion*, trans. Ford Lewis Battles, ed. John T. McNeill, vol. 2 (Philadelphia: Westminster Press, 1960), bk. III, 25.6, p. 997. On mortalism in England, see Norman T. Burns, *Christian Mortalism from Tyndale to Milton* (Cambridge, MA: Harvard University Press, 1972).

21. Lines 47–48. All references to Donne's verse epistles are from Wesley Milgate, ed., *John Donne: The Satires, Epigrams, and Verse Letters* (Oxford: Clarendon Press, 1967).

22. Aquinas, *The Summa Theologica of Thomas Aquinas*, trans. Fathers of the English Dominican Province, vol. 1 (New York: Benziger Brothers, Inc., 1947), pt. 1, Q. 118, art. 2, p. 575.

23. Donne makes a similar declaration in another sermon: "Therefore there is in man a *vegetative*, and a *sensitive* soule, before an *immortall*, and *reasonable* soule, enter" (7:426).

24. Donne, *DEVOTIONS Upon Emergent Occasions*, ed. Anthony Raspa (Montreal: McGill-Queen's University Press, 1975), 93.

25. In the 1651 edition, this letter is assigned to Thomas Lucy, but there is strong reason to believe it was written to Goodyer. According to Roger E. Bennett, it is "one of several of Donne's efforts to encourage Goodere to be constant in his religion" (Roger Bennett, "Donne's Letters from the Continent in 1611–12," *Philological Quarterly* 19 [1940]: 66–78, 75n40). M. Thomas Hester, one of the editors of the forthcoming edition of Donne's letters, agrees with this conclusion.

26. *Letters to Severall Persons of Honour*, 13.

27. Augustine, *De Vera Religione*, xiv, 27, as cited in *The Catholic Encyclopedia*, ed. Charles G. Herbermann, 15 vols. (New York: Encyclopedia Press, 1913), vol. 11, p. 314.

28. *The Literal Meaning of Genesis*, trans. John Hammond Taylor, S.J., 2 vols. (New York: New Man Press, 1982), vol. 2, bk. 7, chap. 26, p. 27.

29. Among other examples, see *The City of God:* "For the corruption of the body, which weighs down the soul, is not the cause but the punishment of the first sin; and it was not the corruptible flesh that made the soul sinful, but the sinful soul that made the flesh corruptible" (Augustine, *The City of God*, trans. Marcus Dods, D.D. [New York: Random House, 1950], bk. 14, chap. 3, p. 444).

30. 1:177. See also 5:348–49.

31. See Elaine Scarry, "Donne: 'But yet the body is his booke,'" in *Literature and the Body: Essays on Populations and Persons*, ed. Elaine Scarry (Baltimore: John Hopkins University Press, 1988), 70–105; Michael Schoenfeldt, "Thinking Through the Body: Corporeality and Interiority in Donne," in *La poesie metaphysique de John Donne*, ed. Claudine Raynaud (Tours: Université françois Rabelais, 2002), 25–35; and Nancy Selleck, "Donne's Body," *Studies in English Literature* 41 (Winter 2001): 149–74.

32. Augustine addresses the problem of cannibalism for personal resurrection in *The City of God* (bk. 22, chap. 12, p. 837).

33. Hardwick, *A History of the Articles of Religion*, Article 8, p. 287.

34. John Milton, *Paradise Lost*, ed. Gordon Teskey (W. W. Norton & Co., 2005), 5:497–99.

35. Donne, *Pseudo-Martyr* (London, 1610), 17.

36. See my discussion of Donne's epitaph for Anne in chapter 2.

37. On Donne's attitude toward his poetry, see his letter to Sir Robert Ker, in which he wishes that Ker had requested a sermon rather than an elegy from Donne on the occa-

sion of the Marquess of Hamilton's death (in Edmund Gosse, *The Life and Letters of John Donne* [New York: Dodd, Mead and Company, 1899], 2:215). See also his verse epistle to Rowland Woodward, in which he admits, albeit backhandedly, his love of writing poems: "Though to use, and love Poetrie, to mee, / Betroth'd to no'one Art, be no'adulterie; / Omissions of good, ill, as ill deeds bee" (7–9).

38. The letter is addressed "*To my worthy friend* F.H.," but the identity of the recipient is unknown (*Letters,* 228).

I. LETTERS

1. Cited in Stephen Gaselee, "The Soul in the Kiss," *Criterion* 2 (April 1924): 349, 352, 351. Gaselee ascribes the first quotation to Plato.

2. *Doctor Faustus,* scene 12, 83–84, vol. 1 of *The Norton Anthology of English Literature,* 7th ed., M. H. Abrams and Stephen Greenblatt, gen. eds. (New York: W. W. Norton, 2000).

3. For the epistle's date, see *John Donne: The Satires, Epigrams, and Verse Letters,* 225–26.

4. The letter was addressed in the 1651 *Letters to Severall Persons of Honour* to "Sir G.M.," but Roger E. Bennett persuasively argues that the letter was written to Goodyer, and that John Donne Jr., who edited the 1651 edition, frequently substituted unknown initials for Goodyer's to make the collection seem more diverse. (Bennett's opinion about this letter is confirmed by M. Thomas Hester.) According to Bennett, nearly half of the 129 letters in the volume are believed to have been written to Goodyer (Roger E. Bennett, "Donne's '*Letters to Severall Persons of Honour,*'" *PMLA* 56 [1941]: 136).

5. Annabel Patterson has convincingly showed more similarities in Donne's and Cicero's letters than this passage from Donne would suggest. See Patterson, "Misinterpretable Donne: The Testimony of the Letters," *John Donne Journal* 1, nos. 1–2 (1982): 39–53.

6. *Letters to Severall Persons of Honour,* 60.

7. A modern edition is currently being completed and will be published by Oxford University Press. I am very indebted to its principal editor, M. Thomas Hester, who has been immensely generous in sharing many of his findings with me.

8. For an account of this medieval practice, see Jean Robertson, *The Art of Letter Writing* (Liverpool: University Press, 1942).

9. William Fulwood, *The Enimie of Idlenesse* (London, 1568), Aiiiv.

10. Cited in Justus Lipsius, *Principles of Letter-Writing,* ed. and trans. R. V. Young and M. Thomas Hester (Carbondale and Edwardsville, IL: Southern Illinois University Press, 1996), 9.

11. Justus Lipsius, *Principles of Letter-Writing,* 9. Lipsius's treatise was never published in English, but it was translated and "borrowed" by John Hoskyns in his *Directions for Speech and Style* (1600?). This text, too, was never published, but its section on letter writing was reprinted by Ben Jonson in *Timber, or Discoveries* (London, 1641).

12. Seneca, *Epistles (Ad Lucilium epistulae morales),* trans. Richard M. Gummere, 3 vols. (1917; Cambridge: Harvard University Press, 1989), 2:137.

13. Erasmus, *De conscribendis epistolis,* 1521, in vol. 25 of *Collected Works of Erasmus,* ed. J. K. Sowards (Toronto: University of Toronto Press, 1985), 50; Juan Luis Vives,

De conscribendis epistolis, vol. 3 of *Selected Works of J. L. Vives*, ed. Charles Fantazzi, gen. ed. C. Matheeussen (Leiden and New York: E. J. Brill, 1989), 23.

14. Vives, *De conscribendis epistolis*, 22.

15. *Epistles (Ad Lucilium epistulae morales)*, 263–64.

16. Cicero, *Letters to Atticus*, ed. and trans. D. R. Shackleton Bailey, 4 vols. (Cambridge: Harvard University Press, 1999), 1:59.

17. *Enimie of Idleness*, 72.

18. *Letters from Petrarch*, trans. Morris Bishop (Bloomington and London: Indiana University Press, 1966), 23.

19. For the addressee of this letter, see note 25 in the introduction. On Donne's interest in ecstasy, see René Graziani, "John Donne's 'The Extasie' and Ecstasy," *Review of English Studies* (May 1968): 121–36; and Austin Warren, "Donne's 'Extasie,'" *Studies in Philology* 55 (1958): 472–80.

20. According to the *Oxford English Dictionary*, there is no record whatever of using the term in the seventeenth century or earlier to refer to a shared experience.

21. Donne quotes Plotinus in an undated sermon preached at St. Paul's on Psalm 90:14 (*The Sermons of John Donne*, 5:287).

22. Plotinus, *The Enneads*, trans. Stephen MacKenna (London: Penguin Books, 1991), 334.

23. Bald states that their letters span 1609–30 (*John Donne, A Life*, 277).

24. There is no evidence about how these letters were delivered, but the letters suggest that a regular delivery was arranged from the Rose in Smithfield on Tuesdays. M. Thomas Hester has confirmed this as the likely arrangement.

25. Evelyn M. Simpson, *A Study of the Prose Works of John Donne* (Oxford: Clarendon Press, 1924), 292.

26. *Letters*, 73–74. This letter is assigned to "Sir G.F." but like so many of the letters in the 1651 edition was almost certainly intended for Goodyer. For an extensive discussion of Donne's use of atomic conceits in his verse and prose, see David A. Hedrich Hirsch's article "Donne's Atomies and Anatomies: Deconstructed Bodies and the Resurrection of Atomic Theory," *Studies in English Literature* 31 (1991): 69–94.

27. On Hill, see my introduction.

28. Charles E. Merrill Jr., editor of a facsimile edition of the 1651 *Letters*, speculates that this letter was written to George Garrard (Merrill, ed., *Letters to Severall Persons of Honour* [New York: Sturgis & Walton, 1910], 309). According to I. A. Shapiro, the letters addressed "to yourself" occurred when Donne made up a packet of letters to various friends and then asked one of his friends to deliver the other letters included in the packet. This cover letter, as it were, would be addressed "to yourself," whereas the letters included in the packet would each be individually addressed ("The Text of Donne's *Letters to Severall Persons*," in *Review of English Studies* 7 [1931]: 292).

29. Merrill, ed., *Letters to Severall Persons of Honour*, 281.

30. After her marriage to Sir Henry Kingsmill at the end of 1610, Donne's correspondence with Bridget White seems largely to have fallen off. Bald remarks that "nothing further is known of their relations until 1624, when Donne wrote her a long letter of consolation on the death of her husband" (*John Donne, A Life*, 187).

31. For a history of the role of the secretary in early modern England, see Jonathan

Goldberg, *Writing Matter: From the Hands of the English Renaissance* (Stanford: Stanford University Press, 1991).

32. For evidence that this letter, which was addressed in the 1651 edition to "Sir G.F.," was actually intended for Goodyer, see Bennett, "Donne's Letters from the Continent in 1611–12," 71–72.

33. See Gerard, *The Autobiography of a Hunted Priest*, trans. Philip Caraman (New York: Pellegrini & Cudahy, 1952), 119. The advantage of orange juice not evaporating once heated is that Gerard can always know whether his message has been read.

34. On the "newslessness" of Donne's letters, see John Carey, "John Donne's Newsless Letters," *Essays and Studies* 34 [1981]: 45–65. Carey's characterization of the letters as "by and large, extremely dull—indeed perversely and elaborately dull" seems inconsistent with even his own insights in the article, and certainly ignores the tremendous complexity of these texts. For a powerful critique of Carey's work on Donne more broadly, see Patterson, "Misinterpretable Donne: The Testimony of the Letters."

35. Fulwood, *The Enimie of Idlenesse*, 73.

36. *Letters*, 121. I have resisted the temptation to emend "piety" to "pretty," as the manuscript clearly states "piety." Hester has confirmed this reading.

37. The National Archives, SP. 84/91/219. The letter is dated 31 August 1619. Despite Donne's claims to be making his first introduction to Carleton, there is ample evidence that Carleton knew exactly who Donne was: as early as February 1609, Chamberlain wrote to Carleton: "Newes here is none at all but that John Dun [Donne] seeks to be preferred to be secretarie of Virginia" (Bald, *John Donne, A Life*, 162).

38. 254. For the letter's address to Goodyer, see Bennett, "Donne's Letters from the Continent," 68, 70–75.

39. See, for example, Donne's two letters to Nicholas Carey in the British Library (Add MS 29598), which each have an outside paper with inscriptions "To the R. Worshipful Sir Nicholas Carey, Kt., at Bevington," along with Donne's (broken) seal. See also Donne's letter to Thomas Roe, dated 1 Dec. 1622, in the National Archives (SP 14/134/59) whose "envelope" is addressed "To the Right Honorable Sr. Thomas Roe, Ambassador for his majestie of Great Britanie, to the Grand Seigneur."

40. See in particular David Aers and Gunther Kress's chapter, "Darke Text Need Notes: Versions of Self in Donne's Verse Epistles," in *Literature and Society in England 1580–1680*, ed. David Aers, Bob Hodge, and Gunther Kress (Dublin: Gill and Macmillan, 1981). Aers and Kress argue that an explicitly social basis underlines Donne's metaphysical conceits in the verse epistle, and that nearly all of his metaphysics can be understood within the context of Donne's larger social agenda.

41. One exception to this generalization is Margaret Maurer, who rightly argues that "the content of the verse letters suggests that Donne composed them in the same spirit of discourse, homily, or ingenious trifle that he claims infiltrates his prose letters" ("John Donne's Verse Letters," *Modern Language Quarterly* 37 [1976]: 238). However, despite this claim, Maurer does not herself discuss the two genres together, but isolates them in her own criticism. Hence "John Donne's Verse Letters" treats, as its title suggests, the verse epistles, and a second article, "The Poetical Familiarity of John Donne's Letters" (*Genre* 15 [1982]: 183–202), discusses the parallel styles of Donne's poetry and letters, but does not address the thematic continuities in the prose letters and the verse epistles.

42. I am not including here the joint epistle written by Donne and Goodyer, "A Letter written by Sir H. G. and J. D. *alteris vicibus*," in which Goodyer mentions the soul in one of his stanzas: "Thus our twin'd soules send forth these buds of love" (9). In the twenty-two epistles I am including, there are a total of fifty-one mentions of the soul.

43. "A Letter to the Lady Carey, and Mrs Essex Riche," line 32; "To the Countesse of Bedford," lines 22–24.

44. Jonson, *Masque of Beautie*, 368–71. In Donne's *Paradoxes and Problems*, he asks, "Why hath the common Opinion afforded Women Soules?" Jonson almost certainly refers to this in his notes to the lines I have quoted from his masque: "There hath beene such a profane *paradoxe* published" (cited in Milgate, 247–48, note to line 2).

45. "To Sir Henry Goodyer, ('Who makes the Past, a patterne for next yeare')," lines 13–14.

46. Here, as elsewhere in the letters, Donne uses "mind" interchangeably with "soul," although on certain occasions he does differentiate the two. For the differentiation of the two, see the letter to Goodyer in which he defines three parts of the self: To Sir H.G. "If I knew that I were ill, I were well; for we consist of three parts, a Soul, and body, and Minde: which I call those thoughts and affections and passions, which neither soul nor body hath alone, but have been begotten by their communication, as Musique results out of our breath and a Cornet" (70).

47. *Sermons*, 4:227. See Helen Gardner, "Appendix A: Donne's Views on the State of the Soul after Death," in *The Divine Poems* (Oxford: Clarendon Press, 1978), 114–17. For the immortality of soul by preservation and not by nature, see, for example, *Sermons* 2:201.

48. Bald, *John Donne, A Life*, 74–75.

49. Milgate points out that of Morpheus's many brothers, only two had the power to give dream-shapes: Phantasus and Phobetor, or Icelus, and Phantatsus's powers were limited to inanimate forms (*The Satires, Epigrams, and Verse Letters*, 218n1.3).

2. *SONGS AND SONNETS*

1. Helen Gardner, ed., *The Elegies, and The Songs and Sonnets* (Oxford: Clarendon Press, 1965), xvii; "The Argument about 'The Ecstasy,'" in *Essential Articles for the Study of John Donne's Poetry*, ed. John R. Roberts (Hamden CT: Archon Books, 1975), 256.

2. Christopher Ricks, "Donne after Love," in *Literature and the Body: Essays on Populations and Persons*, ed. Elaine Scarry.

3. On the *congé d'amour*, see Italo Siciliano, *François Villon et les thèmes poétiques du moyen âge* (Paris: Librairie Armand Colin, 1934).

4. Heather Dubrow, *Echoes of Desire: English Petrarchism and Its Counterdiscourses* (Ithaca, NY: Cornell University Press, 1995), 211–14.

5. Andrew Marvell, *The Poems of Andrew Marvell*, ed. Nigel Smith (London and New York: Pearson Educated Limited, 2003), lines 15–16, 63–64.

6. Emphasis mine; lines 20–21.

7. *Letters to Severall Persons of Honour*, 121; cited also in the third section of chapter 1 above.

8. Cited in Gardner, "The Argument about 'The Ecstasy,'" 239. Pound quotes the

poem in full, giving notes only on the word "concoction" ("Technical alchemical term") and "alloy" ("i.e. that makes metal fit for a given purpose"), and then provides his commentary.

9. Arthur Marotti, *John Donne, Coterie Poet* (Madison: University of Wisconsin Press, 1986), 197.

10. This verb has long been a textual crux. In the 1633 *Poems*, which follows several of the so-called Group I manuscripts of Donne's verse, the verb is printed "interanimates," not "interinanimates," and the OED cites this poem as the first use of this verb ("interinanimates" is not listed at all in the OED). In the rest of the extant manuscripts, the verb is "interinanimates," however, and modern editors have defended this version based both on the preponderance of manuscript support and on its accordance with the line's meter—"interanimates" leaves us one syllable short. We might add to this philological and metrical evidence some theological evidence from Donne's writings more broadly.

11. The OED lists an example from Donne's lyric "The Primrose" as the first usage of "sex" to mean "the distinction between male and female in general": "should she / Be more than woman, shee would get above / All thought of sexe, and thinke to move / My heart to study her, and not to love." It is not clear whether "The Extasie" was written before or after "The Primrose."

12. Although without regard to its meaning line 50 is rhythmically regular—it consists of four iambs—"bodies" on its own is a trochee.

13. Donne makes this point more clearly in a 1619 sermon: "the spirits in a man which are the thin and active part of the blood, and so are of a kind of middle nature, between soul and body, those spirits are able to doe, and they doe the office, to unite and apply the faculties of the soul to the organs of the body, and so there is a man" (2:261–2).

14. Eliot, *The Varieties of Metaphysical Poetry*, 112.

15. Grierson, *The Poems of John Donne*, 2: xlvii.

16. Aristotle, *De Anima*, trans. Hugh Lawson-Tancred (London: Penguin Books, 1986), ii 1, 412b8–13.

17. I disagree here with Gardner's conclusion in "The Argument about 'The Ecstasy,'" 242–43.

18. Gardner writes that "the only proposal which is made in these lines is the perfectly modest one that the lovers' souls, having enjoyed the rare privilege of union outside the body, should now resume possession of their separate bodies and reanimate these virtual corpses" ("The Argument about 'The Ecstasy,'" 242).

19. Ficino, *Marsilio Ficino's Commentary on Plato's Symposium*, trans. Sears Reynolds Jayne (Columbia: University of Missouri Press, 1944), 233.

20. Pico della Mirandola, *Commentary on a Canzone of Benivieni*, trans. Sears Reynolds Jayne (New York: Peter Lang, 1984), bk. 3, ch. 2, 125.

21. Leone Ebreo's *Dialoghi d'amore* was published posthumously in 1535 in Italian and was first translated into English in 1937. Although we have no definitive proof that Donne knew this text, its immense popularity and wide circulation, coupled with Donne's self-declared "hydroptique" appetite for reading, makes it very likely. Gardner makes this point convincingly in "The Argument about 'The Ecstasy,'" 510n16.

22. Leone Ebreo, *The Philosophy of Love*, trans. F. Friedeberg-Seeley and Jean H. Barnes (London: Soncino Press, 1937), 55.

23. *Libro di natura d'amore* (Venice 1531), cited in Donald L. Guss, *John Donne, Petrarchist* (Detroit: Wayne State University Press, 1966), 140.

24. Plato, *Symposium*, trans. Christopher Gill (New York: Penguin, 1999), 49; 211b–c.

25. In A. J. Smith, ed., *John Donne: Essays in Celebration* (London: Metheun, 1972), 129.

26. For the Italian text with an English translation, see Ezra Pound, *Translations* (New York: New Directions Books, 1963), 132–35.

27. *Julius Caesar*, from *The Norton Shakespeare*, Stephen Greenblatt, gen. ed. (New York: W. W. Norton & Co.), 5.1.112–15, 118–20. All references to Shakespeare are from this edition.

28. See Nicholas J. Perella, *The Kiss, Sacred and Profane* (Berkeley: University of California Press, 1969), 164–70.

29. From the poem "Bi liebe lac," in *Poets of the Minnesang*, ed. Olive Sayce (Oxford: Clarendon, 1967), 177; cited in Perella, *The Kiss, Sacred and Profane*, 123.

30. Baldassare Castiglione, *The Book of the Courtier*, trans. Sir Thomas Hoby (1561) (London: David Nutt, 1900), 355–56.

31. The kiss in Christian mysticism was typically linked to the kiss of death—the mystic kiss produces the lover's death at the moment of his or her union with Christ. See Perella, *The Kiss, Sacred and Profane*, 63–70.

32. See Grierson, *The Poems of John Donne*, 1:68, for a list of manuscripts with variant titles.

33. *De rerum natura*, trans. W. H. D. Rouse (Cambridge, MA: Harvard University Press, 1953), bk. 3, 597–98.

34. Robert Watson seems absolutely right to conclude that the lovers make the equivalent of a suicide pact: *The Rest Is Silence* (Berkeley: University of California Press, 1994), 192.

35. I am indebted to Theodore Redpath for his reading of this stanza, and in particular for his gloss of line 8—"when a tear falls, that thou falls which it bore" (*The Songs and Sonets of John Donne* [London: Metheun, 1956], 59). I follow Redpath and Gardner in emending Grierson's "falst" for the MS reading "falls." Gardner, *The Elegies, and The Songs and Sonnets* (Oxford: Clarendon Press, 1965), 196, note to line 8.

36. *Letters*, 43. See my introduction above.

37. On rings, see H. C. Smith, *Jewellery* (London: Methuen, 1908); cited in Juliet Fleming, *Graffiti and the Writing Arts* (London: Reaktion Books, 2001), 55.

38. Ficino, *Commentary on Plato's Symposium*, 146.

39. I am following Gardner's emendation of the punctuation in line 32, which follows the 1633 text. Grierson has a period following "so." See Gardner, *The Elegies, and The Songs and Sonnets*, 191–92.

40. *John Donne: Life, Mind, and Art* (London: Faber and Faber, 1981), 196.

41. I am indebted to Anselm Haverkamp for this observation. Haverkamp writes that in the Valedictions, "die Stimme verebbt, das Gedicht übrigbleibt, und stehen bleibt der Name" (the voice fades away, but the poem remains, and with it: the name). From "Die Schrift im Glas: A Valediction by John Donne," in *Homo medietas: Aufsätze zu Reli-*

giosität, Literatur und Denkformen des Menschen vom Mittelalter bis in die Neuzeit: Festschrift für Alois M. Haas zum 65. Geburtstag, ed. Claudia Brinker von der Heyde und Niklaus Largier (Bern: Peter Lang, 1999), 382.

42. Marotti, for example, says that the first stanzas introduce the fear that death will make their separation permanent, "an anxiety that is a common valedictory theme." (*John Donne, Coterie Poet,* 176)

43. John Freccero, "Donne's 'Valediction: Forbidding Mourning,'" *ELH* 30, no. 4 (Dec. 1963): 335–76, 367.

44. I borrow the English translation from Guss, *John Donne, Petrarchist,* 74.

45. It is used in "Lovers infinitenesse," "The Message," and "Twicknam Garden."

46. The original Latin and an English translation are printed in the beautiful facsimile edition produced by the Folger Library, *John Donne's Marriage Letters in the Folger Shakespeare Library,* ed. M. Thomas Hester, Robert Parker Sorlien, and Dennis Flynn (Washington, D.C.: Folger Shakespeare Library, 2005), 62. I have made some small changes to the translation they provide.

3. *THE ANNIVERSARIES*

1. Michel de Montaigne, *The Complete Works of Montaigne,* trans. Donald M. Frame (Stanford: Stanford University Press, 1957), 386.

2. Augustine, *The Literal Meaning of Genesis,* trans. John Hammond Taylor (New York: Newman Press, 1982), vol. 2, bk. 12, chap. 35, pp. 228–29, pl. 34, col. 483; cited in Caroline Bynum, *The Resurrection of the Body in Western Christianity, 200–1336* (New York: Columbia University Press, 1995), 97n138. Bernard of Clairvaux, *Bernard of Clairvaux: Selected Works,* trans. G. R. Evans (New York: Paulist Press, 1987), 84; cited in Bynum, 164–65. See also Dante's expression of this in the *Paradiso:* "Tanto mi parver subiti e accorti / e l'uno e l'altro coro a dicer 'Amme' / che ben mostrar disio d'i corpi morti" (So sudden and eager both the one and the other chorus seemed to me in saying 'Amen,' that truly they showed desire for their dead bodies) (*Paradiso,* trans. Charles Singleton [Princeton: Princeton University Press, 1975], canto XIV, 61–63).

3. John E. Booty, ed. *The Book of Common Prayer, 1559: The Elizabethan Prayer Book* (Charlottesville: University Press of Virginia; Folger Shakespeare Library, 1976), 312.

4. Thomas Becon, *The Catechism of Thomas Becon with Other Pieces* (Cambridge: Cambridge University Press, 1844), 576; Henry Bullinger, *The Decades of Henry Bullinger: The Fourth Decade* (Cambridge: Cambridge University Press, 1851), 379; Nicholas Ridley, Letter 33, in *The Works of Bishop Ridley,* ed. Henry Christmas (Cambridge: Cambridge University Press, 1841), 425.

5. Louis Martz, *The Poetry of Meditation* (New Haven: Yale University Press, 1954), 236–48; Barbara Lewalski, *Donne's Anniversaries and the Poetry of Praise: The Creation of a Symbolic Mode* (Princeton: Princeton University Press, 1973), 300.

6. P. G. Stanwood, "'Essential Joye' in Donne's Anniversaries," *Texas Studies in Literature and Language* 13 (1971): 231–32; A. C. Partridge, *John Donne: Language and Style* (London: Deutsch, 1978), 101; Terry Sherwood, *Fulfilling the Circle: A Study of John Donne's Thought* (Toronto: University of Toronto Press, 1984), 88; John Carey, *John Donne: Life, Mind, and Art,* 164.

7. Harold Love addresses the relationship between spirit and matter as central to the concerns of *The First Anniversarie*, although he does not connect this to Donne's larger interests in dualism. Hence he concludes that in *The Second Anniversarie*, Donne is "forced to abandon the provocative indeterminacy of the spirit-matter relationship that is central to *The First Anniversary* for a neater but far less stimulating vessel analogy" ("The Argument of Donne's *First Anniversary*," *Modern Philology* 64 [Nov. 1966]: 125–31).

8. Augustine, *Writings of Saint Augustine*, trans. Wilfrid Parsons (New York: Fathers of the Church, Inc., 1955), vol. 12, letter 166, chap. 10, p. 16.

9. See Jerome's reply, in which he declares that he could not reply, "not because I found anything blameworthy . . . but because in the words of the blessed apostle, 'Each person abounds in his own ideas.'" Reprinted in Augustine, *Letters 156–210: The Works of Saint Augustine*, trans. Roland Teske, ed. Boniface Ramsey (Hyde Park: New City, 2004), 122–23.

10. Based on the arguments made by the editors of the Donne *Variorum*, Grierson, and Bald, I assume that "A Funerall Elegie" was composed before *The First Anniversarie*. See the textual introduction to *The Anniversaries and the Epicedes and Obsequies*, vol. 6 of *The Variorum Edition of the Poetry of John Donne*, gen. ed. Gary A. Stringer, text ed. Ted-Larry Pebworth, John T. Shawcross, Gary Stringer, and Ernest W. Sullivan II (Bloomington: Indiana University Press, 1995), 38; Grierson, *Poems* (2:178); and Bald, *John Donne, a Life* (240). Both the editors of *The Variorum Edition* and Grierson print "A Funerall Elegie" after *The First Anniversarie*, following the order in which the first edition of 1611 printed the poems, but this does not reflect what they understand to be the probable order of composition.

11. See Grierson, *Poems*, 2:194. Milgate comments in his edition that the opening lines of "A Funerall Elegie" suggest "the opening of an epitaph to be spoken over the grave, or pinned to the funeral 'hearse'" (*John Donne: The Epithalamions, Anniversaries, and Epicedes* [Oxford: Clarendon Press, 1978], 152).

12. For an introduction to elegy, see Peter Sacks, *The English Elegy: Studies in the Genre from Spenser to Yeats* (Baltimore and London: Johns Hopkins University Press, 1985), 1–37.

13. Ben Jonson, "Ben Jonson's Conversations with William Drummond of Hawthornden," in *Ben Jonson*, ed. C. H. Herford, Percy Simpson, and Evelyn Simpson, 11 vols. (Oxford: Clarendon Press, 1925), 1:128–78. Donne's response is also recorded by Drummond.

14. Critics over the centuries have in effect risen to Jonson's challenge, proposing alternative figures behind Elizabeth to make the poem more palatable. In place of the Virgin Mary, William Empson declared that "the only way to make the poem sensible is to accept Elizabeth Drury as the Logos" (*Some Versions of Pastoral* [London: Chattus & Windus, 1935], 84). Marjorie Nicholson, in turn, understood the hidden subject of the poem to be Queen Elizabeth, whose name the young girl conveniently shared (*The Breaking of the Circle: Studies in the Effect of the "New Science" upon Seventeenth Century Poetry* [Evanston: Northwestern University Press, 1950], 69–70, 79–88). In her book-length study of the *Anniversaries*, Lewalski identified Elizabeth Drury as a symbol of a regenerate soul, a redeemed Protestant everyman who deserves the praise she is given precisely because, and not despite, her lack of accomplishments or merits (*Donne's An-*

niversaries and the Poetry of Praise, 193–94). Most recently, Edward Tayler has critiqued Lewalski's argument, and proposed a more philosophical (rather than theological) understanding of what Donne meant by "Idea" in his monograph *Donne's Idea of a Woman: Structure and Meaning in the Anniversaries* (New York: Columbia University Press, 1991), 10–18.

15. See Martz, *Poetry of Meditation.*

16. Lucretius, *De rerum natura,* 2:654–56, pp. 238–39. Grierson, *Poems,* 2:273.

17. See Hirsch, "Donne's Atomies and Anatomies: Deconstructed Bodies and the Resurrection of Atomic Theory," 69–94.

18. Edward LeComte, in *Grace to a Witty Sinner: A Life of Donne,* suggests that Donne would have seen the beheading of a noble, possibly of Essex himself (New York: Walker, 1965), 133. Cited in *Variorum Edition,* 6:462.

19. See Anthony Low, "The 'Turning Wheele': Carew, Jonson, Donne and the First Law of Motion," *John Donne Journal* 1 (1982): 69–80, for a provocative reading of the final line of this passage: "For there is motion in corruption."

20. See lines 3–6: "For who is sure he hath a Soule, unlesse / It see, and judge, and follow worthinesse, / And by Deedes praise it? hee who doth not this, / May lodge an Inmate soule, but 'tis not his."

21. Martz, who is committed to the devotional clarity of *The Second Anniversarie* as a meditative work, accurately characterizes these lines as expounding the central theme of the poem. But what Martz fails to recognize is that Donne's soul does not yet possess the thirst for God that the passage describes. He makes this mistake because his evidence is entirely external to the poem—we are referred, for example, to St. Bernard's "Anima sitiens Deum," in which the soul desires its union with God, but not to comparable moments in Donne (*Poetry of Meditation,* 239–40).

22. Donne characterizes his own thirst for learning as "Hydroptique" in a letter to Goodyer (*Letters,* 51). See my introduction for a discussion of this letter.

23. Sherwood, *Fulfilling the Circle,* 88; cited in *Variorum Edition,* 6:468.

24. John Davies, *Nosce teipsum,* in *The Poems of Sir John Davies,* ed. Clare Howard (New York: Columbia University Press, 1941), lines 613–24.

25. See Howard's commentary in Davies, *Poems,* 20.

26. John Woolton, *A Treatise of the Immortalitie of the Soule* (London: 1576), fol. 19b, 25b–26.

27. Thomas Browne, *Religio Medici,* ed. James Winny (Cambridge: Cambridge University Press, 1963), 44–45.

28. John Milton, *Complete Prose Works of John Milton,* 8 vols., gen. ed. Don M. Wolfe, rev. ed., vol. 6, ed. Maurice Kelley (New Haven: Yale University Press, 1980), 6:321.

29. In 1603, Donne's contemporary H. Crosse uses the term to insult the London theater—"A play is like a Sincke in a Towne," he declares, "where unto all the filth doth runne"—but outside of Donne's poem, there are no recorded uses of the overwhelmingly pejorative term to describe the site of the soul's creation ("Sink," def. I1a, *Oxford English Dictionary,* 2nd ed., 1989).

30. "Who makes the Past, a Patterne for next yeare," lines 29–30.

31. In Donne's library we find a copy of Paracelsus's *Chirurgia Magna, in duos tomos*

digesta, a Latin translation of *Die Grosse Wundarznei* and several shorter medical tracts, published in 1573. On Donne's library, see Geoffrey Keynes, *A Bibliography of Dr. John Donne*, 4th ed. (Oxford: Clarendon Press, 1973), Appendix IV, "Books from Donne's Library." For Donne's relationship to Paracelsus, see W. A. Murray, "Donne and Paracelsus: An Essay in Interpretation," *Review of English Studies* 25, no. 2 (1949): 115–23.

32. Milgate, *The Satires, Epigrams, and Verse Letters*, 104, lines 5–6.

33. Ibid., 104, lines 27–28.

34. 5:348. This quotation is from a separate sermon, on Psalm 6:2–3, which is undated. The Whitsunday sermon is conjecturally assigned to 1624.

35. I am indebted here to Harold Love, who, contrary to the dominant critical consensus, argued that Elizabeth's death was caused by the death of the world, rather than being the cause for it. ("The Argument of Donne's *First Anniversary*," 127).

36. Richard Steele mentions them in *The Spectator* in 1711 as an ideal description of a woman; Jane Austen's brother Henry applies them to his sister Jane; and Ralph Waldo Emerson remarks that passion "beholds its object as a perfect unit" (all cited in *Variorum Edition*, 6:498).

37. See my discussion of "gold to ayery thinnesse beate" in chapter 2.

38. See John Klause, "The Montaigneity of Donne's *Metempsychosis*," in *Renaissance Genres: Essays on Theory, History, and Interpretation*, ed. Barbara Lewalski, 418–43 (Cambridge: Harvard University Press, 1986).

39. Tayler, *Donne's Idea of a Woman*, 60–61, 162n13.

40. Spenser, *The Faerie Queene*, ed. A. C. Hamilton (New York: Longman Group Ltd., 1977), I.x.63.1–3.

41. For a history of the trumpet image and its relationship to Donne's role as prophet, see Raymond-Jean Frontain, "Donne's Protestant *Paradiso*: The Johannine Vision of the *Second Anniversary*," in *John Donne and the Protestant Reformation: New Perspectives*, ed. Mary Arshagouni Papazian, 113–42 (Detroit: Wayne State University Press, 2003), especially pp. 118–24.

42. John Booty, ed., *The Book of Common Prayer, 1559: The Elizabethan Prayer Book*, 292.

4. HOLY SONNETS

1. Annabel Patterson, "Donne's Re-formed *La Corona*," *John Donne Journal* 23 (2004): 69–93.

2. See the commentary "Dating and Order" and the "General Textual Introduction" to vol. 7 of *The Variorum Edition of the Poetry of John Donne, The Holy Sonnets*, part 1, Gary A. Stringer, gen. ed. (Bloomington: Indiana University Press, 2005). I am very grateful to Gary Stringer for sharing the manuscript of this edition with me in advance of its publication. For an alternative dating of the poems, proposing that they may have been written in the 1590s, see Dennis Flynn, "'Awry and Squint': The Dating of Donne's Holy Sonnets," *John Donne Journal* 7 (1988): 35–46.

3. In Donne, *The Divine Poems*, ed. Helen Gardner, 2nd ed. (Oxford: Clarendon Press, 1978), xxxvii–liii.

4. OED, v2, def. 3.

5. Donne, *Biathanatos*, ed. Ernest W. Sullivan II (Newark: University of Delaware Press, 1984), 29.

6. See my discussion of Donne's desire for an active death in chapter 6.

7. Donne, *Biathanatos*, 130.

8. Jorge Luis Borges, "Biathanatos," in *Selected Non-Fictions*, ed. Eliot Weinberger (New York: Penguin Books, 1999), 333–36.

9. Donne, *Biathanatos*, 130.

10. Donne, *Sermons*, 5:266. Potter and Simpson tentatively date the sermon to 1622.

11. Donne, *Divine Poems*, ed. Helen Gardner, xlv–xlvi. Grierson also adopts this version. I cite the manuscript reading provided in the *Variorum*, vol. 7, pt. 1, p. 7.

12. Milton, *Paradise Lost*, 5:857–58.

13. For a philosophical treatment of the "as if," see H. Vaihinger, *The Philosophy of "As If": A System of the Theoretical, Practical and Religious Fictions of Mankind*, trans. C. K. Ogden, 2nd. ed. (London: Routledge, 1968).

14. For a sampling of these opinions, see the *Variorum* commentary on this poem, under the heading "Opinions," vol. 7, pt. 1, 239–61.

15. OED, v2, def. 1 and 2.

16. There is an extensive critical history of reading God as a metalsmith or tinkerer in these opening lines. See, among others, J. C. Levenson, "Holy Sonnets, XIV," *Explicator* 11 (1953): item 31 (cited in *Variorum*, 242); William W. Heist, "Donne on Divine Grace: Holy Sonnet No. XIV," *Papers of the Michigan Academy of Science, Arts, and Letters* 53 (1968): 311–29; and Elias Eschwartz, "Donne's 'Holy Sonnets, XIV,'" *Explicator* 26 (1976): item 27.

17. Milton launches an argument similar to Donne's in *De Doctrina Christiana:* "There is a good deal of controversy about what the original matter was. On the whole the moderns are of the opinion that everything was formed out of nothing (which is, I fancy, what their own theory is based on!). In the first place is it certain that neither the Hebrew verb [*bara*] nor the Greek [*epoihsen*] nor the Latin [*creare*] means 'to make out of nothing.' On the contrary, each of them always means 'to make out of something.' Gen. i. 21, 27: *God created . . . which the waters brought forth abundantly, he created them male and female. . . .* It is clear, then, that the world was made out of some sort of matter" (*Complete Prose Works of John Milton*, 6:305–6).

18. Donne, *Essays in Divinity*, ed. Evelyn M. Simpson (Oxford: Clarendon Press, 1952), 28.

19. Cited in *Variorum*, vol. 7, pt. 1, 264–65. I am especially indebted to the glosses from A. G. Hooper and C. J. D. Harvey, *Poems for Discussion: With Commentaries and Questions* (Cape Town: Oxford University Press, 1958).

20. Cited in E. N. Tigerstedt, "The Poet as Creator: Origins of a Metaphor," *Comparative Literature Studies* 5 (1968): 464.

21. In the *Devotions*, Donne explains the salutary effects of a similar fear as he lies on his sickbed: "How *fully* then, O my abundant God, how *gently*, O my sweet, my easie God, dost thou unentangle mee, in any scruple arising out of the consideration of thy feare? Is not this that which thou intendest, when thou sayst, *The secret of the Lord is with them that fear him;* The secret, the mistery of the right use of fear" (32).

22. Donne, *The Divine Poems*, ed. Helen Gardner, 67, note to line 13.

23. Latimer, *Sermons and Remains of Hugh Latimer* (Cambridge: Cambridge University Press, 1844), 45.

24. *The Sermons of Edwin Sandys, D.D.* (Cambridge: Cambridge University Press, 1841), 352.

25. For a full account of this, see Anne Ferry, *The "Inward" Language: Sonnets of Wyatt, Sidney, Shakespeare, Donne* (Chicago: University of Chicago Press, 1983), 229.

26. Modern editors have made a compelling case for why "assures," the verb used in all reported manuscripts, is to be preferred. See Grierson, *Poems of John Donne*, 2:234; and *Divine Poems*, ed. Helen Gardner, 71.

27. William Empson, *Seven Types of Ambiguity*, rev. ed. (1930; New York: New Directions, 1947), 146. Empson includes this footnote to his reading: "I leave in my expression of distaste for the poem, but it has little to do with the ambiguity in question."

28. R. V. Young, *Doctrine and Devotion in Seventeenth-Century Poetry: Studies in Donne, Herbert, Crashaw, and Vaughan* (Cambridge: D. S. Brewer, 2000), 26–28.

29. Stanley Fish, "Masculine Persuasive Force: Donne and Verbal Power," in *Soliciting Interpretation: Literary Theory and Seventeenth-Century English Poetry*, ed. Elizabeth D. Harvey and Katharine Eisaman Maus (Chicago: University of Chicago Press, 1990), 247.

30. See Anthony Bellette's fine treatment of the relationship between the formal and devotional aims in his "'Little Worlds Made Cunningly': Significant Form in Donne's *Holy Sonnets* and '*Goodfriday, 1613*,'" *Studies in Philology* 72 (1975) 322–47.

5. DEVOTIONS

1. For an overview of both the Protestant and Jesuit readings of the *Devotions*, see Mary Papazian, "Donne, Election, and the *Devotions upon Emergent Occasions*," *Huntington Library Quarterly* 55 (1992): 603–19.

2. For a critique of this Ignatian reading, see Janel Mueller, "The Exegesis of Experience: Dean Donne's *Devotions upon Emergent Occasions*," *Journal of English and German Philology* 67 (1968): 1–19.

3. Cited in Becon, *Prayer and Other Pieces of Thomas Becon* (Cambridge: Cambridge University Press, 1844), 31–32. Originally published by John Day (London, 1551).

4. John Booty, ed., *The Book of Common Prayer, 1559: The Elizabethan Prayer Book*, 301.

5. For a persuasive account of the sixteenth-century conception of illness as divine blessing, see Jonathan Goldberg, "The Understanding of Sickness in Donne's *Devotions*" (*Renaissance Quarterly* 24, no. 4 [Winter 1971]: 507–17).

6. This work was composed sometime before 1553. See Derrick Sherwin Bailey, *Thomas Becon and the Reformation of the Church in England* (Edinburgh: Oliver and Boyd, 1952), 140–47.

7. Becon, *Prayer and Other Pieces of Thomas Becon*, 94.

8. Article 17 reads: "Predestination to life is the everlasting purpose of God, whereby, before the foundations of the world were laid, He hath constantly decreed by His counsel secret to us, to deliver from curse and damnation those whom He hath chosen in Christ

out of mankind, and to bring them by Christ to everlasting salvation as vessels made to honour" (Hardwick, *A History of the Articles of Religion*, 297).

9. Lancelot Andrewes, *Two Answers to Cardinal Perron, and Other Miscellaneous Works* (Oxford: John Henry Parker, 1967), 182.

10. Jeremy Taylor, *Holy Living and Holy Dying*, vol. 2 (Oxford: Clarendon Press, 1989), chap. 3, sect. 4.4.

11. Taylor, 95. See also Proverb 3:11: "My son, refuse not the chastening of the Lord, neither be grieved with His correction."

12. Richard Greenham, *The Words of the Reverend and Faithful Servant of Jesus Christ*, 4th ed. (1605, 159), cited in Andrew Wear, "Puritan Perceptions of Illness in Seventeenth-Century England," in *Patients and Practitioners: Lay Perceptions of Medicine in Pre-industrial Society*, ed. Roy Porter (Cambridge: Cambridge University Press, 1985), 55–99.

13. On the "preternatural," see Lorraine Daston, "Preternatural Philosophy," in Daston, ed., *Biographies of Scientific Objects* (Chicago: University of Chicago Press, 2000).

14. See my discussion of Holy Sonnet V, "I am a little world made cunningly" in chapter 4. On the early modern attitude toward man as microcosm, see Leonard Barkan, *Nature's Work of Art: The Human Body as Image of the World* (New Haven: Yale University Press, 1975).

15. On self-ministering, see Donne's "Hymne to God, my God, in my sicknesse," which concludes, "And as to others soules I preach'd thy word, / Be this my Text, my Sermon to mine owne, / Therfore that he may raise the Lord throws down" (28–30).

16. Clara Lander makes this particular point about the urine in her article, "A Dangerous Sickness Which Turned to a Spotted Fever," *Studies in English Literature* 11, no. 1 (Winter 1971): 89–108.

17. See Jonathan Sawday's illuminating discussion of Donne's secrecy, *The Body Emblazoned: Dissection and the Human Body in Renaissance Culture* (London and New York: Routledge, 1995), 33–36 and *passim*.

18. *Letters*, 241–42. The addressee of this letter is unknown.

19. Augustine, *The Confessions*, trans. William Watts, 2 vols. (Cambridge, MA: Harvard University Press, 1951), 2:239.

20. See Nancy G. Siraisi, *Medieval and Early Renaissance Medicine: An Introduction to Knowledge and Practice* (Chicago: University of Chicago Press, 1990); Owsei Temkin, *Galenism: Rise and Decline of a Medical Philosophy* (Ithaca: Cornell University Press, 1973).

21. See chapter 2.

22. As we shall see in chapter 6, this position was by no means atypical for patristic and medieval theologians, but it was not ordinarily embraced by the Church of England.

23. See OED for these usages: definition 1a, "Appearance; outward form. (*Obs*)"; 3a, "The outward appearance or aspect, the visible form or image, *of* something, as constituting the immediate object of vision. *Obs.* (Common in 17th cent.)." Donne's interest in optics is borne out not only by internal references within his works, but also by his ownership of a book published in 1606 by Petrus Ramus and Fridericus Risnerus, *Opticae Libri Quatuor*, which treats questions of refraction and reflexive light. Donne's copy of this volume survives in the collection from his personal library at the Middle Temple Library in London.

24. *Letters*, 249.

25. See Selleck, "Donne's Body," for an account of Donne's selfhood as intentionally unstable. Within this model, illness becomes a "solution."

6. *DEATHS DUELL*

1. Bald explains that the sermon was entered in the Stationer's Register without a title, and that its title was borrowed or lifted from a volume by Walter Colman, whose original title was also *Deaths Duell*, but which was subsequently altered to *La Dance Macabre, or Death's Duell*. It would seem that Roger Michell, the publisher of Donne's sermon, could not resist taking Colman's title for Donne's work (Bald, *John Donne, A Life*, 529n1). Gardner proposes that Donne himself arranged for the publication of his last sermon with the engraving of Donne in his shroud as its frontispiece (*Divine Poems* [Oxford: Clarendon Press, 1952], 113).

2. M. Thomas Hester dates this letter Dec. 10, 1630, in his introduction, *Letters to Severall Persons of Honour*.

3. Walton, *Life of Donne*, 231–32.

4. Bald, *John Donne, A Life*, 312.

5. Over the course of his career, Donne preached thirty-six sermons at court. See the appendix listing these sermons in Peter McCullough, "Donne as Preacher at Court: Precarious 'Inthronization,'" in *John Donne's Professional Lives*, ed. David Colclough (Cambridge: D. S. Brewer, 2003), 203–4. I am indebted throughout this chapter to McCullough's groundbreaking work on the conditions of preaching in the seventeenth century, and I am very grateful for his generosity in discussing his research with me.

6. Bald, *John Donne, A Life*, 318–19.

7. On Donne's preaching when a pulpit was temporarily vacant, see Bald, *John Donne, A Life*, 328. On James I's penchant for hearing sermons during his hunting trips, see McCullough, *Sermons at Court* (Cambridge: Cambridge University Press, 1998), 125–26.

8. McCullough, "Donne as Preacher at Court: Precarious 'Inthronization,'" 198–200.

9. Jeanne Shami, *John Donne and Conformity in Crisis in the Late Jacobean Pulpit*, Studies in Renaissance Literature (Cambridge, UK: D. S. Brewer, 2003).

10. McCullough draws our attention to the court chaplain's practice of preaching two sermons on Sunday—one to the royal family and office holders, and one to the staff. He also persuasively establishes that the title of this sermon, "to the houshold" (a title unprecedented not only for Donne but for all extant sermons from this period), must mean that it was the early morning Sunday sermon for household staff members at Whitehall (McCullough, "Donne as Preacher at Court: Precarious 'Inthronization,'" 184–86).

11. OED, "hearken," second edition, 1989, definitions 4 and 3.

12. Shuger, *Habits of Thought in the English Renaissance* (Berkeley: University of California Press, 1990), 178.

13. Donne's sermon was more political than usual, and was interpreted to be under the influence of Abbot's recent contra-Laudian actions. For more details, see Bald, *John Donne, A Life*, 491–94; McCullough, "Donne as Preacher at Court: Precarious 'Inthronization,'" 199–200.

14. Cited in Bald, *John Donne, A Life*, 494.

15. Joan Webber, *Contrary Music: The Prose Style of John Donne* (Madison: University of Wisconsin Press, 1963). See also Peter McCullough, "Donne as Preacher," in *Cambridge Companion to John Donne* (Cambridge: Cambridge University Press, 2006), 167–76.

16. Richard Bernard, *The Faithfull Shepheard; or, The Shepheards Faithfulnesse* (London, 1607), 72.

17. Andrew Hyperius, *The Practis of Preaching, otherwise called, The Pathway to the Pulpet*, englished by John Ludham, vicar of Wetherffeld (London, 1577), 43a.

18. T. S. Eliot, *Selected Essays* (New York: Harcourt, Brace, 1950), 292.

19. Walton, *Life of Donne*, 225.

20. *Letters to Severall Persons of Honour*, 308. Bald dates this letter April 2, 1627 (*John Donne, A Life*, 493), and the editors of *John Donne: Selected Prose* simply date it "April, 1627" (*Selected Prose*, chosen by Evelyn Simpson, ed. Helen Gardner and Timothy Healy [Oxford: Clarendon Press, 1967], 161–62).

21. Bald, *John Donne, A Life*, 494n1.

22. Augustine, *The City of God*, bk. 13, chap. 10, p. 419.

23. Seneca, *Ad Lucilium epistulae morales*, 1:176–77. I am indebted to Marcus Dods for this reference (*The City of God*, 419n13).

24. Donne is listed in the OED as the second author to use this word, but the first entry is from Florio's 1611 Italian-English dictionary, *Queen Anna's New World of Words*.

25. Bald, *John Donne, A Life*, 563.

26. See chapter 1, above.

27. Bald, *John Donne, A Life*, 563.

28. See earlier discussion of this sermon, in my introduction and in chapter 2.

29. Article 4: "Christe dyd truely aryse agayne from death, and toke agayne his body, with flesh, bones, and all thinges apparteyning to the perfection of mans nature, wherewith he ascended into heaven, and there sitteth, untyll he returne to judge all men at the last day" (Hardwick, *A History of the Articles of Religion*, 281).

30. See William P. Haugaard, *Elizabeth and the English Reformation* (Cambridge: Cambridge University Press, 1968), 251–52, and Felicity Heal, *Reformation in Britain and Ireland*, 305–10 (Oxford: Oxford University Press, 2003).

31. John E. Booty, ed., *The Book of Common Prayer, 1559: The Elizabethan Prayer Book*, 310.

32. Carolyn Bynum, *The Resurrection of the Body in Western Christianity, 200–1336* (New York: Columbia University Press, 1995); The Holy Bible (London, 1611).

33. Dale B. Martin, *The Corinthian Body* (New Haven: Yale University Press, 1995). Martin challenges John A. T. Robinson's classic treatment in *The Body: A Study in Pauline Theology* (Philadelphia: Westminster Press, 1977).

34. Tertullian, *Concerning the Resurrection of the Flesh*, trans. A. Souter (London: Society for Promoting Christian Knowledge, 1922), 145.

35. *City of God*, bk. 22, chap. 14, p. 837.

36. Peter Lombard, *Sentences*, bk. 4, 44, chaps. 1–3, unpublished translation by Robert O'Brien (1970).

37. The text of the Fourth Lateran Council reads: "*Qui omnes cum suis propriis cor-*

poribus resurgent, quae nunc gestant" (Norman P. Tanner, ed., *Decrees of the Ecumenical Councils,* vol 1. [London: Sheed and Ward, 1990], 230, lines 30–31).

38. For the reasons behind the shift away from the materialist position in the early 1300s, see Bynum, *The Resurrection of the Body in Western Christianity, 200–1336,* 135ff.

39. See in particular Mary Ramsay's *Les Doctrines Medievales Chez Donne* (London: Oxford University Press, 1917).

40. Here my interpretation differs dramatically from Stanley Fish's account in *Self-Consuming Artifacts,* which remains one of the surprisingly few sustained readings of this famous sermon. Fish wants us to see Donne's erasure of self into the Word, his "becom[ing] indistinguishable from the Word he preaches." "He loses his identity exactly at the point where we are blessed with the loss of ours," Fish concludes (*Self-Consuming Artifacts* [Berkeley: University of California Press, 1972], 70).

41. Cited in McCullough, *Sermons at Court,* 34.

42. *Reports on the Manuscripts of Lord de l'Isle and Dudley preserved at Penshurst Place in Royal Commission on Historical Manuscripts* (London: H.M. Stationery Office, 1925–), 6:99.

43. Unfortunately there is no way to know definitively where *Deaths Duell* was preached. "The Declaration of the Accompte of Sir William Uvedale, Knight, Treasurer of the Kinges Majesties Chamber," 1630–31, acknowledges payments to several yeomen and grooms of the chamber for "making ready Whitehall for his Majesty" over the course of the year, but does not specify what preparations were made for the specific day that Donne was preaching. (See item A01/393/69 in the National Archives, London, for this record.)

44. McCullough, *Sermons at Court,* 44.

45. Joseph Koerner, *The Reformation of the Image* (Chicago: University of Chicago Press, 2004), 226.

46. Cited in Koerner, *The Reformation of the Image,* 176–77.

47. See the illustration in McCullough, *Sermons at Court,* 44.

48. *The Book of the Craft of Dying,* ed. Frances M. M. Comper (New York: Arno Press, 1977), 61.

49. See Gardner, "Dean Donne's Monument in S. Paul's," in *Evidence in Literary Scholarship: Essays in Memory of James Marshall Osborn,* by René Wellek and Alvaro Ribeiro (Oxford: Clarendon Press; New York: Oxford University Press, 1979), 34–36.

50. Bald also sees the monument as a resurrection figure, although he draws different conclusions from my own (*John Donne, A Life,* 535–36).

51. Gardner, "Dean Donne's Monument," 36–40.

INDEX

Works not attributed to another author are by Donne.